THE BOOK OF EPHESIANS

BOOKS OF THE BIBLE
VOLUME 8
GARLAND REFERENCE LIBRARY OF THE HUMANITIES
VOLUME 1466

BOOKS OF THE BIBLE
HENRY O. THOMPSON, *Series Editor*

THE BOOK OF PSALMS
An Annotated Bibliography
Thorne Wittstruck

I CORINTHIANS
An Annotated Bibliography
Watson E. Mills

THE BOOK OF REVELATION
An Annotated Bibliography
Robert L. Muse

THE BOOK OF DANIEL
An Annotated Bibliography
Henry O. Thompson

THE BOOK OF RUTH
An Annotated Bibliography
Mishael Maswari Caspi

THE BOOK OF EPHESIANS
An Annotated Bibliography
William W. Klein

THE BOOK OF EPHESIANS
AN ANNOTATED BIBLIOGRAPHY

WILLIAM W. KLEIN

GARLAND PUBLISHING, INC.
NEW YORK AND LONDON
1996

Library of Congress Cataloging-in-Publication Data

Klein, William W. (William Wade)
    The Book of Ephesians : an annotated bibliography / William W. Klein.
        p.   cm. — (Books of the Bible ; vol. 8) (Garland reference library
    of the humanities ; vol. 1466)
        ISBN 0-8153-0364-5 (alk. paper)
        1. Bible N.T. Ephesians—Bibliography.   I. Title.   II. Series.
    III. Series: Garland reference library of the humanities ; vol. 1466.
    Z7772.P1K54   1996
    [BS2695.2]
    016.227'5—dc20   95-20253
                                                                            CIP

#325900036

Printed on acid-free, 250-year-life paper
Manufactured in the United States of America

for Phyllis, Alison, and Sarah

"I pray that out of his glorious riches he may strengthen you with power through his Spirit in your inner being, so that Christ may dwell in your hearts through faith."
Ephesians 3:16-17

Advisory Board

CONTENTS

Series Preface

It is a personal and professional pleasure to commend Dr. William W. Klein's annotated bibliography to the public. The Book of Ephesians has had a varied and continuing impact on the Western world and through Christian culture, the whole world. Klein has arranged the entries for the bibliography in what one might call "The Best of Two [or more] Possible Worlds." The "introductory" section points the reader to the background studies of the text as a whole, while the chapter on commentaries gives immediate access to publications that give both introductions and a general treatment of the entire Epistle. Many will come looking for material on individual verses. By arranging the entries for the chapters and verses of Ephesians itself, Klein has given the user of this bibliography a kind of carte blanche— there it all is, open, ready to seek and find. But others need to know the issues, the themes, the debates, the history, the theology related to Ephesians. These are lined up for ready access. One could almost say there are several bibliographies here, each designed to meet particular needs.

Dr. Klein's thorough search will facilitate the study, understanding and appreciation of Ephesians. In turn, this volume will give entré to the entire body of Paul's writing including the debates over what he did or did not write. The arrangement of the entries thus does what a bibliography of this type is supposed to do. It will guide users to the several approaches for special study or general interest.

This volume is one of a series of Bible bibliographies. They should be of value to anyone interested in the biblical text—teachers, students, professional clergy, the laity, undergraduate and graduate students—and several fields of disciplines of study—Bible, Church History, Literature,

History of Religions. The annotated bibliographies will serve as reference works in libraries for colleges, theological schools, the public, religious groups, individuals.

The projected series was planned to include the Judeo-Christian Scriptures (canon, rule of faith). Jews call the Hebrew Scriptures the Tenak or Tanakh, from the first letters of the three sections: Torah (Instruction or Law), Nabiim (Prophets) and Kethubim (Writings; Hebrew for "cut" as in preparing a reed or quill pen). Christians call this collection of Scriptures the Old Testament (OT). The Christian Bible includes the New Testament (NT). Jews and Protestant Christians have the same books in the Tenak or OT, but they are arranged in different orders. Roman Catholic and Eastern Orthodox Christians have fifteen (more or less) additional Writings call deuterocanonical, "second canon," or Apocrypha ("Hidden"). Hopefully the series will include them all.

The writers are drawn from across doctrinal perspectives and across the Judeo-Christian perspective. Each person has had academic freedom. That includes the arrangement of the entries to facilitate the reader's usage of the volume. The freedom includes what selections to include. The understanding of the latter is that the result would reflect the field of study for the book presented. The collection is comprehensive for the post-World War II years with greater selectivity prior to that. This does not mean everything ever published, probably an impossible goal. It does mean available, though not necessarily in the compiler's own hands, e.g., doctoral dissertations. The annotation is selective.

Users can be helpful to the series. Please share new materials, items missed in the general search, or appearing later than the volume's coverage. Please correct factual errors. Perfection may be only an ideal but it remains a goal.

As in giving birth, editing involves labor and sometimes labor pains. The end of the process, however, is joy and the joy remains. It is a special privilege to thank Dr. Klein for his work on this volume. Without his persistence and study, this book would not exist. The thank you spreads out to other authors and the editorial board and all who have helped make the series viable. This of course includes Garland

Publishing for producing this series. A very special thank you to Editor Phyllis Korper, for commissioning the series, for editorial advice and directions, for a listening ear, a friendly voice. Final thank you's go out to Assistant Editor Jennifer Sorenson and all who brought the final manuscript into print, production, distribution, and into the hands of you the reader.

Henry O. Thompson
Series Editor

AUTHOR'S INTRODUCTION

A review of other volumes in this series shows that their authors adopt a variety of organizational plans. One might make a case for one of a variety of systems to make the wealth of sources available to would-be researchers of Ephesians. One seemed to be most useful here—to present the sources, first, by two genres of publications written on biblical books, and then, second, by the kinds of ways students and scholars actually go about their study of a book of the Bible.

Initially, then, we present sources that treat the so-called issues of *Introduction*, those topics and concerns that interpreters must consider to put the letter of Ephesians in its historical, cultural, and literary settings. The next chapter catalogues the wealth of *commentaries* written on Ephesians.

Approaching the letter itself, the next series of chapters moves through the epistle passage by passage, enumerating sources that investigate parts or the whole of each logical literary unit.

The final section of the book moves *topically* through important subjects that are pertinent to a study of Ephesians. They will inevitably overlap with some of the prior entries. In these instances most often we will simply cross reference prior annotations. The topics include such things as: literary issues including the letter's structure, genre, style, vocabulary, and textual transmission, its relation to Colossians and the rest of the Pauline corpus; Ephesians' relations to other writings or movements (e.g., gnostic beliefs and texts, Qumran, other parts of the New Testament and Old Testament); the presence of various hymnic, confessional, and catechetical formulations; the letter's historical setting including issues surrounding its authorship (including pseudonymity and its place in the canon), the institution of slavery and the so-called "Household codes"; and, finally, its thought or theology including the important phrase "in Christ."

The question of the date of the sources included here should be addressed. The author has attempted to concentrate on sources written in the last fifty years or so, though not exclusively so. The selection strives to be relatively complete for this most recent half century. The entries are the ones that researchers might reasonably find, at least in major theological libraries. Selected sources prior to World War II are included—those that the author deemed especially important or useful. Either they were groundbreaking, they made a significant contribution to Ephesian studies, or they have remained the topic of ongoing discussion or research. The compilation includes sources in several modern western languages, though readers will see that the majority languages are English, German, and French.

Readers will quickly see how wide-ranging and prevalent have been the debates and controversies surrounding these six chapters. Though its authorship is hotly disputed, the epistle remains, even for many who doubt that the Apostle wrote it, the "quintessence of Paulinism." Though some volumes in this Garland bibliography series have included a brief "Introduction" to the various issues surrounding their respective books, I will not follow their lead. Such a task has been done extremely well by many others. If readers desire an overview of the major issues concerning Ephesians they would be served well by consulting the introductory pages in one of the key recent commentaries: Barth, Bruce, Lincoln, or Schnackenburg, among others, are excellent places to start. Alternatively, readers might secure one of the books listed in the "Introduction" chapter. Toward the "conservative" side of the spectrum, see the volumes by Carson, et al., Gundry, Guthrie, or L. T. Johnson. In the more "liberal" direction see Collins, Keck, Kümmel, or Roetzel.

The author wishes to pay tribute to several others who facilitated this project. First, thanks to the Administrative Committee of Denver Seminary who provided a research grant that helped fund part of this project. Second, the staff of the Cary S. Thomas Library of Denver Seminary—especially research librarian Robin Ottoson and Wyne Lundy of the interlibrary loan department—provided enormous technical help in locating the multitude of sources such a project required. Many thanks to them. Finally, two research assistants helped me track down and understand a number of the entries in this volume. My student Richard Scovel provided expert assistance. His work was careful, accurate, and judicious. Through an independent study on Ephesians we together learned much about the message of this poignant letter. A Denver Seminary graduate, Julia Raiss Slayback, also served as a research assistant. I acknowledge my gratitude to these colleagues.

It was a privilege to read and learn so much about this letter during these recent years. May these small efforts introduce many others to the Epistle's life-changing insights. Some of those insights impacted my own household, helping to shape my own *Haustafel*. For this reason I dedicate this book to the three women in my household: my wife Phyllis and my daughters Alison and Sarah. May these words from Ephesians characterize each of us:

$$\ldots \text{ἐδυναμοῦσθε ἐν κυρίῳ}$$

$$\text{καὶ ἐν τῷ κράτει}$$

$$\text{τῆς ἰσχύος αὐτοῦ.}$$

Ephesians 6:10

ABBREVIATIONS

For the exhaustive and authoritative listing of abbreviations see S. Schwertner, *Internationales Abkürzungsverzeichnis für Theologie und Grenzgebiete / International Glossary of Abbreviations for Theology and Related Subjects.* Berlin/New York: de Gruyter, 1974.

General Abbreviations

A.D.	Anno Domine, "The Year of our Lord," often replaced by C.E.
B.C.	Before Christ, often replaced by B.C.E.
B.C.E.	Before the Common Era = the Christian B.C., Before Christ.
ca.	*circa,* about
C.E.	Common Era = Christian A.D.
cf.	*confer,* about
chap.(s)	chapter(s)
contra	in contrast to
DSS	Dead Sea Scrolls
ed.	edited by, editor(s)
e.g.	*exempli gratia,* for example
esp.	especially
et al.	*et alii,* and others
ET	English translation
f., ff.	following [verse(s); page(s)]

fem.	feminine
FS	*Festschrift* = commemorative volume
Ger.	German
Gr.	Greek
Heb.	Hebrew
i.e.	*id est,* that is
LXX	Septuagint
MS(S)	manuscript(s)
MT	Masoretic text of the Old Testament
n.d.	no date
N.F.	*Neue Folge* = new series
no.	number
n.s.	new series
NT	New Testament
OT	Old Testament
p., pp.	page, pages
par.	parallel (to)
pl.	plural
Q	*Quelle* (Ger. "sayings" source for the Gospels)
rev.	revised, reviser, revision
tr.	translator, translated by
UBS	United Bible Societies
v., vv.	verse(s)
viz.	*videlicet,* namely
vol.	volume

Periodicals, Reference Works, and Serials

AER	*American Ecclesiastical Review*
AnBib	*Analecta biblica* (Rome)
ANRW	*Aufstieg und Niedergang der römischen Welt* (Berlin)
ASNU	*Acta seminarii neotestamentici upsaliensis* (Uppsala)
AsSeign	*Assemblée du Seigneur* (Bruges)

ATANT	*Abhandlungen zur Theologie des Alten und Neuen Testaments* (Zürich)
AThR	*Anglican Theological Review* (Evanston, IL)
BETS	*Bulletin of the Evangelical Theological Society*; name changed to *JETS* (see below)
BHTh	*Beiträge zur historischen Theologie* (Tübingen)
BhZNW	*Beihefte zur ZNW*
Bib	*Biblica* (Rome)
BibLeb	*Bibel und Leben* (Düsseldorf)
BSac	*Bibliotheca Sacra* (NY, London, Andover; now Dallas)
BiTod	*Bible Today* (Collegeville, MN)
BJRL	*Bulletin of the John Rylands Library* (Manchester, UK)
BLit	*Bibel und Liturgie* (Klosterneuburg)
BT	*The Bible Translator* (London)
BTB	*Biblical Theology Bulletin* (Rome; Jamaica, NY)
BVC	*Bible et vie Crétienne* (Paris; Bruges)
BWANT	*Beiträge zur Wissenschaft vom Alten und Neuen Testament* (Lepizig; Stuttgart)
BZ	*Biblische Zeitschrift* (Frieburg; Paderborn)
CBQ	*Catholic Biblical Quarterly* (Washington, DC)
CSEL	*Corpus scriptorum ecclesiasticorum Latinorum*
CTh	*Cahiers théologiques* (Neuchâtel)
CTM/Q	*Concordia Theological Monthly/Quarterly* (St. Louis, MO; Fort Wayne, IN)
CulB	*Cultura biblica* (Madrid, Segovia)
CurTM	*Currents in Theology and Mission* (Chicago)
DB (Supp.)	*Dictionnaire de la Bible*, 5 vols, ed. L. Vigouroux; *DB Supplément* ed. L. Pirot et al. Paris: Letouzey et Ané, 1928-.
EcuR	*Ecumenical Review* (Geneva)
ErJb	*Eranos Jahrbuch*
EstBi	*Estudios bíblicos* (Madrid)
ETR	*Études théologique et religieuse* (Montpelliar)
EV	*Esprit et Vie* (Langres)
EvJ	*Evangelical Journal* (Myerstown, PA)
EvQ	*Evangelical Quarterly* (Exeter, UK)
EvRT	*Evangelical Review of Theology*
EvT	*Evangelische Theologie* (Munich)

Exp	*The Expositor* (London)
ExpT	*Expository Times* (Edinburgh; Banstead, Surrey, UK)
FRLANT	*Forschungen zur Religion und Literatur des Alten und Neuen Testaments* (Göttingen)
GeistL	*Geist und Leben* (Würzburg; Munich)
Greg	*Gregorianum* (Rome)
GTJ	*Grace Theological Journal* (Winona Lake, IN)
HNT	*Handbuch zum Neuen Testament* (Tübingen: Mohr-Siebeck)
HPR	*Homiletic and Pastoral Review* (New York)
HTR	*Harvard Theological Review* (Cambridge, MA)
HTS	*Hervormde Teologiese Studies* (Pretoria)
IDB (Supp.)	*Interpreter's Dictionary of the Bible*, 4 vols., ed. G. A. Buttrick (Nashville: Abingdon, 1962) and *Supplementary Volume*, ed. K. Crim (Nashville: Abingdon, 1976)
Int	*Interpretation* (Richmond, VA)
JAC	*Jahrbuch für Antike und Christentum* (Munich)
JBL	*Journal of Biblical Literature* (Atlanta, GA)
JETS	*Journal of the Evangelical Theological Society* (Jackson, MS)
JQR	*Jewish Quarterly Review* (Winona Lake, IN)
JSNT	*Journal for the Study of the New Testament* (Sheffield, UK)
JSOT	*Journal for the Study of the Old Testament* (Sheffield, UK)
JTS	*Journal of Theological Studies* (Oxford; London, UK)
KEKNT	*Kritisch-exegetischer Kommentar über das Neue Testament*
KJV	King James Version of the Bible, 1611
LJ	*Liturgisches Jahrbuch* (Munich)
LXX	Septuagint
LumVie	*Lumière et Vie* (Saint-Albert-Leysse, Savoie)
MethQR	*Methodist Quarterly Review*
NEB	New English Bible (Cambridge/Oxford, et al.)
Neot	*Neotestamentica* (Pretoria, SA)
NIDNTT	*New International Dictionary of New Testament Theology* (Grand Rapids: Zondervan; Exeter: Paternoster)

NIV	New International Version (International Bible Society; Zondervan)
NovT	*Novum Testamentum* (Leiden)
NovT Supp.	*Supplements to Novum Testamentum* (Leiden: Brill)
NRT	*Nouvelle revue théologique* (Tournai; Louvain)
NTS	*New Testament Studies* (Cambridge, UK)
PaCl	*Palestra del clero* (Rovigo)
PG	*Patrologia Graeca (Patrologiae Cursus Completus: Series Graeca,* ed. Jacques-Paul Migne, 162 vols. Paris: Migne, 1857-66.)
PL	*Patrologia Latina (Patrologiae Cursus Completus: Series Latina,* ed. Jacques-Paul Migne, 221 vols. Paris: Migne, 1844-64. Supplement ed. A. Hamman, 3 Paris: Garnier Frères, 1958-66.)
RAC	*Reallexikon für Antike und Christentum* (Stuttgart)
RB	*Revue Biblique* (Paris; Jerusalem)
RCB	*Revista de cultura Bíblica* (São Paulo, Brazil)
RCR	*Revue des communautés religieuses*
RE	*Review and Expositor* (Lousiville, KY)
REA	*Revue des études Augustinniennes* (Paris)
RechBib	*Recherches bibliques*
RestQ	*Restoration Quarterly* (Abiline, TX)
RevRef	*Revue réformée* (Saint-Germain-en-Laye)
RGG	*Die Religion in Geschichte und Gegenwart* (Tübingen: Mohr, 1909-13 [1st ed., 5 vols.; 1927-32, 2d ed., 5 vols.; 1957-65, 3d ed., 7 vols.)
RHPR	*Revue d'histoire et de philosophie religieuses* (Strasbourg; Lausanne)
RHR	*Revue de l'histoire des religions* (Paris)
RivB	*Rivista Biblica Italiana* (Rome)
RQum	*Revue de Qumran* (Paris)
RSPT	*Revue des sciences philosophiques et théologiques* (Paris)
(N)RSV	(New) Revised Standard Version (New York: National Council of Churches)
RThR	*Reformed Theological Review* (Hawthorn, Victoria)
SBT	*Studies in Biblical Theology* (London: SCM)
ScEs	*Science et esprit*
SCR	*Scripture* (London)

ScuolC	*Scuola Cattolica* (Milan)
SJT	*Scottish Journal of Theology* (Edinburgh)
SNTSMS	*Society for New Testament Studies Monograph Series* (Cambridge, UK)
SPAW	*Sitzungsberichte der preussischen Akademie der Wissenschaften*
StEv	*Studia Evangelica* (Berlin)
StPa	*Studia Patavina* (Padua)
StTh	*Studia theologica* (Lund, Sweden)
SUNT	*Studien zur Umwelt des Neuen Testaments* (Göttingen)
SvTk	*Svensk Teologisk Kvartalskrift* (Lund)
SWJT	*Southwestern Journal of Theology* (Fort Worth, TX)
TB	*Theologische Beiträge* (Wuppertal)
TDig	*Theology Digest* (St. Louis, MO)
TDNT	*Theological Dictionary of the New Testament* (Grand Rapids: Eerdmans)
ThT	*Theology Today* (Princeton, NJ)
TLZ	*Theologische Literaturzeitung* (Leipzig)
TRev	*Theologische Revue* (Munich)
TrinJ	*Trinity Journal* (Deerfield, IL)
TS	*Theological Studies* (Washington, DC; New York)
TSK	*Theologische Studien und Kritiken* (Hamburg)
TTZ	*Trierer theologische Zeitschrift* (Trier)
TU	*Texte und Untersuchungen* (Berlin)
TynB	*Tyndale Bulletin* (Cambridge, UK)
TZ	*Theologische Zeitschrift* (Vienna; Basel)
UUÅ	*Uppsala Universitetsårsskrift* (Uppsala)
VD	*Verbum Domini* (Rome)
VigChr	*Vigiliae Christianae* (Amsterdam; Leiden)
Wor	*Worship* (Collegeville, MN)
WTJ	*Westminster Theological Journal* (Philadelphia)
WUNT	*Wissenschaftliche Untersuchungen zum NT* (Tübingen)
ZEE	*Zeitschrift für evangelische Ethik* (Gütersloh)
ZKT	*Zeitschrift für katholische Theologie* (Innsbruck)
ZNW	*Zeitschrift für die Neutestamentliche Wissenschaft und die Kunde der alteren Kirche* (Berlin; Hawthorne, NJ)
ZRG	*Zeitschrift für Religions- und Geistesgeschichte* (Erlangen)
ZTK	*Zeitschrift für Theologie und Kirche* (Tübingen)

Books of the Bible

Old Testament			New Testament	
Gen	2 Chr	Dan	Mt	1 Tim
Exod	Ezra	Hos	Mk	2 Tim
Lev	Neh	Joel	Lk	Titus
Num	Esth	Amos	Jn	Phlm
Deut	Job	Obad	Acts	Heb
Josh	Psa (Pss)	Jonah	Rom	Jas
Judg	Prov	Mic	1 Cor	1 Pet
Ruth	Eccl	Nah	2 Cor	2 Pet
1 Sam	Song	Hab	Gal	1 Jn
2 Sam	Isa	Zeph	Eph	2 Jn
1 Kgs	Jer	Hag	Phil	3 Jn
2 Kgs	Lam	Zech	Col	Jude
1 Chr	Ezek	Mal	1 Thes	Rev
			2 Thes	

THE BOOK OF EPHESIANS

Chapter 1

INTRODUCTORY ISSUES

1. Alexander, N. "The Epistle for Today," in *Biblical Studies.* FS W. Barclay, ed. J. R. McKay and J. Miller. Philadelphia: Westminster, 1976, 99-118.

   After discussing the relevance of NT epistles for people today, and after evaluating each epistle in turn as possible candidates, Alexander settles upon Ephesians as the one NT epistle most relevant and needed for people today. It stimulates the ongoing ecumenical movement and brings disparate people together in Christ.

2. Barker, G. W., Lane, W. L., and Michaels, J. R. *The New Testament Speaks.* New York: Harper and Row, 1969.

   This well-informed and argued volume presents the case for a conservative assessment of the letter, defending the Pauline authorship of both Colossians and Ephesians.

3. Barrett, C. K. Paul. *An Introduction to His Thought.* Louisville, KY: Westminster/John Knox, 1994.

A simplified introduction to Paul's career, the controversies that surrounded his apostolic ministry, the essentials of his theology (and those of the Deutero-Paulines, including Ephesians). Though he does not come right out and say so, Barrett comes very close to finding that the letter is so thoroughly Pauline, perhaps Paul was indeed the author. The book concludes with a short section on the significance of Paul's theology for today.

4. Barry F. R. *St. Paul and Social Psychology. An Introduction to the Epistle to the Ephesians.* Oxford and New York: Oxford Univ. Press, 1923.

5. Baulès R. *L'Insondable Richesse Du Christ.* Paris: Cerf, 1971.

Following a brief defense of Pauline authorship and other introductory issues, the author offers a detailed plan of the entire letter. Succeeding chapters analyze key themes in the epistle such as: God the Father, Christ as Lord not only of the church but the entire universe, salvation as a reality to be communicated to others, and the mystery of God revealed in the Gospel.

6. Beker, J. C. *Heirs of Paul: Paul's Legacy in the New Testament and in the Church Today.* Philadelphia: Fortress, 1991.

The author evaluates Paul's influence and legacy as they developed in the "Deutero-Pauline" literature, among which Ephesians occurs. The Pauline tradition was adapted by these later writers—a process that must go on today as well. Beker believes that Col and Eph are much more indebted to Paul's letters than to Pauline legend. Yet the adaptation of the Pauline tradition in Eph demonstrates that it grows out of a period much later than that of the historical Paul.

7. Best, E. *Ephesians.* Sheffield, UK: Sheffield Academic Press, 1993.

A brief study that examines introductory issues, surveys the content of the letter, and focuses attention on its theology, especially its application to church and Christian living.

8. Bowen, C. R. "The Place of Ephesians Among the Letters of Paul." *AThR* 15 (1933) 279-299.

9. Bowman, J. W. "The Epistle to the Ephesians." *Int* 8 (1954) 188-205.

The author expounds the content and themes in this expansive epistle prior to taking up the introductory issues briefly. He finds it to be a round-robin letter genuinely from Paul's pen, though with no immediate situation in view.

10. Bruce, F. F. "St. Paul in Rome. 4. The Epistle to the Ephesians." *BJRL* 49 (1966-67) 303-22.

Without getting into such issues as the book's authorship, Bruce attempts to show that Eph sums up the leading themes of Paul's epistles and the central motive of Paul's ministry among the Gentiles. In short, it stands as "The Quintessence of Paulinism."

11. _____. *Paul: Apostle of the Heart Set Free.* Grand Rapids: Eerdmans, 1977.

In this excellent "life of Paul," the author defends the Pauline character of Ephesians, locating its origin during Paul's imprisonment in Rome.

12. Cantinat, J. "Épître aux Éphésiens." In *Les Épîtres de Saint Paul Expliqueés.* Paris: Gabalda, 1960, 167-179.

Short study providing a review of introductory issues followed by brief summaries of each section of the epistle.

13. Carson, D. A., Moo, D. J., and Morris, L. *An Introduction to the New Testament.* Grand Rapids: Zondervan, 1992.

First-rate evangelical study adopting conservative conclusions on introductory issues, including the traditional view on the origin of Ephesians.

14. Cash, W. W. *Helps to the Study of Ephesians.* London: Church
     Missionary Society, 1936.

15. Casper, J. "Paulus grüsst seine erste Gemeinde in Europa." *BiLit* 14
     (1939-40) 46-51.

16. Childs, B. S. *The New Testament as Canon: An Introduction.*
     London: SCM, 1984; Philadelphia: Fortress, 1985.

     The author rehearses the major critical issues surrounding the letter
     but refuses to allow such unresolved debates to detract from the
     canonical function of the letter. To decide the book's importance on
     the basis of its relation to the historical Paul, if at all—as many
     critical scholars do—subverts the purpose of the canon, according to
     Childs. He says, "The function of the canon is to establish the shape
     of the vehicle through which the true Pauline witness to the gospel
     is made" (323). He goes on, "The central problem lies in evaluating
     the role and the validity of this extended witness of the apostle Paul
     which the canonical process has received, nourished, and shaped"
     (327-28).

17. Collins, R. F. *Introduction to the New Testament.* London: SCM;
     Garden City, NY: Doubleday, 1983.

     Readable and comprehensive Catholic introduction to the formation
     of the NT and the critical methods used to understand it. In the
     process Collins denies Pauline authorship to Ephesians.

18. _____. *Letters that Paul Did Not Write: The Epistle to the
     Hebrews and the Pauline Pseudepigrapha.* Good News
     Studies 28. Wilmington, DE: Michael Glazier, 1988.

     Not a critical introduction to these books, this work seeks the
     message to the NT epistles not coming directly from Paul's pen.
     Ephesians lies among the Pauline pseudepigrapha.

19. Conybeare, W. J. and Howson, J. S. *The Life and Epistles of St.
     Paul.* Grand Rapids: Eerdmans, repr. 1976.

A classic "life of Paul" that opts for the traditional position of Pauline authorship of Ephesians.

20. Cotter, A. C. "The Epistles of the Captivity." *CBQ* 11 (1949) 370-380.

After discarding H. Wedell's suggestion that instances of prison language in Phil, Phlm, Col, and Eph are merely metaphorical, attempts to establish the provenance of the "captivity epistles." Rejects Caesarea (G. Paulus) and Ephesus (A. Deissmann) in favor of Rome (traditional view). Concludes with certainty that Col, Phlm, and Eph were written during the same captivity, and that Phil was composed during Paul's first Roman captivity. Concludes that it is highly probable that all four were written during the same imprisonment.

21. Dacquino, P. "I destinatari della lettera agli Efesini." *RivB* 6 (1958) 102-10.

Attempts to catalogue the positive elements from the various theories for the destination for the letter, and then to attempt to reconcile them. Concludes that the letter was found preserved at the church of Ephesus, the mother church of the Christian communities of Asia. It was a doctrinal treatise written to circulate among these various churches threatened by the doctrines countered in Colossians.

22. _____. "Interpretatio Epistolae ad Eph. in luce finis intenti." *VD* 36 (1958) 338-49.

Pursues the purpose of the author of Ephesians concluding that he wrote to reassert Christ's unique function and dignity in the life of the church which he redeemed against the backdrop of views promoting the importance of angels as mediators.

23. Dahl, N. A. "Ephesians, Letter to the." *IDB Supp.* (1976) 268-69.

Adopts the theory that Col and later Eph were written by members of a `Pauline' school that continued to flourish after Paul's death, perhaps in Ephesus. Eph represents a type of Greek letter that substituted for a public speech rather than for private conversation. The epistolary style established contact between sender and recipients.

24. _____. "Interpreting Ephesians: then and now." *TDig* 25 (1977) 305-15.

Dahl traces two of the various trajectories of interpreting Ephesians from ancient times to modern: one along the lines of Gnosticism and the other as an example of early Catholicism. In either case, one is constrained to reject Pauline authorship.

25. Dominy, B. B., ed. *SWJT* 22 (1979) 4-73.

Four articles on Ephesians occur in this issue including: an introduction to Ephesians, F. D. Howard; the theology of Ephesians, B. Corley; ethics in Ephesians, N. L. Baker; and preaching from Ephesians, D. B. Harbuck.

26. Danker, F. W. "Ephesians, Epistle to the." *ISBE* 2 (1982) 109-14.

Concise article on the essential issues of introduction. Senses the weight of the arguments against authenticity and urges consideration of alternate explanations for the production of the letter. In the end he opts for Pauline authorship.

27. DuBose, H. M. "The Epistle to the Ephesians." *MethQR* 66/2 (1917) 241-47.

28. Duncan, G. S. "The Epistles of the Imprisonment in Recent Discussion." *ExpT* 46 (1934-35) 293-298.

Explains the position developed more fully in his St. Paul's Ephesian Ministry where contending that the so-called prison epistles derive from Paul's imprisonment in Ephesus, not Rome. Here Duncan abandons a minor point he made in the book, that Rom 16 was originally addressed to Ephesus. Rather, Rom 16 indicates that some friends formerly from Ephesus now reside in Rome.

29. Easton, B. S. "Dr. Goodspeed's Work on Ephesians." *AThR* 16 (1934) 27-31.

30. Fischer, K. M. *Tendenz und Absicht des Epheserbriefs.* Göttingen: Vandenhoeck & Ruprecht, 1973.

31. Fitzmyer, J. A. *According to Paul. Studies in the Theology of the Apostle.* Rahway, NJ: Paulist, 1993.

Enlightening series of studies on Paul's spiritual journey, his Jewish background in relationship to the Law, his career correlated to the Acts chronology, "*Abba* and Jesus' Relation to God," Paul and preaching, plus studies of three interesting Pauline texts.

32. Freed, E. D. *The New Testament. A Critical Introduction.* Belmont, CA: Wadsworth, 1986.

Includes his discussion of Ephesians among the disputed books along with Colossians and 2 Thessalonians. He takes a neutral position, in fact leaving the issue of authorship undecided due to the balance of the evidence arguing that this may be the most responsible position.

33. Fuller, R. H. *A Critical Introduction to the New Testament.* London: Duckworth, 1966.

34. Goguel, M. "Esquisse d'une solution nouvelle du probleme de l'épître aux Ephesiens." *RHR* 111 (1935) 254-84; 112 (1935) 73-99.

35. Gundry, R. H. *A Survey of the New Testament.* 3d. ed. Grand Rapids: Zondervan, 1994.

Adopts a conservative position on authorship placing Ephesians among the Pauline prison epistles. It was a circular epistle addressed to various churches in Asia Minor surrounding Ephesus.

36. Guthrie, D. *New Testament Introduction.* 4th rev. ed. Leicester and Downers Grove: Inter-Varsity, 1990.

Comprehensive British evangelical introduction that provides the

most copious modern defense of the traditional Pauline authorship
position.

37. Harrison, E. F. *Introduction to the New Testament*. Revised ed.
     Grand Rapids: Eerdmans, 1971.

Taking on the various objections to authenticity posed by Nineham,
Baur, Moffatt, Percy, Mitton, and Goodspeed, the author defends
Pauline authorship.

38. Hort, F. J. A. *Prolegomena to St. Paul's Epistle to the Romans and
     the Ephesians*. London and New York: Macmillan, 1895.

In the author's university lectures presenting the various introductory
surrounding Ephesians, he affirms traditional views including the
Pauline authorship. An old classic to be sure.

39. Johnson, L. T. *The Writings of the New Testament*. Philadelphia:
     Fortress; London: SCM, 1986.

Though confessing the difficulty of the issues, the author concludes
that the special circumstances eliciting the letter could well account
for its divergence from what we have come to expect from Paul. It
may well come from within Paul's circle of associates or followers,
if not directly from his own pen.

40. Johnston, G. "Ephesians." *IDB*. Nashville: Abingdon, 1962. II:
     108-114.

41. Keck, L. E. *Paul and His Letters*. 2d ed. Philadelphia: Fortress,
     1988.

In discussing the problem of Paul in the NT, the author locates
Ephesians in the nongenuine category.

42. Keck, L. E., and Furnish, V. P. *The Pauline Letters*. Nashville:
     Abingdon, 1984.

Popular introduction to Paul's epistles that locates Ephesians in the

Deutero-Pauline category.

43. Knox, W. L. "The Ephesian Continuator," in *St. Paul and the Church of the Gentiles.* Cambridge: Cambridge University Press, 1961, 182-203.

    Knox considers a number of factors that lead him to conclude that the Pauline origin of Eph is impossible, though this does not diminish the value of the letter. Borrowing Paul's name gave Ephesians the requisite sanction in the early church. Knox proceeds to show how Pauline thought was drawn out and applied to the changing needs of the church in later decades following Paul's life.

44. Koester, H. *Introduction to the New Testament*, 2 vols. Philadelphia: Fortress, 1982.

    Locates Ephesians in the section entitled "The Transformation of Pauline Theology." He views the Pauline authorship of Ephesians as "completely impossible," though it borrows extensively from genuine Pauline letters. Not a true letter, Ephesians represents a laborious and ornate elaboration of Paul's theology in a later period.

45. Kümmel, W. G. *Introduction to the New Testament.* Rev. ed. Trans. H. C. Kee. Nashville: Abingdon, 1975.

    The author of this standard, moderate German introduction denies any possibility that Paul could be the author. Rejects theory that the letter was originally destined for Laodicea (see Col 4:16).

46. Longenecker, R. N. "On the Form, Function, and Authority of the New Testament Letters," in *Scripture and Truth,* ed. D. A. Carson and J. D. Woodbridge. Grand Rapids: Zondervan, 1983, 101-114.

    Discusses the various types of letters in the ancient world including pastoral and tractate letters, plus such issues as amanuenses and anonymity and pseudonymity. Longenecker considers Ephesians to be a tractate letter (with Romans, Hebrews, James, 1 Peter, and 1 John).

47. Martin, R. P.   "Epistle in Search of a Life-Setting."   *ExpT* 79
     (1967-68) 296-302.

     Suggests that Luke published Ephesians under Paul's aegis, either
     during his final imprisonment or soon after his death. Ephesians
     constitutes, then, a compendium of Paul's teaching and liturgical
     elements designed to show the nature of the church and the life in
     Christ.

48. _____. *New Testament Foundations.* Vol. 2.   Grand Rapids:
     Eerdmans and Exeter: Paternoster, 1978, 223-40.

     In this introduction the author restates the thesis developed in the
     previous article.

49. Marxsen, W. *Introduction to the New Testament.* Tr. G. Buswell.
     Philadelphia: Fortress, 1968.

     Discusses the various introductory issues concerning Eph including
     the sources behind Eph and its `setting in life.' The author wished
     to stand in the Pauline tradition and adopted, developed further, and
     interpreted many of Paul's ideas in pursuing his task. Questions
     whether Ephesians should even be classified as a letter.

50. McCall, D. K., ed. "Ephesians." *RE* 76 (1979) 463-567.

     This issue contains the following articles: "Introduction to
     Ephesians," by J. B. Polhill; "A study outline of Ephesians," by J.
     B. Polhill; "To the praise of his glory: Ephesians 1," by N. H.
     Keathley; "The grace of God and the life of the church: Ephesians
     2," by P. D. Simmons; "The church's great ministry: Ephesians 3,"
     by J. L. Blevins; "A life worthy of the calling: Ephesians 4:1-24,"
     by D. E. Garland; "Ethical dualism and church discipline: Ephesians
     4:25-5:20," by R. A. Culpepper; "The domestic code and final
     appeal: Ephesians 5:21-6:24," by F. Stagg; "Ephesians — a
     manifesto for the mission of the church," by H. H. Culpepper; and
     "Preaching from Ephesians," by W. P. Tucke.

51. Moffatt, J. *An Introduction to the Literature of the New Testament.*

3rd ed. Edinburgh: T. & T. Clark; New York: Scribner's, 1918.

Includes Ephesians among the homilies and pastoral letters in the NT. Moffatt favors the authenticity of Col and the "sub-Pauline origin of Ephesians" (375). Most likely, employing a copy of Col, a follower of Paul composed this homily (Eph) in Paul's name just as Luke composed the Pauline speeches in Acts. It represented what Paul would have said in a current situation.

52. Morton, A. Q. et al. *A Critical Concordance to the Letter of Paul to the Ephesians.* Wooster, Ohio: Biblical Research Assoc., 1980.

Part of the Computer Bible project, this work is set up to deal with critical problems concerning matters of language, text, morphology, grammar, and syntax. It supplies forward and reverse indexes giving word counts, word frequencies and frequency profiles, and forward and reverse key words in context concordances.

53. Parker, J. *The Epistle to the Ephesians.* London: Hodder and Stoughton; New York: George Doran, nd.

Various popular expositions on features the author finds in Ephesians.

54. Perrin, N., and Duling, D. C. *The New Testament: An Introduction.* 2nd ed. New York: Harcourt, Brace Jovanovich, 1982.

Finds the difficulties in maintaining Pauline authorship to be insurmountable. This work finds the "cover letter" theory of Goodspeed and Mitton to make sense.

55. Puskas, Jr. C. B. *The Letters of Paul.* Collegeville, MN: M. Glazier, 1993.

Following a discussion of the genre of ancient letters and a chronology of Paul's life, the author evaluates the background and contents of Paul's letters in chronological order. Puskas' analysis includes all the alleged Pauline letters, including Ephesians, the pastoral letters, and Hebrews. He favors a post-Pauline origin of Ephesians due to its: well-developed themes, dependency on Colossians, and distinctive vocabulary. Puskas provides a fascinating comparative study of Ephesians including in tables comparisons to many of the other Pauline letters plus Luke-Acts, 1 Peter, Qumran literature, and Gnostic writings. He opines that the liturgical and hortatory features in Ephesians may suggest it was a baptismal homily adapted for general circulation.

56. Ridouard, A. and Gourbillon, J. G. "Rendons grâce au Seigneur: Pour la louange de sa gloire. La lettre aux Ephesiens." *Cahiers Évangiles* 30 (1958) 34-40.

57. Robert, A. and Feuillet, A., ed. *Introduction to the New Testament,* trans. P. W. Skeham et al. New York: Desclée, 1965. ET of Vol. 2 of *Introduction à la Bible,* 2 vols. Paris: Desclée et Cie, 1957-59.

L. Cerfaux wrote the section on Eph, evaluating both the hypotheses of authenticity and non-authenticity. After considering the merits of various alternatives he opts for authenticity. He concludes that "Eph is the swan song of Paul the theologian" (509).

58. Roetzel, C. J. *The Letters of Paul.* 3d ed. Philadelphia: Westminster, 1991.

Readable introduction to many issues surrounding the writing of Paul's epistles, the book rejects that Ephesians could come from Paul himself.

59. Rowston, D. J. "Changes in Biblical Interpretation Today: the Example of Ephesians." *BTB* 9 (1979) 121-25.

Evangelical scholar R. P. Martin's view of the Lukan authorship of Eph provides a case study indicating, Rowston hopes, the end of theological labeling based on one's view vis-a-vis "traditional authorship of a New Testament document." Helpfully traces the background of Martin's position that Luke is the amanuensis of Eph—composed during Paul's Roman imprisonment, in relation to the hypotheses of Goodspeed and Mitton and the work of P. R. Jones.

60. Sampley, J. P. and Francis, F. O. *Pauline Parallels.* Rev. ed. Philadelphia: Fortress, 1984.

This study tool consists of a sequential presentation of the ten chief letters attributed to Paul (includes Eph but not the pastorals). Arranged in canonical order the book presents sense units for each letter indicating where they have parallels in the other letters.

61. Schenke, H.-M., and Fischer, K. M. *Einleitung in die Schriften des Neuen Testaments,* 2 vols. Gütersloh: Gerd Mohn, 1978.

62. Smith, D. *The Life and Letters of St. Paul.* New York and London: Harper, n.d.

In this massive tome the author presents a chronology of Paul's life, inserting along the way the letters in their appropriate places. He believes Paul wrote Ephesians as an encyclical to the churches of Asia, probably in the beginning of A.D. 62.

63. Stockhausen, C. K. *Letters in the Pauline Tradition: Ephesians, Colossians, 1 Timothy, 2 Timothy, and Titus.* Wilmington, DE: M. Glazier, 1989.

64. Thiessen, H. C. *Introduction to the New Testament.* Grand Rapids: Eerdmans, 1943.

Conservative scholar defends Pauline authorship on both external and internal grounds. Thiessen supports the view that Ephesians was an encyclical to the churches of Asia consisting chiefly of Gentiles while including some Jews. He provides a brief response to Goodspeed.

65. Tyson, J. B. *The New Testament and Early Christianity.* New York: Macmillan; London: Collier Macmillan, 1984.

The author was a disciple of Paul who wrote Ephesians to introduce the entire collection of Paul's letters (Goodspeed's thesis). Ephesians stands within the Pauline tradition, but it expresses a further development of that tradition.

66. Wikenhauser, A. *New Testament Introduction.* Tr. J. Cunningham. New York: Herder & Herder, 1958.

Originally in German this work assesses the various introductory issues concerning Eph. Considering the various arguments against the letter's authenticity, Wikenhauser concludes that the most natural and best founded theory affirms Paul as the author both Col and Eph. Yet we can't rule out the possibility that Paul commissioned a disciple to write Eph.

67. Ziesler, J. A. *Pauline Christianity.*   Oxford: Oxford University Press, 1990.

This represents a succinct guide to various issues relating to Paul's letters. The author relegates Ephesians to the position of Deutero-Pauline.

Chapter 2

COMMENTARIES

68. Abbott, T. K. *A Critical and Exegetical Commentary on the Epistles to the Ephesians and to Colossians,* International Critical Commentaries. Edinburgh: T. & T. Clark 1897; 5th ed., 1946.

Argues that the apostle Paul wrote Ephesians, an encyclical letter, while in prison in Rome and that differences between the letter and other Paulines have been exaggerated. The work follows the standard format of the ICC volumes. Abbott includes a listing of commentaries on Ephesians going back to the sixteenth century.

69. Allan, J. A. *The Epistle to the Ephesians.* Torch Bible Commentaries. London: SCM, 1959.

Short study that presents in brief scope the important introductory issues (rejects Pauline authorship based on Mitton's arguments) and brief comments on the letter's verses. The study includes seven essays on important topics.

70. Baker, C. F. *Understanding the Body of Christ: A Pauline Trilogy.* Grand Rapids: Grace Bible College, 1985.

71.   Barclay, W. *The Letters to the Galatians and Ephesians.* The Daily
       Study Bible. Philadelphia: Westminster, 1958.

       A devotional, practical walk through these letters following brief
       introductions.   Barclay adopts traditional views of the origin of
       Ephesians.

72.   Barnes, A. *Notes on the New Testament, Ephesians, Philippians and
       Colossians.* Reprint. Grand Rapids: Baker, 1950.

       Written in a day when Barnes could write, "It has never been denied
       that the apostle Paul was the author of this epistle" (viii).   Many
       devotional thoughts occur in this pre-critical study.

73.   Barry, A. "Ephesians" in *A Bible Commentary for English Readers,*
       Vol. 8, "Ephesians to Revelation," ed. C. J. Ellicott.   London:
       Cassell, 1896, 9-60.

       Defends the traditional positions on the letter.

74.   _____. *A Philosophy from Prison: A Study of the Epistle to the
       Ephesians.* London: SCM, 1926.

75.   Barth, M. *Ephesians.* Anchor Bible. 2 vols. New York: Doubleday,
       1974, 1986.

       Masterful and thorough analysis of the letter, section by section.
       Provides a thorough discussion of the authorship issue concluding
       that the traditional view that attributes it to Paul is still better than
       the alternatives.   After his exegesis of each section, the author
       provides numerous "comments" that pursue key issues in more depth.
       Certainly one of the best treatments of the letter.

76.   Beare, F. W.   "The Epistle to the Ephesians,"   *The Interpreter's
       Bible,* Vol. 10.   Nashville: Abingdon, 1953, 597-749.

       Rejects Pauline authorship; very useful comments within the confines
       of the IB.

77. Beet, J. A. *A Commentary on St. Paul's Epistles to the Ephesians, Philippians, and Colossians.* 3d ed. London: Hodder & Stoughton, 1902.

78. Bengel, J. A. "Ephesians." *Gnomon of the New Testament,* Vol. 4, 1773; trans. J. Bryce. Edinburgh: T. & T. Clark, 1863, 61-118.

    Provides comments on the Greek text of the epistle.

79. Benoit, P. *Les Épîtres de Saint Paul aux Philippiens, a Philemon, aux Colossiens, aux Éphésiens.* Paris: du Cerf, 1959.

80. Billerbeck, P. and Strack, H. L. *Kommentar zum NT aus Talmud und Midrasch.* 5 volumes. Munich: Beck'sche, 1926, III: 579-618.

    Follows the standard S-B approach of attempting to shed light on the text from Jewish backgrounds. Requires ability to read German.

81. Blackwood, A. W. *The Epistles to the Galatians and Ephesians.* Grand Rapids: Baker, 1962.

    Seeks to provide homiletical comments and ideas for the busy pastor. For each text the author provides the historical setting, the expository meaning, the doctrinal value, the practical aim, and a homiletical form.

82. Boice, J. M. *Ephesians: An Expositional Commentary.* Grand Rapids: Ministry Research Library, 1988.

    Homiletical style commentary.

83. Bouttier, M. *L'Épître de saint Paul aux Éphésiens.* Commentaire du Nouveau Testament, deuxieme serie 9b. Genève: Labor et Fides, 1991.

    Following a discussion of various introductory issues, he presents, section by section, his own French translation, analyses, exposition, notes, and bibliography. Believes the author attempted to interpret Paul and so evidences both Pauline evidences and deviations from Paul. Assumes that the author had Colossians before him as he wrote. Doubts that one element from the cultural milieu can explain the total background to the letter; instead different elements influence the writer at various points. The book concludes with several essays on important themes of the letter.

84. Bratcher, R. G. and Nida, E. A. *A Translator's Handbook on Paul's Letter to the Ephesians.* Help for Translators. London: New York and Stuttgart, United Bible Societies, 1982.

Using the Today's English Version and RSV as bases, the authors explain how each verse functions and help translators render the sense into whatever target language with which they are working.

85. Braune, K. "The Epistle of Paul to the Ephesians," in *A Commentary on the Holy Scriptures,* ed. J. P. Lange. New York: Scribner's, 1870, 1887.

Includes a discussion of both introductory issues and a detailed analysis of the Greek text of Ephesians. Defends traditional positions on the origin of the letter.

86. Bristow, B. B. *Commentary on Ephesians.* Abilene, TX: Quality Publications, 1987.

Very short study.

87. Brooks, N. *Ephesians: Outlined and Unfolded.* Franklin Springs, GA: Advocate Press, 1984.

Originally appeared as a series of lessons in *The Pentecostal Holiness Advocate.*

88. Bruce, F. F. *The Epistle to the Ephesians.* London: Pickering and Inglis, 1961.

Brief, fairly popular approach, expanded considerably in his NICNT volume (see next entry). Adopts a traditional approach.

89. _____. *The Epistles to the Colossians, to Philemon, and to the Ephesians.* In The New International Commentary on the New Testament. Rev. ed. Grand Rapids: Eerdmans, 1984.

Fine medium-level approach that interacts with most issues in the body of the text while comments on the Greek text are relegated to footnotes. Very serviceable, though it lacks the detail found in other commentaries. Takes a conservative view of authorship and most other points.

90. Cable, J. H. *The Fullness of God. An Exposition of Ephesians from the Greek.* Chicago: Moody, 1945.

Popular presentation of the message of Ephesians with references to the Greek text.

91. Caird, G. B. *Paul's Letters from Prison.* Oxford: Oxford University Press, 1976.

Considers the case for the various options for the prison from which the letters derive, concluding that the Roman option remains the best. Likewise, Caird considers the traditional position assigning the authorship of Ephesians to Paul still the best alternative. The commentary itself contains a surprising amount of detail within the confines of this short volume. Helpful analyses.

92. Campbell, E. R. *Ephesians.* Silverton, OR: Canyonview, 1986.

A verse by verse commentary based on the Greek text. Includes the biblical text in English.

93. Cambier, J. *Vie chrétienne en Église. L'Épître aux Éphésiens lue aux chrétiens d'aujourd'hui.* Tournai: Desclée et Cie, 1966.

94. Chadwick, H. "Ephesians," *Peake's Commentary on the Bible,* ed. M. Black and H. H. Rowley. London: Van Nostrand Reinhold; Nashville: Nelson, 1962, 980-84.

Chadwick considers the question of authorship at the same time one of the least important questions about the epistle and one of the most fascinating and baffling. In the end, he considers the sides to be delicately balanced and, perhaps, leaning to authenticity. The one-volume approach allows only minor comments.

95. Chafer, L. S. *The Ephesian Letter.* Findlay, Ohio: Dunham, 1935; New York: Loizeaux, 1959.

Compilation of fifteen magazine articles on sections in the letter, some exegetical and others devotional.

96. Clark, G. H. *Ephesians.* Jefferson, MD: Trinity, 1985.

A devotional commentary on brief units of the text that explains key terms and ideas with a special focus on proper translation. Includes the author's own translation of Ephesians.

97. Collins, R. F. *Letters That Paul Did Not Write. The Epistle to the Hebrews and the Pauline Pseudepigrapha.* Good News Studies 28. Wilmington, DE: Glazier, 1988.

In the topical section on authorship, this work discusses the authorship issue of the letters whose Pauline authorship is widely disputed by scholars in decreasing order of certainty: Hebrews (least likely to come from Paul), the Pastorals, Ephesians, Colossians, and 2 Thess. Beyond authorship, he considers their content, historical setting, theology and the portrait of Paul each portrays.

98. Conzelmann, H. "Der Brief an die Epheser." In *Die Briefe an die Galater, Epheser, Philipper, Kolosser, Thessalonicher und Philemon,* ed. J. Becker, H. Conzelmann, and G. Friedrich. 14th ed. Göttingen: Vandenhoeck & Ruprecht, 1976, 86-124.

Standard German critical approach that rejects Pauline authorship. Only brief discussion of introductory issues and the text permitted within the confines of this commentary series.

99. Criswell, W. A. *Ephesians: an Exposition.* Grand Rapids:

Zondervan, 1974.

A compilation of thirty-six sermons on Ephesians edited for publication by the long-term pastor of First Baptist Church of Dallas.

100. Cundy, I. *Ephesians - 2 Thessalonians.* London: Ark, 1981.

Very short commentaries on these epistles of Paul.

101. Dahl, N. A. "Ephesians," *Harper's Bible Commentary,* ed. J. L. Mays. San Francisco: Harper and Row, 1988, 1212-19.

Assumes that an anonymous author, a personal disciple of Paul, possibly a Jew, wrote Ephesians in Paul's name to Christians in Asia Minor. They were in danger of fragmentation and of losing their Pauline heritage.

102. _____, et al. *Kurze Auslegung des Epheserbriefes.* Göttingen: Vandenhoeck & Ruprecht, 1965, 7-83.

103. Dale, R. W. *The Epistle to the Ephesians.* London: Hodder & Stoughton, 1901.

The author here presents in edited version what were originally lectures to a popular audience. He rejects a Calvinistic interpretation of Paul's election language in Eph 1.

104. Davies, J. L. *The Epistles of St. Paul to the Ephesians, the Colossians, and Philemon.* London: Macmillan, 1884.

105. Detzler, W. A. *Living Words in Ephesians.* Grand Rapids: Baker; Welwyn, UK: Evangelical, 1981.

Popular approach, homiletical and practical in focus.

106. Dibelius, M., and Greeven, H. *An die Kolosser, Epheser, an Philemon.* Tübingen: Mohr, 1973.

Rejects Pauline authorship.

107. Dunnam, M. D. *Galatians, Ephesians, Philippians, Colossians, Philemon,* vol. 8, *The Communicator's Commentary,* gen. ed. L. J. Ogilvie. Waco, TX: Word, 1983, 137-249.

Popular presentation of the message of these letters with applications and illustrations along the way.

108. Eadie, J. A. *A Commentary on the Greek Text of the Epistle of Paul to the Ephesians.* 3d ed. Edinburgh: T. & T. Clark 1883.

Learned exposition of the text from a thoroughly Reformed orientation.   Supports Pauline authorship, responding to the objections used against that position at the end of the last century. One of the last defenses that the letter was written to the church at Ephesus.   Thoroughly conversant with ancient sources and the contemporary literature of the day.

109. Ellicott, C. J. *St. Paul's Epistle to the Ephesians.* 5th ed. London: Longman, 1884.

With virtually no introduction, the author adopts Pauline authorship and writes a critical commentary on the Greek text of the epistle. Emphasizes words and parallels with little explanation of meaning or theology.

110. Erdman, C. R. *The Epistle of Paul to the Ephesians.* Philadelphia: Westminster, 1931.

In the scope of 130 pages, the author presents a popular exposition of the letter based on the supposition of Pauline authorship.

111. Ernst, J. *Die Briefe an die Philipper, an Philemon, an die Kolosser, an die Epheser.* Regensburg: F. Pustet, 1974.

Following ten pages of bibliography, this volume provides introductions and commentary on these four letters. For Ephesians, the author treats theology as a major component of the introduction. The language of Eph makes Pauline authorship unlikely. Provides a table comparing Col and Eph as to parallels and unique features, and discusses the reception of Eph and its addressees. The commentary section itself covers 144 pages, includes the German text of the epistle, plus five excurses on important topics. An excursus on "Haustafel" occurs in the commentary on Col.

112. Ewald, P. *Die Briefe des Paulus an die Epheser, Kolosser und Philemon.* 2d ed. Leipzig: Deichert, 1910.

113. Findlay, G. G. *The Epistle to the Ephesians.* 4th ed. New York: A. C. Armstrong, 1899. Also in *The Expositor's Bible,* vol. 40. London: Hodder & Stoughton; New York: A. C. Armstrong, 1903.

    Defends Pauline authorship and that Ephesians represents a circular letter sent to several churches in Asia Minor. Proceeds in short sections to explain the meaning and significance of the text.

114. Foulkes, F. *The Epistle of Paul to the Ephesians.* Tyndale New Testament Commentaries. 2d ed. Leicester, UK: InterVarsity Press; Grand Rapids: Eerdmans, 1989.

    Typical of the TNTC series, this short treatment takes a conservative position on the background issues—here finding Paul the author writing from Rome.

115. Frost, B. *Ephesians - Colossians. A Dogmatic and Devotional Commentary.* London: Mowbray; New York: Morehouse-Gorham, 1946.

116. Gaebelein, A. C. *Unsearchable Riches. An Analytical Exposition of the Ephesian Epistle.* New York: Publication Office "Our Hope," 1928.

    Popular exposition of a dispensational variety.

117. Gaugler, E. *Der Epheserbrief.* Auslegung ntl. Schriften 6. Zurich: EVZ, 1966.

    Comes down on the side of Pauline authorship.

118. Gerstner, J. H. *The Epistle to the Ephesians.* In Shield Bible Study
      Series. Grand Rapids: Baker, 1958.

      Short popular-level study guide briefly defending Pauline authorship.

119. Getz, G. A. *Looking up when you feel down: based on Ephesians
      1 - 3.* Ventura, CA: Regal, 1985.

      Popular, practical exposition.

120. Gnilka, J. *Der Epheserbrief.* Freiburg, Basel, Wien: Herder, 1971;
      4th ed., 1990.

      Following an extensive bibliography, Gnilka provides an extensive
      discussion of key introductory issues. His discussion of the text is
      full and informed by numerous sources—mostly German. The book
      includes six excurses on crucial issues including the Weltbild, the
      phrase 'in Christ,' ecclesiology, and eschatology.

121. Gore, C.   *St. Paul's Epistle to the Ephesians.   A Practical
      Exposition.* London: Murray, 1905.

122. Govett, R.   *What Is the Church? or the Argument of Ephesians.*
      London, 1889. [Repr. as *Govett on Ephesians.*   Miami
      Springs, FL: Conley & Schoettle, 1981.]

      Popular-level exposition of the letter verse by verse.

123. Graham, W.   *Lectures on St. Paul's Epistle to the Ephesians.*
      London: Partridge & Co., 1870.

      Eschewing any introduction, the author presents a popular exposition
      of the meaning of the letter, assuming Pauline authorship. Extensive
      cross-referencing to other parts of the Bible.

124. Griffith, L. *Ephesians: A Positive Affirmation.* Waco, TX: Word,
      1975.

      Contains the substance of three series of sermons entitled: Such is the Gospel; Live up to your Calling; and The Whole Armor of God. A popular-level homily that moves section by section through the epistle in twenty-one brief chapters. Not much value here.

125. Guthrie, D. *Exploring God's Word. Bible Guide to Ephesians, Philippians and Colossians.* London: Hodder & Stoughton; Grand Rapids: Eerdmans, 1984.

Provides outlines for the sections in these three letters, showing both what the texts say and how their principles can be applied to daily life.

126. Gutzke, M. G. *Plain Talk on Ephesians.* Grand Rapids: Zondervan, 1973.

Popular exposition on the entire letter.

127. Habeck, I. J. *Ephesians: Amazing Grace.* Milwaukee: Northwestern, 1985.

This plainly-written, verse-by-verse commentary maintains an exegetical-theological focus, offering little structural attention for a work of its level (assumes an intermediate knowledge of Koine). Each section is preceded with the Greek text and the author's literal translation. Self-consciously slights citing other commentators or grammarians while including various interpretations. Emphatically asserts Pauline authorship.

128. Harbour, B. L. *Living Abundantly. Living the New Testament Faith, Ephesians.* Nashville: Broadman, 1992.

An evangelical, devotional approach that takes the biblical text section by section in thirteen chapters. No interaction with other scholarship or critical issues, though some attention to (transliterated) Greek. Very anecdotal.

129. Harless, G. C. A. von. *Commentar über den Brief Pauli an die Epheser.* 2d ed. Erlangen: Heider, 1834.

130.   Harris, R. L. et al. eds. *The New Testament Study Bible: Galatians -*
        Philemon, vol. 8, *The Complete Biblical Library.* Springfield,
        MO: Complete Biblical Library, 1986.

131.   Harrison, N. B. *His Very Own. Paul's Epistle to the Ephesians.*
        Chicago: Bible Institute Colportage Assn., 1930.

        Brief popular explanation employing extensive outlines of the letter.

132.   Haupt, E. *Die Gefangenschaftsbriefe. Der Brief an die Epheser,*
        vol. 8, *KEKNT.* 8th rev. ed. Göttingen: Vandenhoeck &
        Ruprecht, 1902.

        Decides for Pauline authorship.

133.   Havener, I. *First Thessalonians, Philippians, Philemon, Second*
        Thessalonians, Colossians, Ephesians. Collegeville, MN:
        Liturgical Press, 1983.

        Short biblical commentaries on these various epistles of Paul.

134.   Haynes, W. A. *The Beautiful Word Pictures of the Epistle to the*
        Ephesians. Caney, KS: Busy Man's Bible Co., 1911.

        Popular treatment that emphasizes the etymological meaning of
        Greek words as if that holds the key to the epistles meaning.

135.   Hendriksen, W. *Ephesians.* Grand Rapids: Baker, 1967.

        This Reformed Evangelical scholar argues for Pauline authorship.
        Tends toward dogmatism though occasional nuggets occur in this
        volume.

136.   Hitchcock, G. S. *The Epistle to the Ephesians. An Encyclical of St.*
        Paul. London: Burns and Oates, 1913.

137.   Hobbs, H. H. *New Men in Christ.* Waco, TX: Word, 1974.

        Short study on a popular level yet interacts with key literature in a responsible manner.

138. Hodge, C. *Commentary on the Epistle to The Ephesians.* London: James Nisbet, 1876. [Repr. London: Marshall Pickering, 1991.]

Assumes Pauline authorship; strong Reformed orientation. Many superb insights to be sure.

139. Hoppe, R. *Epheserbrief, Kolosserbrief.* Stuttgart: Katholisches Bibelwerk, 1987.

Of the 81 pages given to Eph, seven cover the typical introductory concerns followed by brief comments on the various sections of the letter interspersed with four excurses, including one on *Die "Haustafeln."* Doubts that the letter could derive from Paul's pen.

140. Hort, F. J. A. *Prolegomena to St. Paul's Epistles to the Romans and the Ephesians.* London: Macmillan, 1895.

Views Ephesians originally as a circular letter written for several churches in Asia Minor.

141. Houlden, J. L. *Paul's Letters from Prison.* Pelican NT Commentaries. Harmondsworth and Baltimore: Penguin, 1970, 1977.

Following a general introduction to the captivity epistles, the author introduces and comments on each of the four letters in turn. Houlden concludes that Ephesians derives from a Christian leader writing thirty to fifty years after Paul's death. Attributing his letter to Paul, then, involved the deception of pseudonymity. The commentary that follows is brief.

142. Hubbard, W. M. *Bible Studies in Layman's Terms.* 5 vols. Knoxville, TN: W. M. Hubbard, 1988.

Volume 2 provides comments on 1 Corinthians and Ephesians.

143.   Huby, J. *Épîtres de la captivité.* 19th ed. Paris: Beauchesne, 1947.

144.   Hugedé, N. *L'Épître aux Éphésiens.* Geneva: Labor et Fides, 1973.

Eschewing an extended introduction for one that produces little insight for understanding the text, in four brief pages the author adopts the traditional Pauline origin of the letter from a Roman imprisonment. Devotes 236 pages to a careful exegesis of the letter, interacting with major, almost exclusively European, sources. Much comparison to material in Colossians.

145.   Hughes, A. *The Whole Armour of God.* Grand Rapids: Zondervan, 1939.

Following a fourteen-page introduction of the whole of Ephesians, the bulk of the book unpacks in a popular fashion the author's understanding of the section in chapter 6 on the armor of God.

146.   Hughes, R. K. *Ephesians: The Mystery of the Body of Christ.* Wheaton, IL: Crossway, 1990.

Thirty sermons covering the entire letter by a well-informed preacher.

147.   James, R. *Jesus Christ in Ephesians: a Devotional Commentary on Ephesians.* Nashville: The Upper Room, 1987.

148.   Ironside, H. A. *In The Heavenlies.* New York: Loizeaux, 1937. [Repr. as *Galatians and Ephesians (In the Heavenlies).* Neptune, NJ: Loizeaux, 1981.]

Twenty-six practical expository lectures based on the letter.

149.   Johnson, Jr., E. S. *Galatians and Ephesians.* Nashville: Graded Press, 1988.

150.   Johnston, G. *Ephesians, Philippians, Colossians, and Philemon.* Century Bible, new ed. Ed. H. H. Rowley and M. Black. London: Thomas Nelson, 1967.

Begins with a terse introduction followed by the RSV with commentary printed at the foot of the pages and referenced by verse numbers. Some interaction with other sources. Rejects Pauline authorship.

151. Kelly, W. *Lectures on the Epistle of Paul, The Apostle, to the Ephesians.* London: Morrish, n.d.

Following the author's own translation of the letter, he gives a running explanation of its meaning, chapter by chapter.

152. Kent, H. A. *Ephesians. The Glory of the Church.* Chicago: Moody, 1971.

Study of the letter on a popular level that does not seriously consider modern literature or positions.

153. Kinsey, B. *The Bride's Pearl: A Commentary on Ephesians.* Hazelwood, MO: Word Aflame, 1993.

154. Lawson, E. L. *Galatians, Ephesians.* Standard Bible Studies. Cincinnati: Standard, 1987.

Twenty short, expository chapters follow the biblical text nearly sequentially, though not verse-by-verse. Little serious interaction with critical questions and sources, but does seek to clarify word meanings (transliterated Greek). Written in a conversational style, full of illustrations (many footnoted) and applications.

155. Lee, Witness. *Life-Study of Ephesians.* 2d ed. Anaheim, CA: Living Stream Ministry, 1984, 1990.

156. Lenski, R. C. H. *Interpretation of St. Paul's Epistles to the Galatians, to the Ephesians, and to the Philippians.* Columbus, Ohio: Wartburg, 1937.

Not a circular letter, Ephesians was written by Paul to the church at Ephesus. Lenski's non-critical commentary follows a brief introduction.

157. Lightfoot, J. B. *Notes on the Epistles of St. Paul.* London: Macmillan, 1895. [Repr. Grand Rapids: Zondervan, 1957.]

Contains notes on the Greek text of Eph. 1:1-14 only. Adopts the view that the letter was originally a circular letter to churches in Asia Minor. Lightfoot is guilty of false etymologizing.

158. Lincoln, A. T. *Ephesians.* Word Biblical Commentary, vol 42. Dallas: Word, 1990.

A masterful treatment, and very thorough, that addresses all the key issues in the helpful WBC format. Decides against Pauline authorship after a detailed investigation. Concludes that a Jewish-Christian admirer of Paul wrote in his name. Doubts that the secretary theory sufficiently accounts for the divergences from Paul's pattern of writing.

159. Lindemann, A. *Der Epheserbrief.* Zurcher Bibelkommentaire, vol. 8. Zurich: Theologischer Verlag, 1985.

160. Loane, M. L. *Three Letters from Prison: Studies in Ephesians, Colossians, and Philemon.* Waco, TX: Word, 1972.

Brief studies—short sermons—in Ephesians, Colossians, and Philemon following short discussions of introductory issues.

161. Lock, W. The Epistle to the Ephesians. In Westminster Commentaries. London: Methuen, 1929.

163. MacArthur, J. *Ephesians.* In The MacArthur New Testament Commentary. Chicago: Moody, 1986.

This well-known pastor writes a very brief, popular introduction followed by an almost sermonic commentary, section by section. The use of the Greek language is simplistic.

163. Macpherson, J. *A Commentary on St. Paul's Epistle to the Ephesians.* Edinburgh: T. & T. Clark, 1892.

164. Mahan, H. T. *Galatians, Ephesians, Philippians, Colossians.* Bible Class Commentary, Vol. 3. Welwyn, Herts, UK: Evangelical Press, 1985.

   Exceptionally brief (31 pp.), verse-by-verse exposition with select biblical words and phrases in bold print. Its loosely theological approach is evidenced by biblical cross-references for nearly every verse. Designed for use in Sunday schools, youth groups, and devotions.

165. Manning, G. R. *Searching for Rainbows: A Commentary on Ephesians.* Columbus, GA: Brentwood Christian Press, 1988.

166. Marberry, T. *Galatians through Colossians.* Nashville: Randall House, 1988.

   Commentaries on these four epistles.

167. Martin, R. P. "Ephesians," *Broadman Bible Commentary,* Vol. 11. Nashville: Broadman, 1971, 125-77.

168. _____. *Ephesians, Colossians, Philemon.* In Interpretation. Atlanta: John Knox, 1991.

   This eminent scholar produces brief introductions to these epistles. The Interpretation series has the goal of helping preachers and teachers explain the NT. Martin believes a disciple of Paul penned Ephesians to extend Paul's influence to a later generation. The commentary is done section by section, not verse by verse.

169. Masson, C. *L'Épître de Paul aux Éphésiens.* Commentaire du Nouveau Testament 9. Neuchâtel: Delachaux et Niestle, 1953, 133-230.

   Rejects Pauline authorship.

170. Mather, T. L. *Heavenly Things: Outlines of the Epistle to the Hebrews, the Epistle to the Ephesians, the Judgment of the World and the Holy City of Jerusalem in the Book of*

Revelation. Port Credit, Ont.: Berean Foundation, 1987.

171. Meinertz, M., and Tillmann, F. *Die Gefangenschaftsbriefe.* 4th ed.
      Bonn: Hanstein, 1931, 50-106.

172. Meyer, F. B. *Ephesians: A Devotional Commentary.* London:
      Marshall, Morgan & Scott, 1953.

      Develops the devotional impact of various themes in the letter.

173. Meyer, H. A. W. *Critical and Exegetical Handbook to the Epistle
      to the Ephesians and the Epistle to Philemon.* Edinburgh: T.
      & T. Clark 1880; New York: Funk and Wagnalls, 1884. Tr.
      W. P. Dickson, from *KEKNT* 9, 6th German ed. Göttingen:
      Vandenhoeck & Ruprecht, 1886.

174. Mitton, C. L. *Ephesians.* In The New Century Bible Commentary.
      Grand Rapids: Eerdmans and London: Marshall Morgan &
      Scott, 1973; London: Oliphants, 1976.

      Rejects Pauline authorship, believing that the difficulties presented by
      assuming direct Pauline authorship are insuperable. Mitton is
      persuaded by Goodspeed's reconstruction of the background to
      Ephesians. Yet the unknown author presents "a brilliant and
      comprehensive summary of Paul's main theological emphases" (p.
      11). The book is characterized by persuasive exegesis and clear
      writing. Very useful.

175. Morris, L. *Expository Reflections on the Letter to the Ephesians.*
      Grand Rapids: Baker, 1994.

      More a devotional guide than a commentary, the study divides the
      letter into twenty-one sections, anywhere from four to thirteen verses
      each. A combination of the author's verse-by-verse translation plus
      interpretation of a devotional, homiletical nature. Includes comments
      on key words and grammar. Only minimal interaction with other
      sources.

176. Moule, C. F. D. *Ephesians.* Cambridge: Cambridge University Press, 1935.

177. Moule, H. C. G. "The Epistle to the Ephesians," *Cambridge Bible for Schools and Colleges,* ed. J. J. S. Perowne. Cambridge, UK: Cambridge University Press, 1893.

Following a brief discussion of an introductory nature—assuming Pauline authorship along the way—the author provides succinct but helpful notes about features of the text of Ephesians. Nine appendices take up various historical, theological, and textual issues.

178. _____. *Ephesian Studies.* London: Thynne & Co., 1900.

Eighteen chapters that move section by section through virtually the entire scope of the letter. Argues that both Ephesians and Colossians derive from the same moment in Paul's ministry. Employs the Greek text in his analyses.

179. Moulton, H. K. *Colossians, Philemon and Ephesians.* London: Epworth, 1963.

Introduces all three prison epistles together and, though recognizing the considerable problems, assumes their Pauline authorship. Part of the Preacher's Commentaries series, the book's comments follow verse by verse through the text, though the short scope of the book forces them to be extremely brief.

180. Murray, J. O. F. *Commentary on Ephesians.* In the Cambridge Greek Testament for Schools and Colleges, gen. ed. R. St. J. Parry. Cambridge: Cambridge University Press, 1914.

Encompasses an extensive introduction (103 pp.), the Greek text according to Westcott and Hort (10 pp.), terse notes, phrase by phrase, on the Greek text of Ephesians (97 pp.), and additional notes—especially on significant words and phrases (27 pp.). Murray's careful and extensive analysis of the issues leads to his adoption of the epistle's authenticity as a Pauline letter.

181. Mussner, F. *Der Brief an die Epheser.* In Ökumenischer Taschenbuchkommentar zum Neuen Testament, 10. Gütersloh: Gerd Mohn; Wurzburg: Echter-Verlag, 1982.

Begins with a selected survey of significant literature concerning Ephesian studies followed by twenty pages of introduction covering numerous topics, including tradition history, relations to other NT writings, liturgical and paraenetic traditions, lexicography, the letter's theology, its history of religions background, authorship, and the addressees. There follows Musser's commentary of the letter section by section, albeit brief due to the limitations of the series. The book ends with a few pages devoted to the ecumenical message of the letter.

182. Olbricht, T. H. *Ephesians - Colossians. The Message of the New Testament.* Abilene, TX: Biblical Research, 1983.

A brief introduction is followed by a thirty-eight-page "landscape-overview" of Ephesians divided into six chapters (not corresponding to the canonical ones). Sermonic in nature, despite its brevity.

183. Olshausen, H. *Biblical Commentary on The New Testament,* Vol. 5. New York: Sheldon, 1860, 9-154.

Following a brief introduction that settles on Pauline authorship, the author conducts an analysis of the letter verse by verse. Comments are based on the Greek text and interact extensively with numerous authors along the way. Amazingly thorough discussion of the important issues in the text.

184. Patzia, A. G. *Ephesians, Colossians, Philemon.* In The New International Biblical Commentary. Peabody, MA: Hendrickson, 1990. [Revision of Good News Commentary, New York: Harper and Row, 1984.]

An evangelical exposition of Ephesians, very useful if on the short side. Agrees that the question of authorship is at an impasse but sees no inherent reason why the issue should divide "conservatives" and "liberals." That is, Patzia believes that some follower of Paul could well be responsible for Ephesians and that such a conclusion need not imply it was a forgery. He makes a good case for understanding on both sides while stressing the well-recognized Pauline marks of the letter in any case.

185. Penner, E. *The Power of God in a Broken World: Studies in Ephesians.* Winnipeg, MB: Kindred, 1990.

An evangelical, lay commentary that develops the author's thesis that God's power to the believer is Ephesian's main theme (cf. 1:18-19). An introductory chapter precedes twelve sections that take passages in order, each providing an interpretive translation, concluding response questions, and bold outline headings in the body of the text. Interacts with a dozen or so select sources.

186. Pfammatter, J. *Epheserbrief, Kolosserbrief.* Wurzburg: Echter Verlag, 1987, 1990.

After a brief four-page introduction (Eph was written by a Paulinist) and a short bibliography, this study cites the German text of the epistle on each page with brief comments below. The same format follows for Colossians.

187. Phillips, J. *Exploring Ephesians.* Neptune, NJ: Loizeaux, 1993.

188. Pokorný, P. *Der Brief des Paulus an die Epheser.* Berlin: Evangelische Verlagsanstalt, 1992.

Provides an extensive introduction to important introductory issues. First considers the text and language. There follows a section that investigates the various sources and traditions that the writer took over in writing the epistle (including Colossians, OT quotes, and the Pauline tradition). Also investigates the religious background that formed the milieu in which the letter was written (includes the Qumran traditions, Gnostic and Hellenistic Judaism, and eschatology), the nature of the addressees, and the authorship issue (written by someone in the Pauline tradition between A.D. 80-90). The commentary itself is thorough and interacts extensively with recent sources.

189. Powell, I. *Exciting Epistle to the Ephesians.* Grand Rapids: Kregel, 1989.
      Verse-by-verse exposition of the KJV. Concluding the discussion of each chapter in Ephesians is a summary and several self-contained "homilies" (several reprinted from the author's other books) whose connection with the commentary is not always apparent. Some word studies (transliterated Greek) and even more stories.

190. Rienecker, F. *Der Brief des Paulus an die Epheser.* 8th ed. Wuppertel: Brockhaus, 1984.

      After a short eight-page introduction, provides an analysis of the epistle that treats virtually every verse. Adopts a traditional view that Paul wrote the letter during his Roman imprisonment, that it comprises an encyclical letter to the churches in the region around Ephesus, and that the "community of Jesus Christ" is its major theme. Only limited interaction with other literature.

191. Robertson, A. T. *Word Pictures in the New Testament,* Vol. 4, *Letters of Paul.* Nashville: Broadman, 1931, 516-52

      In the style of the entire series, Robertson provides an extremely brief introduction (2 pages) in which he opts for Pauline authorship. There follows his verse by verse comments on the Greek text with a heavy stress on grammatical analysis and word definitions. Helpful, though potentially dangerous also, to beginning students, for Robertson leaves the impression that matters are more easily explained than they really are. Must be used in concert with other tools.

192. Robinson, J. A. *St. Paul's Epistle to the Ephesians.* 2d ed. London: Macmillan, 1904. [Repr. London: Clark, 1922.]

      Assuming that Paul wrote the letter, the author proceeds to provide his own translation and exposition before engaging in a critical analysis of the Greek text. The volume ends with his discussion of the meaning of key topics in the letter. Much value here.

193. Roon, A. van. *De Brief van Paulus aan de Epheziërs.* Nijkerk:

Callenbach, 1976.

Commentary in Dutch that provides no introduction to the letter prior to the analysis. Considerable interaction with, mostly, continental sources.

194. Rossier, B. L. *Prison Epistles; Praise from Prison: Studies in Ephesians, Philippians, Colossians and Philemon.* New Wilmington, PA: House of Bon Giovanni, 1987.

195. Russell, L. M. *Imitators of God: A Study Book on Ephesians.* New York: United Methodist Church, 1984.

Feminist theologian Russell does for Ephesians what E. Tamez does for James, with the difference that this work more specifically arises from and addresses the experiences of women. Adopts a four-fold hermeneutical approach that considers at each state of the canonical text the context of (1) Ephesians, (2) us [American women like Russell?], (3) oppressed women, and (4) the Bible more broadly. To accomplish the third goal, the experiences of an oppressed South Korean worker and a battered woman from New Haven, CT are included. Following a section covering introduction proper and methodology, six chapters correspond to the modern Ephesian text and conclude with application questions.

196. Salmond, S. D. F. "The Epistle to the Ephesians," vol. 3 of *The Expositor's Greek Testament.* 5 volumes, gen. ed. W. R. Nicoll. London: Hodder and Stoughton; Grand Rapids: Eerdmans, 1903, 201-395.

Extensive analysis of the various introductory issues surrounding the production of the letter in which Salmond takes up the various objections to authenticity. Acknowledging the differences between Ephesians and other Pauline literature, Salmond sides strongly with the traditional view that Paul penned the letter. The commentary itself includes the Greek text with his analysis of each phrase or feature requiring explanation. The analysis is very thorough.

197. Sampley, J. P. et al. *Ephesians, Colossians, 2 Thessalonians, The*

Pastoral Epistles, in the Proclamation Commentaries. Philadelphia: Fortress, 1978, 9-39.

The short space allotted by the volume allows Sampley minimal space to treat introductory issues. In simple terms he shows why Pauline authorship presents problems and concludes that though Paul probably did not write Ephesians, most likely one of his close followers wrote on his behalf. Though the series title identifies this as a commentary, in reality Sampley proceeds through the letter isolating and discussing key themes that the author develops in the epistle.

198. Schick, E.   *Christus ja, Kirche nein!?   Die Antwort des Epheserbriefs.* Kevelaer: Butzon und Bercker, 1985.

199. Schlatter, A. *Die Briefe an die Galater, Epheser, Kolosser und Philemon.* Stuttgart: Calwer, 1963, 152-249.

200. Schlier, H. *Der Brief an die Epheser.* Düsseldorf: Patmos, 1957; 7th ed., 1971.

Adopts Pauline authorship in this volume, though in his book *Christus,* p. 39, he calls the position of Pauline authorship "cumbersome." Conjectures that the letter was an encyclical written to several communities.

201. Schnackenburg, R. *Der Brief an die Epheser.* Evangelisch-Katholischer Kommentar zum Neuen Testament, vol 10. Zurich: Benzinger and Neukirchen-Vluyn: Neukirchener, 1982.

The original German whose translation into English appeared in 1991. See next entry.

202. _____. *Ephesians: A Commentary.* Edinburgh: T. & T. Clark, 1991. ET of 1982 German ed.

Surprisingly short (17 pages) discussion of introductory issues that sets the tone for the entire work: concise and to the point. Notes that most of his fellow Catholics now agree that Ephesians is post-

Pauline. He concurs that such a pseudepigraphal conclusion is hermeneutically demanded. Not that the author lacked self-confidence or was a forger, he conceals his identity since his object is to communicate and interpret the Pauline tradition. Probably the letter originated about A.D. 90 and was sent to churches in Asia Minor, perhaps the same ones that received Colossians. Schnackenburg approaches each section of the letter by citing key literature, providing an analysis, engaging in his verse-by-verse exegesis, and concluding with a summary. Includes an excursus on the church in Ephesians. Includes "comments by the Protestant partner," viz., Eduard Schweizer. Well worth consulting.

203. Scott, E. F. *The Epistles to the Colossians, to Philemon, and to the Ephesians.* Moffatt New Testament Commentary, vol. 10. London: Hodder and Stoughton, 1930, 117-257.

The space limitations allow only an eighteen-page introduction in which Scott opts for Pauline authorship. Employing the English text, the author provides a running commentary on the epistle.

204. Shedd, R. *Táo Grande Salvaçáo.* Sâo Paulo, Brazil: Abu Editora, 1978.

Popular level commentary in Portuguese produced by a prominent missionary statesman and educator in Brazil. A brief introduction adopts traditional views setting the stage for the seventy-four-page commentary. The discussion proceeds section by section through the letter.

205. Simpson, E. K., and Bruce, F. F. *The Epistles of Paul to the Ephesians and to the Colossians.* In New International Commentary on the New Testament. Grand Rapids: Eerdmans, 1957.

Follows the established format of this series. This entry on Ephesians by Simpson is clearly inferior and was subsequently replaced by an edition done fully by F. F. Bruce (on both Ephesians and Colossians; see above).

206. Soden, H. von. *Die Briefe an die Kolosser, Epheser, Philemon; die Pastoralbriefe.* Hand-Commentar zum Neuen Testament, 3. 2d ed. Freiburg and Leipzig: Mohr, 1893.

207. Staab, K. and Freundorfer, J. *Die Thessalonicherbriefe und die Gefangenschaftsbriefe.* 3d ed. Regensburg: Pustet, 1959.

208. Stoeckhardt, G. *Commentary on St. Paul's Letter to the Ephesians.* St. Louis: MO: Concordia, 1952.

Systematically responding to the objections to Pauline authorship, the author believes the traditional view to be superior to all alternatives. Rejecting the encyclical view, the author believes Paul wrote the letter to the Ephesian church and sent it through Tychicus. Strongly Reformed in its orientation.

209. Stott, J. R. W. *The Message of Ephesians: God's New Society.* 2d ed. Leicester, UK and Downers Grove, IL: InterVarsity, 1991.

Popular yet thoughtful and engaging study by the well-known evangelical pastor-scholar.   Provides helpful insights into the significance of the letter for Christians today.

210. Strauss, L. *Devotional Studies in Galatians and Ephesians.* New York: Loizeaux, 1957.

As the title indicates, this is a popular and devotional commentary— almost a sermon—on these two epistles. No interaction with other sources.

211. Summers, R. *Ephesians: Patterns for Christian Living.* Nashville: Broadman, 1960.

212. Swain, L. *Ephesians.*   New Testament Message, vol. 13. Wilmington, DE: Glazier, 1980.

Swain remains open on the authorship question, though he expresses a preference for authenticity amidst a very brief four-page introduction. The commentary proceeds by paragraphs or sections through the epistle. This short study in this Roman Catholic series focuses not on the langauge or original text of the letter but on its theological message for people today. A few excurses are interspersed throughout.

213. Synge, F. C. *St. Paul's Epistle to the Ephesians.* London: S.P.C.K., 1941, 1954.

With no introduction, this short analysis of Ephesians presumes Pauline authorship. It explains the book in terms of the theme of unity which the author believes pervades the letter. The author addresses features in the Greek text upon occasion.

214. Taylor, W. F., and Reumann, J. H. P. *Ephesians, Colossians.* Augsburg Commentary on the New Testament. Minneapolis: Augsburg, 1985.

Writing the section on Ephesians, Taylor, writing for laypersons, students, and pastors, focuses on the meaning of the text, not so much its application. Recognizing that any discussion of authorship today must deal in probabilities, Taylor believes it more probable that Paul did not author Ephesians. More likely, one of Paul's Jewish followers wrote it; it is pseudonymous, and that would not have been a "dirty word" in the ancient world. Taylor proceeds to comment briefly by paragraphs or sections.

215. Taylor, W. H. *Galatians, Ephesians.* Kansas City, MO: Beacon Hill, 1981.

216. Thompson, G. H. P. *The Letters of Paul to the Ephesians, to the Colossians, and to Philemon.* The Cambridge Bible Commentary on the New English Bible. Cambridge: Cambridge University Press, 1967.

The authors in this series aim to provide the results of modern scholarship to the general reader, especially teachers and students. Thompson questions the validity of the category of pseudonymity as applied to Ephesians, and after addressing the various problems and issues concludes that Ephesians could well come from Paul himself, perhaps with its unique features due to the freedom Paul gave to his secretary. The commentary provides the text of the NEB followed by brief comments verse by verse.

217. Trenchard, E. and Wickham, P. *Una exposición de la epístola a los Efesios.* Cursos de estudio bíblico. Madrid: Editorial Literatura Biblica, 1980.

218. Tucker, W. L. *"With Him," or Studies in the Epistle to the Ephesians.* New York: Book Stall, 1917. [Repr. *Studies in Ephesians.* Grand Rapids: Kregel, 1983.]

Popular exposition of the letter, heavily weighted on chapter 1.

219. Turner, S. H. *The Epistle to the Ephesians.* New York: Dana & Co., 1856.

220. University of Navarre, Faculty of Theology, ed. *St. Paul's Captivity Epistles,* The Navarre Bible. Dublin: Four Courts, 1992. [Originally published as *Epistolas de la cautividad,* vol. 8 of Sagrada Biblia, 1986.]

The biblical text occurs in English (RSV) and Latin (New Vulgate), with the English commentary translated from the original Spanish. Notes for Ephesians, Philippians, Colossians, and Philemon draw on the writings of the Magisterium, various Fathers and Doctors of the church, important spiritual writers, and J. Escrivá de Balaguer.

221. Vaughan, C. *Ephesians. A Study Guide Commentary.* Grand Rapids: Zondervan, 1977.

As the title says, this attempts to guide readers or groups in their own study of the letter. This popular treatment provides study questions at the end of each section.

222. Veloso, M. *Prison Papers From a Captive Ambassador.* Boise: Pacific Press Publication Assn., 1985.

Non-technical, but fairly focused studies originally designed for

(Seventh-Day Adventist) Sabbath schools. Progresses through Ephesians in thirteen chapters with practical titles (e.g., "How to Create Unity"). Written in a pithy, conversational style.

223. Weed, M. R. *The Letters of Paul to the Ephesians, the Colossians, and Philemon.* The Living Word Commentary, gen ed. E. Ferguson. Austin, TX: Sweet, 1971.

Fourteen pages of introduction and sixty-eight of comments comprise the space devoted to Ephesians. After considering the problems involved, Weed concludes that Pauline authorship remains the best alternative. The volume includes the text of the RSV. The few references to the Greek text are transliterated. The verse by verse comments provide brief explanations of the texts' meaning.

224. Westcott, B. F. *St. Paul's Epistle to the Ephesians.* London: Macmillan, 1906.

This towering figure of the last century affirms Pauline authorship following his critical discussion of ancient sources and internal evidence. He lays out in parallel columns correspondences between Ephesians and Colossians, and Ephesians' relations to other NT texts. He provides a critical commentary on the Greek text of Ephesians and ends with sections on the Latin text of the letter, the texts of Wycliffe (1380) and Tyndale (1534) in parallel columns, plus an appendix containing various notes and word studies.

225. Wette, W. M. L. de. *Kurze Erklärung der Briefe an die Kolosser, an Philemon, an die Epheser und an die Philipper.* Kurzgefasstes exegetisches Handbuch zum Neuen Testament, II, 4. Leipzig: Weidmann, 1843.

226. Wiersbe, W. *Be Rich.* Wheaton, IL: Scripture Press, 1986.

Popular exposition with practical insights.

227. Willis, W. R. *Ephesians.* Wheaton, IL: Victor Books, 1987.

Personal growth Bible studies, this work consists of twelve studies on the unity and diversity in the body of Christ.

228. Wilson, G. B. *Ephesians.* Edinburgh: Banner of Truth, 1978.

Brief and popular treatment that is informed by responsible sources. Reformed and conservative in its orientation.

229. Wuest, K. S. *Ephesians and Colossians.* The Greek New Testament for the English Reader. Grand Rapids: Eerdmans, 1953, 1981.

Seeks to make insights from the Greek text of the letters accessible to non-specialists. Guilty of occasional "over-exegesis" in his word studies: too prone to commit word study fallacies. Yet he includes some valuable insights along the way. Assumes Pauline authorship.

230. Wood, A. S. "Ephesians," in *Expositor's Bible Commentary,* vol. 11, ed. F. E. Gaebelein. Grand Rapids: Zondervan, 1978, 1-92.

The target audience of the series is preachers, teachers, and Bible students; the stance of the authors is evangelical; and the translation employed is the NIV. Wood considers both the cases for and against Pauline authorship concluding that only an overwhelmingly conclusive counterargument could disturb the traditional view. He fails to find that case and supports authenticity. Wood also surveys all the other significant introductory issues surrounding the letter. The format of the EBC then unfolds providing text and verse by verse exposition and then the more technical notes, usually on the Greek text.

231. Yandian, B. *Ephesians: The Maturing of the Saints.* Tulsa, OK: Harrison House, 1985.

232. Zerwick, M. *Der Brief an die Epheser.* 2d ed. Düsseldorf: Patmos, 1962.

233. _____. *The Epistle of the Ephesians.* Trans. from German by K. Smyth. New York: Crossroad, 1981.

Selected Pre-Modern Commentaries / Studies

234. Ambrosiaster. *Commentaria in epistolan B. Pauli ad Ephesios. PL* 17, 393-426, or *CSEL* 81/3, 69-126.

235. Aquinas, Thomas. *Commentary on Saint Paul's Epistle to the Ephesians.* Vol. 2 of *Aquinas Scripture Series.* Trans. M. L. Lamb. Albany: Magi Books, 1966.

236. Calvin, J. *Comm. in Ep. Pauli ad Ephesios. Corpus reformatorum* 79 (2895), Calvini opera 51, col. 141-240.

237. _____. *Commentaries on the Epistles of Paul to the Galatians and Ephesians.* Tr. W. Pringle. Edinburgh: T. & T. Clark, 1854. Reprinted, Grand Rapids: Eerdmans, 1957.

238. _____. *The Epistles of Paul the Apostle to the Galatians, Ephesians, Philippians, and Colossians.* Tr. T. H. L. Parker; ed. D. W. and T. F. Torrance. Grand Rapids: Eerdmans, 1965.

239. _____. *Sermons on the Epistle to the Ephesians.* Reprinted. London: Banner of Truth, 1973.

240. Chrysostom, Johannes. *Epistolam ad Ephesios. PG* 62, 7-176.

241. _____. *Commentary on the Epistle to Galatians, and Homilies on the Epistle to the Ephesians.* Oxford: J. H. Parker, 1845.

242. Cramer, J. A., ed. *Catenae Graecorum Patrum in Novum Testamentum,* 6. Oxford: Typographia Academica, 1834, 100-225.

243. Damascenus, Johannes. *Epistolam ad Ephesios. PG* 95, 821-56.

244. Ephraim the Syrian. *Commentarii in Epistolas D. Pauli.* Venice:

Typographia Sancti Lazari, 1893, 140-56.

245. Erasmus of Rotterdam. *Novum Testamentum Annotationes.* Basel:
     Froben, 1519, 413ff. Repr. 1540, 591ff.

246. _____. *In Epistolam ad Ephesios.* In Operal VI. Leiden: Brill,
     1705. Republished, London: 1962, 831-860.

247. Fergusson, J. *A Brief Exposition of the Epistles of Paul to the
     Galatians and Ephesians.* London: Higgins, 1659.

248. Goodwin, T. and Bayne, P. *An Exposition of Ephesians.* Repr.
     Sovereign Grace Book Club, 1958-59.

     Puritan preachers produced this exhaustive Calvinist exposition.
     Goodwin (born in 1600) comments in sermons on Eph 1:1-2:10 (in
     824 pages). Bayne died in 1617, and in this edition the last two-
     thirds of his comments on Ephesians, from 2:11-6:18 (671 pages),
     are included.

249. Gregg, J. A. F. "The Commentary of Origen upon the Epistle to the
     Ephesians." *JTS* 3 (1902) 233-44, 398-420, 551-76.

250. Grotius, Hugo. *Annotanones in Novum Testamentum,* II. 1646.
     Repr. Leipzig: Tetzscher, 1757.

251. Jerome (Hieronymus). *Commentaria in Epistolam ad Ephesios.* PL
     26, 439-554.

252. Locke, John. *A Paraphrase and Notes on the Epistles of St. Paul to
     the Galatians, 1 and 2 Corinthians, Romans, Ephesians.* 2
     vol., ed. A. W. Wainwright. Oxford: Clarendon, 1987.

253. Oecumenius of Tricca. *Pauli apostoli ad Ephesios epistola.* PG
     118, 1170-1266.

254. Theodore of Mopsuestia. *In Epistolas B. Pauli Commentarii.* H. B.
     Swete, ed. Cambridge: Cambridge University Press, 1880. I,
     112-96.

255. Theodoret of Cyrus. *Interpretatio epistolae ad Ephesios.* *PG* 82, 505-58.

256. Theophylact. *Commentarius in epistolam ad Ephesios.* *PG* 124, 1031-1138.

257. Wesley, J. *Explanatory Notes upon the New Testament.* Vol. II. Repr., Grand Rapids: Baker, 1983.

Chapter 3

TEXTS: Ephesians 1

Ephesians 1:1-2

258. Aberle, M. V. "Über eine Äusserung des Origenes zu Eph. 1, 1." *TQ* 34 (1852) 108-22.

259. Bartlett, W. "The Saints at Ephesus." *Exp,* 8th series, 18 (1919) 327-41.

   On Eph 1:1.

260. Batey, R. "The Destination of Ephesians." *JBL* 82 (1963) 101.

   Batey suggests that a scribe mistook the original destination "Asia" and wrote it as ουσιν. So Batey recommends a conjectural emendation in 1:1 to return to the original destination of Asia.

261. Best, E. "Ephesians i.1," in *Text and Interpretation.* FS for M. Black, ed. E. Best and R. McL. Wilson.   Cambridge: Cambridge University Press, 1979, 29-41.

A text critical study that seeks to establish a proper approach to making a decision about the original addressees of Ephesians. Best sets out and evaluates the evidence in the manuscript tradition. Though the designation "Ephesians" may not have been a part of the original letter, it must have been appended to it as early as the first collection of the group of letters containing Ephesians. He finds theories like Batey's (above) too complex and far fetched.

262.   _____. "Ephesians 1.1 Again," in *Paul and Paulinism.* FS for C. K. Barrett, ed. M. D. Hooker and S. G. Wilson. London: S.P.C.K., 1982, 273-79.

Takes up again the problems surrounding determining the original text of 1:1 and, hence, the recipients of Ephesians. Best theorizes that originally "in Ephesus" was not a part of the text. But when the letter was brought together with others in the Pauline corpus, a name—parallel to the church names that all the other letters had— was sought. At some stage for some reason we cannot know an unknown Christian community applied the name "Ephesus" and this later found its way into the prescript of 1:1. Best then conjectures from these suppositions how the various textual traditions arose.

263.   _____. "Recipients and Title of the Letter to the Ephesians: Why and When the Designation 'Ephesians'?" *ANRW* 2.25.4. *Geschichte und Kultur Roms im Spiegel der neueren Forschung.* II: *Principat.* Band 25 (4. Teilband): *Religion* (Vorkonstantinisches Christentum: Leben un Umwelt Jesu; Neues Testament [Danonische Schriften und Apokryphen], Forts.), ed. W. Haase. Berlin/New York: de Gruyter, 1987, 3247-79.

Comprehensive discussion surrounding the question of why 'Ephesus' occurs in the address of the majority of manuscripts and as the 'title' in the few whose address does not contain it. Surveys the textual evidence, the early evidence for the knowledge of the letter, the collections of Pauline letters, and the variety of the orders of the letters in the collections. Concludes that Eph originally lacked a geographical designation with an original title: "to the saints." The designations as "Ephesians" probably occurred relatively late in some important Christian center, even Ephesus itself. As to why this became its title, Best urges hesitancy. Perhaps memories of a lost letter to the Ephesians led to its attribution to this one, especially since it was known that Paul had spent considerable time there.

264. Brown, S. "God our father; Ephesians 1:1-2." *Henceforth* 13 (1985) 98-103.

Taking "God our Father" (1:1-2) as the controlling theme of the letter, this three-point homily addresses the sovereignty, mystery, and grace of God. Serves as an invitation to a series on the letter. Reads like a transcript.

265. Dacquino, P. "I destinatari della lettera agli Efesini." *RivB* 6 (1958) 102-110.

On the topic of the addressees of Ephesians.

266. Dahl, N. A. "Adresse und Proömium des Epheserbriefes." *TZ* 7 (1951) 241-64.

A study consisting of two parts, as given in the title. First considers the problem of the addressees of Ephesians, considering the absence of the words "in Ephesus" in the best manuscripts, conjecturing how the initial wording of the epistle came to be what it was. Most likely an encyclical, perhaps the letter was produced in several copies, each with a specific location. Looks with favor upon Goodspeed's hypothesis that the letter originally functioned as an introduction to the Pauline corpus. The section 1:3-14 functions as a eulogy or benediction that introduces the entire letter. Dahl provides his analysis of the structure of this eulogy.

267. _____. "The Particularity of the Pauline Epistles as a Problem in the Ancient Church," in *Neotestamentica et Patristica*. FS O. Cullmann. Leiden: Brill, 1962, 261-71.

Rejects the view that Ephesians is a catholic epistle and argues that it has a specific, epistolary function—sent to a church, or a number of churches, in Asia Minor. Dahl supposes the original geographical designation in 1:1 must have been left out. Perhaps this occurred when Ephesians—along with Romans and 1 Corinthians—were circulated widely. The location was left out to make the letter have wider application.

268. Ewald, P. "Exegetische Miszellen. Zu Eph. 1, 1." *Neue Kirchliche Zeitschrift* 15 (1904) 560-617.

269. Garofalo, S. "Rettifica zu Eph. 1, 1." *Bib* 16 (1935) 342f.

270. Girgensohn, H. "Die Gestalt der Kirche aus der Sicht des Briefes an die Epheser." In *Heilende Kräfte der Seelsorge.* Göttingen, Vandenhoeck & Ruprecht, 1966, 192-98.

Three sections that address the state of the church as viewed in the Ephesian letter. The first part considers God's economy of salvation in Eph 3:1-7. The three persons of the trinity work out together their plan for producing the Church, the community that enjoys God's salvation.

271. Godet, F. "The Epistle to the Gentile Church." *Exp,* 3rd Series, 5 (1887) 376-91.

On the destination of Ephesians.

272. Harnack, A. von. "Die Adresse des Epheserbriefes des Paulus." *SPAW* 37 (1910) 696-709.

Suggested on the basis of Marcion's statement and the note in Col 4:16 that the letter of Ephesians was originally written for the church at Laodicea.

273. Keathley, N. H. "To the Praise of His Glory: Ephesians 1." *RE* 76 (1979) 485-93.

A general exposition of Eph 1 that takes particular notice of its epistolary features. Divides the chapter into an address (vv. 1-2), a *berakah* (vv. 3-14) and a prayer of thanksgiving (vv. 15-23). Touches on several important interpretive issues, interacting with commentators and various versions. A readable overview of the passage.

274. Kessler, P. D. "Unsere Berufung zum göttlichen Leben. Betrachtung über den Prolog des Epheserbriefes." *BLit* 40 (1967) 119-22.

275. Lightfoot, J. B. "The Destination of the Epistle to the Ephesians," in *Biblical Essays.* London: Macmillan, 1893, 375-96.

Catalogs the ancient evidence showing that "Epistle to the Ephesians" was probably not its original designation. He shows, as well, that the tone and content of the epistle itself mitigate against a solely Ephesian designation. Lightfoot concludes that the letter was actually an encyclical letter addressed to the churches lying within a certain area, roughly coextensive with Proconsular Asia. He adopts Ussher's view that in the original letter a vacant space was left after the words "to the saints that are . . ." and in each copy for distribution the name of the individual church was inserted. When later copies were made of the letters the city names were typically omitted and the words run together: "to the saints that are and faithful brethren." Lightfoot concludes by discussing Paul's motive in writing such an encyclical.

276. Lindemann, A. "Bemerkungen zu den Adressaten und zum Anlass des Epheserbriefes." *ZNW* 67/3-4 (1976) 235-51.

The study argues that the phrase "in Ephesus" is the original reading in Eph 1:1. Seeking to give the epistle the theological character of a genuine Pauline letter, the unknown writer addressed the letter to Ephesus because Paul had not. The writer was not a Jewish Christian given the relatively small use of the OT. The letter was written in approximately A.D. 100 and aims to console Asian Christians undergoing persecution (Eph 6:10-20).

277. Lloyd-Jones, D. M. *God's Ultimate Purpose (Ephesians 1:1-23).* Grand Rapids: Baker, 1978.

The first in an eight-volume series spanning Ephesians. Each consists of a series of sermons delivered by this famous medic-turned-preacher at London's Westminster Chapel. Each sermon grows out of a verse or two from the text. In some instances, several individual sermons grow out of a single verse.

278. Percy, E. *Die Probleme der Kolosser- und Epheserbriefe.* 2d rev. ed. Lund: Gleerup, 1964.

Analyzes the language, style, and content of the epistles followed by a detailed comparison of their many points of contact. Focuses on the purpose and addressees of Ephesians. See especially pp. 449-66 on these introductory verses.

279. Roon, A. van. *The Authenticity of Ephesians.* Leiden: Brill, 1974, 72-94.

In reality, pp. 3-99 consider issues surrounding the origin and addresses of Ephesians. But in this section of Chapter V (pp. 72-94), van Roon focuses on the prescript of the letter. He considers the manuscript tradition and the evidence from ancient authors. He suggests that originally the city names of Hierapolis and Laodicea occurred in the text. Later ecumenical motives led to excising the two names to facilitate a wider dissemination of its message. Still later, the name of the city where Paul spent so much time— Ephesus—was inserted either by the Ephesian church itself or by others. Further, van Roon suggests that the sole mention of Paul as author, in distinction to all other letters besides Romans, strongly argues that it came from Paul's pen.

280. Santer, M. "The Text of Ephesians i.l." *NTS* 15 (1969) 247-48.

Objecting to the usual explanations concerning the corrupt text, the author suggests an emendation that posits no particular local reference. The letter—an encyclical—was sent to "those in Christ" probably indicating that a disciple of Paul wrote it.

281. Schenk, W. "Zur Entstehung und zum Verständnis der Adresse des Epheserbriefes." *Theologische Versuche* 6 (1975) 73-78.

Short discussion of the issues surrounding an understanding of the addresses of Ephesians. Characterizes Ephesians as "an edifying tractate" that only has a pretense of being an actual letter.

282. Schmid, J. "Der Epheserbrief des Apostels Paulus." *Biblische Studien* 22, 3/4. Freiburg: Herder, 1928.

See especially pp. 125-29 on the introductory verses.

283. Wilson, J. P. "Note on the textual problem of Ephesians 1:1." *ExpT* 60 (1949) 225-26.

Emends 1:1 by inserting the word "one" that was, that author conjectures, dropped from the original text. It would have read, "to the saints who are one and faithful in Christ Jesus."

284. Zuntz, G. *The Text of the Epistles.* London: Oxford, 1953.

In this meticulous text-critical work on the earliest manuscripts of the NT, Zuntz repudiates Goodspeed's theory that Ephesians was compiled as a covering letter of introduction to the entire Pauline corpus. Zuntz suspects that the original letter did not have a blank space into which a place name was inserted. He argues that logic leads to the conclusion that Ephesus was the original destination for the letter (pp. 276f.).

Ephesians 1:3-14

285.   Ab Alpe, A.   "Instaurare omnia in Christo (Ephes 1, 10)."   *VD* 23 (1943) 97-103.

286.   Ahern, B.   "The Indwelling Spirit, Pledge of Our Inheritance—Eph I.14."   *CBQ* 9 (1947) 179-89.

Engages in a philological study of *arrabon* ("pledge") in general, in Eph 1:14, plus what various commentators, starting with Jerome, said about its use in Eph 1:14. Consistent with the interpretation of the patristic commentators, the word denotes a pledge-guarantee—both the pledge of a future payment plus a down-payment up front. This is a significant word study that refers to related Semitic, Greek, and Latin vocabulary.

287.   Allan, J, A.   "The `In Christ' Formula in Ephesians."   *NTS* 5 (1958-59) 54-62.

The author analyzes the use of "in Christ" in Ephesians in comparison to its uses in Paul's epistles. Based on the prominence and employment of the formula "in Christ" in Ephesians, the study concludes that the author of Ephesians could not be Paul.

288.   Arvedson, T.   *Das Mysterium Christi.*   Uppsala: Wretsmans, 1937.

289.   Barkhuizen, J. H.   "The strophic structure of the eulogy of Ephesians 1:3-14."   *Hervormde Teologiese Studies* 46 (1990) 390-413.

Presents an original proposal of the structure of this hymn after reviewing the work of Cambier, Schattenmann, Kramer, Lang, Coutts, Schnackenburg, and Robbins. Includes three reconstructions of the text investigating the hymnic features plus an extensive bibliography and tables. Provides an excellent history of the structural work done on this text including an evaluation and application of the principles of strophic reconstruction.

290. Barth, M. "Conversion and Conversation: Israel and The Church in Paul's Epistle to the Ephesians." *Int* 17 (1963) 3-24.

Argues that the internal evidence in the letter makes an impressive case for Pauline authorship. The major task of the essay is to show that the Gentiles' adoption into the household of God compares to the prodigal son's reception in his father's house. Key passages in the discussion are Eph 1:11-14, 2:11-20, and 3:5-6. The study includes an outline of the theological implications of the oneness of Jew and Gentile in Christ and concludes with a discussion of the practical consequences of Ephesians' teaching on the church and Israel, one of which is that the church has no business in engaging in a "mission to the Jews."

291. Bartling, V. A. "The Church in God's Eternal Plan. A Study in Ephesians 1:1-14." *CTM* 36/4 (1965) 198-204.

Anticipating the 1965 convention of the Lutheran Church—whose emphasis was missions—this article lays out a basic theology of the church universal after giving a brief introduction to Ephesians. The hymn of 1:3-14 locates the church's origin and meaning in divine grace rather than human design. Verses 9-10 get special attention including discussions of "mystery" and "time." The emphasis is devotional: being a member of the church gives each Christian significant meaning and a purpose in life.

292. Best, E. "Fashions in Exegesis: Ephesians 1:3." In *Scripture: Meaning and Method.* FS A. T. Hanson, ed. B. P. Thompson. Hull, UK: Hull University Press, 1987, 77-91.

Best's discussion of the ways of understanding this verse is found on pp. 77-91.

293. Bover, J. "Doxologiae Epistolae ad Ephesios logica partitio." *Bib* 2 (1921) 458-60.

294. Burney, C. F. "Christ as the APXH of Creation," *JTS* 27 (1926) 160-77.

295. Cambier, J. "La Benédiction d'Eph. 1, 3-14." *ZNW* 54 (1963)
      58-104.

Argues that this section constitutes the doctrinal resume of the entire
epistle. The study engages in a detailed exegesis of this introductory
benediction of the letter. Ends with both literary and doctrinal
conclusions and a structural analysis of the section.

296. Caragounis, C. C. *The Ephesian Mysterion: Meaning and Context.*
      Coniectanea Biblica, New Testament Series, 8. Lund: Gleerup,
      1977, 39-52; 78-96; 143-57.

An expansive study, growing out of a doctoral dissertation, of the
backgrounds of *mysterion* ("mystery") and its uses in Ephesians.
Considers its uses in the mystery religions, philosophy, secular use,
magic, Gnosticism, LXX, pseudepigrapha, and early Christian writers
to ascertain its basic sense and shifts of meaning. Concludes that
mysterion in Ephesians belongs to the long Jewish tradition reflected
in the OT, not the mystery religions. The closest parallels occur in
Daniel and the Qumran literature. Mystery, then, demonstrates God's
eschatological purposes—a unified plan with cosmic dimensions.
The author of Ephesians is conscious of standing in the Danielic
tradition, giving the final word on God's eschatological mystery.

297. Cazelles, H. "Instaurare omnia in Christo (Eph 1, 10)." *Bib* 40/2
      (1959) 342-54.

Written in French, the study pursues God's grand scheme of salvation
hinted at in 1:10. The religion of Israel was a revealed religion.
Israel was a people prepared by God to receive the universal Savior.
Scripture testifies to God's desire to proclaim salvation to the entire
world.

298. Conzelmann, H. "Paulus und die Weisheit." *NTS* 12 (1965-66) 231-
      44.

Pursues the issue of a wisdom tradition in Paul's writings. Posits
that, trained as a theologian, Paul probably established a school, most
likely at Ephesus, in which wisdom was an organizing principle.

Evidence of this schooling in wisdom surfaces in the writings of his later followers, e.g., Hebrews, Ephesians, and the Pastorals. Even certain texts within Paul's acknowledged writings (2 Cor 3:7ff.; 1 Cor 1:18ff.; 2:6ff.; 10:1ff.; 11:2ff.; 13; and Rom 1:18ff. suggest that later editors from his school incorporated wisdom traditions into his writings. Suggests further implications of this thesis for the study of Paul.

299. Coiner, H. G. "The Secret of God's Plan (Eph 1, 9-10). Guidelines for a Theology of Stewardship." *CTM* 34 (1963) 261-77.

Loosely based on Eph 1:9-10, this article broadly discusses God's οἰκονομια ("plan") from Abraham, through the church age, to the end of history. God's *oikonomia* antedates and underlies his divine purposes through history. The study develops implications for Christian stewardship—broadly defined—at length and concludes with a brief bibliography. Strong on application and laden with secondary biblical references.

300. Conchas, D. A. "Redemptio acquisitionis (Eph. 1, 14)." *VD* 30 (1952) 14-29, 81-91, 154-169.

301. Coppieters, H. "La doxologie de la lettre aux Éphésiens: Notes sur la construction syntaxique de Éph. 1, 3-14." *RB* n.s. No. 1 (1909) 74-88.

Discussion of the various literary and grammatical features of this expansive introductory section. Comments on the three parallel sections evident in the Greek text (vv. 3b-4, 5-8a, and 8b-14) interacting with the major commentaries of the time. Concludes with a diagram of the structure of the section.

302. Couch, B. M. "Blessed Be He Who Has Blessed. Ephesians 1:3-14." *International Review of Mission* 77/306 (1988) 213-20.

An English translation of a brief Bible study written in Spanish from a liberationist perspective. Concludes that 1:3-14 is a doxology or summary of the divine plan of salvation contained in a letter which itself is the most mature distillation of Pauline theology. Includes a chart of the passage based on Krugger's semiotic analysis. Decides that the central theme concerns being in Christ as the new life and the new humanity.

303. Coune, M. "Dieu veuille illuminer les yeux de notre (Ép I)." *AsSeign* n.s. 11 (1971) 75-79.

304. _____. "A la louange de sa gloire. Eph 1.3-14." *AsSeign* 46 (1974) 37-42.

The great benediction of this passage divides into proclamation, predestination, redemption, and salvation for all. It recapitulates the essence of the gospel.

305. Coutts, J. "Ephesians 1.3-14 and I Peter 1.3-12." *NTS* 3/2 (1956-57) 115-27.

A form-critical study based on a comparative analysis of these texts in Greek. Both passages are homilies that derive from a common form, namely, liturgical prayer connected with the rite of baptism. Offers a reconstruction of the original prayer underlying the Ephesian passage. Uncovers the relation of Ephesians to 1 Peter and to Colossians.

306. Cunningham, M. K. "Karl Barth's Interpretations and Use of Ephesians 1:4 in his Doctrine of Election. An Essay in the Relation of Scripture and Theology." Ph.D. thesis, Yale University, 1988.

307. Dahl, N. A. "Adresse und Proömium des Epheserbriefes." *ThZ* 7 (1951) 241-64.

See on texts, 1:1-2.

308. Davies, W. D. *Paul and Rabbinic Judaism.* London: SPCK, 1955. 4th ed. Philadelphia: Fortress, 1980, 147-76.

On the subject of Christ as the wisdom of God, Davies argues that for Paul, Jesus' teaching and life assumed the place of the New Torah. Paul came to picture Jesus in terms of the Wisdom of the OT and contemporary Judaism, as seen in such texts as Col 1:15-18; 1 Cor 10:1-4; 1:24; and 1:30. Concludes with a paragraph on the relevance of his conclusions for contemporary theology.

309. Debrunner, A, "Grundsätzliches über Kolometrie im NT." *Theologische Blätter* 5 (1926) 231-34.

310. Deichgräber, R. "Epheser 1, 3-14." In *Gotteshymnus und Christushymnus in der frühen Christenheit. Untersuchungen zu Form, Sprach und Stil der frühchristlichen Hymnen. SUNT* 5. Göttingen: Vandenhoeck & Ruprecht, 1967, 40-43; 64-76.

Discusses various prior studies on early Christian hymnody and proposes criteria for determining genuine hymnic material. Eph 1:3-14 occurs in the section of extended eulogies (along with 1 Pet 1:3-5 and Col 1:12-14). He also discusses examples of God-hymns and Christ-hymns plus similar forms in Ignatius and other NT examples.

311. Denton, D. R. "Inheritance in Paul and Ephesians." *EvQ* 54 (1982) 157-62.

Challenges P. L. Hammer's argument (in *JBL* 79 [1960] 267-72) that ΚΛΗΡΟΝΟΜΙΑ in Ephesians and Paul's *Hauptbriefe* is used in significantly different ways. Appeals to texts excluded by Hammer's methodology and argues that his conclusions derive from a faulty understanding of ΑΡΡΑΒΩΝ (Eph 1:10) and ΣΥΓΚΛΗΡΟΝΟΜΟΣ (Rom 8:17 and Eph 3:6). A focused, well-documented study.

312. Drago, A. "La nostra adozione a figli di Dio in Ef 1,5." RivB 19 (1971) 203-19.

Analyzes 1:5 with a view to establishing the meaning of *huiothesian* (adoption) in its context and in relation to other texts. Adoption is foundational to the developing stages of salvation which God determined for us. It expresses the "state of children" to which God predestined us and which is now being worked out via the Spirit through Christ's merits.

313. Dreyfus, F. "Pour la louange de sa gloire (Ep 1, 12. 14): L'origine
      vetero-testamentaire de la formule." In Paul de Tarse. Apôtre
      du nôtre Temps, ed. L. de Lorenzi. Rome: Abbaye de S. Paul,
      1979, 233-48.

      Studying the hymn of Eph 1:3-14 that begins the letter, the author
      focuses attention on what the author considers the leitmotiv of the
      hymn: praise and glory (vv. 6, 12, 14), in Paul's thought and the
      Ephesian letter. Studies the origin of concepts of glory in Middle-
      Eastern thought. Sees the presence of the transcendent glory and
      perfection of God in the writings of Moses which becomes
      progressively refined and elaborated in the OT (including the stress
      on the importance of God's name) until it finds its way into this
      Ephesian hymn.

314. Dufort, J.-M. "La recapitulation paulinienlle dans l'exégèse des
      Peres." *StEv* 12 (1960) 21-38.

315. Feuillet, A. *Le Christ Sagesse de Dieu d'après les épîtres
      pauliniennes, Études bibliques.* Paris: Gabalda, 1966.

      Very thorough study of Christology in the NT that locates Paul's
      soteriology in the late Jewish Wisdom tradition. In studying "the
      rulers of this age" in various NT texts (including Eph 1:23, 3:18),
      Feuillet decides that Paul did not intend a cosmology but rather a
      Christology that was soteriological by applying wisdom themes to
      Christ (especially Prov 8). Divine wisdom is accessible in Christ.

316. Fischer, K. M. *Tendenz und Absicht des Epheserbriefs.* FRLANT
      111 Göttingen: Vandenhoeck & Ruprecht, 1973.

      This volume addresses the purpose of Eph and in the history-of-
      religions problems raised by the various spiritual traditions in the
      book. Discusses several key topics including the body of Christ (the
      church's unity), the variety of church material, and gnostic
      influences. On this passage see especially pp. 111-18.

317. Flowers, H. J. "Adoption and Redemption in the Beloved. A Study of Ephesians 1, 5-7." *ExpT* 39 (1927-28) 16-21.

Elaborates on three broad ideas contained in these verses: God's eternal purpose in Christ; God's adoption of human beings; and redemption through Christ's blood. A homiletical study that treats the passage as a springboard to sundry topics. Far-reaching and pedantic.

318. _____. "Election in Jesus Christ—A Study of Ephesians 1:3-4." *RE* 26 (1929) 55-67.

319. Gamber, K. "Alteste Eucharistiegebete. 9. Die paulinischen Dankgebete im Epheser- und Kolosserbrief." *Heiliger Dienst* 42/4 1988) 171-76.

A study of the thanksgiving prayers in Eph 1:3-14 and Col 1:12-20 (cf. 1 Pet 1:3-5; 2 Cor 1:3-4). Discovers common themes and formulas used in early Christian eucharistic prayers, with roots in Jewish prayers before them.

320. Gibbs, J. G. *Creation and Redemption: A Study in Pauline Theology.* NovT Supp. 26. Leiden: Brill, 1971.

Concludes that Christ mediates as the nexus between God's creation and redemption (on the basis of a study of Rom 8:19-23, 38-39; 5:12-21; 1 Cor 8:6; Phil 2:6-11; Col 1:15-20; and Eph 1:3-14). The discussion of this latter text occurs on pp. 114-34. Christ exercises cosmic sovereignty and lordship over the church. These themes originate in Paul's Hebraic background rather than within Hellenism.

321. Grelot, P. "La structure d'Éphésiens 1:3-14." *RB* 96/2 (1989) 237-64.

Seeks to explain this interminable sentence which forms a liturgical text or hymn by proposing that the initial phrase of v. 3a constitutes a refrain that is repeated before each of the six stanzas.

322. Groenewald, E. P. "Jesus Jesurun/ἠγαπημένος Eph 1, 6 - Is 44, 2

(LXX)." *Nederduitse Gereformeerde Teologiese Tydskrif* 2/4
(1961) 197-204.

323.   Gromacki, R.   "Ephesians 1:3-14: the Blessings of Salvation."   In
       New Testament Studies in Honor of Homer A. Kent, Jr., ed. G.
       T. Meadors. Winona Lake, IN: BMH Books, 1991, 219-237.

A phrase-by-phrase study of the singular Greek sentence,
emphasizing word meanings, grammar, and theology.   Greek is
confined to parentheses and the whole is quite accessible to those
without it, though some parsings are included in the notes.

324.   Halter, H.   "Eph 1,3-14. Versiegelt mit dem Geist der Verheissung."
       In *Taufe und Ethos: Paulinische Kriterien für das Proprium
       christlicher Moral.* Freiburg: Herder, 1977.

This massive study evaluates twenty-one passages that detail the
existential dimensions of baptism, including several Ephesian texts:
1:3-14 (227-233); 2:1-10; 4:1-6, 17-24; 4:25 - 5:2;5:3-14, 25-27.
Then examines the relation between the indicative of baptism and the
resulting ethical imperatives that grow out of these texts. Baptism
enveloped, for Paul, the total plan of salvation.

325.   Hammer, P. L.   "A Comparison of κληρονομία in Paul and
       Ephesians." *JBL* 79/3 (1960) 267-72.

A comparison of passages in Paul and Ephesians (presumed to be
"deutero-Pauline") with reference to the κληρονομ- word group.
Makes eschatological, Christological, and ecclesiological comparisons of κληρονομία ("inheritance"), κληρονόμος ("heir"), and
συνκληρονόμος ("fellow heir") respectively.   Concludes that
inheritance in Ephesians is future while for Paul it is oriented to the
past. A thought-provoking study whose conclusions D. R. Denton
would challenge (see above).

326.   Harris, W. H.   "'The Heavenlies' Reconsidered: Οὐρανός and
       Ἐπουράνιος in Ephesians." *BSac* 148 (1991) 72-89.

Examines all Ephesian (1:3, 10, 20; 2:6; 3:10, 15; 4:10; 6:9, 12) and some other NT contexts in which these terms occur. Discusses background of both and questions their alleged interchangeability in Ephesians. Concludes that *ouranos* is the more preferred term when it is used in contrast to earth, while *epouranios*—which may encompass the earthly realm (3:10)—more often denotes the place where the ascended Christ dwells (1:3, 20; 2:6).

327. Harrisville, R. A. "Der kosmische Christus im Neuen Testament." In *Das Evangelium und die Bestimmung des Menschen,* ed.V. Vajta. Göttingen: Vandenhoeck &: Ruprecht, 1972, 38-63.

Discusses 1:9-10 in his treatment of the cosmic Christ.

328. Hartin, P. J. "ΑΝΑΚΕΦΑΛΑΙΩΣΑΣΘΑΙ ΤΑ ΠΑΝΤΑ ΕΝ ΤΩ ΧΡΙΣΤΩ (Eph. 1:10)." *A South African Perspective on the New Testament,* ed. J. H. Petzer and P. J. Hartin. Leiden: Brill, 1986, 228-37.

Engages in an exegesis of this phrase from 1:10. It starts with a study of the context of the phrase with the entire letter and proceeds to studies of each of the terms. Concludes that the phrase points to God's eventual plan to sum up or unite all things in Christ as Head. The church has a special role to cooperate with God in bringing to all creation the knowledge of this mystery. The study concludes with some implications for modern science and the relations between diverse peoples.

329. Hofius, O, "'Erwählt vor Grundlegung der Welt' (Eph. 1.4)." *ZNW* 62/1-2 (1971) 123-28.

Discovers backgrounds for the conception of the election of the people of God in Jubilees 2:19ff., the rabbinic interpretations of Psa 74:2, and in Joseph and Aseneth 8:9.

330. Hoyt, H. A. "The Purpose and Program of the Prophetic Word." *GTJ* 4 (1983) 163-71.

Studies the purpose and program of prophecy as suggested by Rev 4:11; Eph 1:11; and 3:11. The author traces God's glory in Eden, with Israel's patriarchs, the tabernacle and temple, the incarnation, the church, the second coming and finally in the eternal state.

331. Innitzer, Th. "Der 'Hymnus' im Epheserbrief (1,3-14)." *ZKT* 28 (1904) 612-21.

332. Jayne, D. "'We' and 'You' in Eph. 1:3-14." *ExpT* 85 (1974) 151-52.

After considering the likely options, the author takes 'we' to be the Senders of the letter and 'you' to be the Recipients.

333. Jankowski, A. "L'espérance messianique d'Israël selon la pensée paulinienne, en partant de *Proelpizein* (Ep I, 12)." In *De la Tôrah au Messie*. FS H. Cazelles, ed. M. Carrez, J. Doré, and P. Grelot. Paris: Desclée, 1981, 475-81.

Seeks to pursue the theme of the mysterious presence of Christ in the historic people of God in the OT, particularly as that presence is found in the messianic hope of Israel in Paul's thinking. The point of departure for the study is the verb *proelpizein* (to hope previously) found in Eph 1:12 which he studies both within and outside of Pauline and NT writings. The divine election of people in Christ before the foundation of the world (Eph 1:4) explains the nature of "who were the first to hope in Christ" (1:12).

334. Joüon, P. "Notes philologiques sur quelques versets de l'Épître aux Éphésiens (1,12; 2,1-3; 2,15; 3,13.15; 4,28; 5,18.19; 6,9.19-20)." *Revue des Sciences Religieuses* 26 (1936) 455-56.

Brief technical notes.

335. Kerr, A. J. "APPABΩN." *JTS* 39/1 (1988) 92-97.

Discusses the proper translation of this concept in its various uses, including Eph 1:14. Concludes that "a first installment" best conveys the original sense to modern readers.

336. Krahe, Maria-Judith. "Psalmen, Hymnen und Lieder, wie der Geist

sie eingibt: Doxologie als Ursprung und Ziel aller Theologie."
In *Liturgie und Dichtung II: Interdisziplin und Reflexion,* Pictas
Liturgica Series, ed. H. Becker and R. Kaczynski. St. Ottilien:
EOS Verlag Erzabtei St. Ottilien, 1983, 923-57.

Contains a bibliography.

337. Krämer, H. "Zur sprachlichen Form der Eulogie Eph. 1.3-14." *Wort
und Dienst* N.F. 9 (1967) 34-46.

338. Kruse, C. "Il significato di περιποίησις in Eph. 1.14." *RivB* 16
(1968) 465-94.

Concludes that the term has an active sense used epexegetically with
ἀπολύτρωσιν. Parallel to his deliverance of Israel from Egypt, in
redemption God obtains a new people. The Greek Father understood
περιποίησις to be an act of God.

339. Lamarche, P. "Étude d'Éphésiens 1,3-23." In *Christ vivant. Essai
sur la Christologie du Nouveau Testament.* Paris: Cerf, 1966,
73-82.

Proceeds from the speeches of Acts through the Epistles and Gospels
to the Fourth Gospel to outline the NT's teaching on Christology.

340. Lang, F. "Die Eulogie in Epheser 1, 3-14." In *Studien zur
Geschichte und Theologie der Reformation.* FS E. Bizer, ed.
L. Abramowski and J. F. G. Goeters. Neukirchen-Vluyn:
Neukirchener Verlag, 1969, 7-20.

A study of this section that divides into four components: the
passage's formal arrangement or structure; its assertions of content
and *Sitz im Leben*; its history of religions background; and the place
of this eulogy at the outset of the letter itself. He concludes that this
sections functions as the basis or foundation (*Grundlage*) of the
entire Ephesian epistle.

341. Lemmer, H. R. "Reciprocity between Eschatology and Pneuma in
Ephesians 1:3-14." *Neot* 21 (1987) 159-82.

Using techniques of discourse analysis, the author studies 1:3-14 finding a reciprocal connection between eschatology and the Spirit throughout the passage. An appendix includes a diagram of the Greek text of the passage analyzed according to his discourse analysis. In the course of the study, he defends the Pauline authorship of Ephesians.

342. Lightfoot, J. B. *Notes on Epistles of St. Paul.* London: Macmillan, 1895, 307-24.

Commentary discussion of 1:1-14.

343. Lincoln, A. T. "A Re-Examination of 'The Heavenlies' in Ephesians." *NTS* 19 (1973) 468-83.

Studies each use of the concept of "heavenlies" deciding that a local sense best fits all the uses. Ephesians views heaven in a Pauline eschatological perspective in which the two ages currently overlap. So, the believers experience spiritual benefits because they are in the "heavenlies" in Christ.

344. Lohmeyer, E. "Das Proömium des Epheserbriefes." *Theologische Blätter 5* (1926) 120-25.

345. Lyonnet, S. "La benédiction de Eph. 1, 3-14 et son arrière-plan judaïque." In *A la Rencontre de Dieu.* FS A. Gelin, ed. M. Jourjon, et al. Le Puy: Editions Xavier Mappus, 1961, 341-52.

346. MacArthur, Jr. J. *Chosen for Eternity. A Study of Election.* Chicago: Moody, 1989.

A very short study of 1 Pet 1:1-2 and Eph 1:3-14 on the topic of God's election to salvation.

347. MacDonald, W. G. "The Biblical Doctrine of Election." In *The Grace of God, the Will of Man: A Case for Arminianism,* ed. C. H. Pinnock. Grand Rapids: Zondervan, 1989, 207-29.

An exposition of Eph 1:3-14 occurs in the midst of an argument on the subject of election, since it is "the most definitive passage" on this subject (pp. 219-26). The focus of election is in Christ and before creation. Election limited to Israel in the OT need not demand that election is limited to Christians in the NT, for "the church actually predates Israel!" Provides a diagram of the passage in Greek.

348. Mackay, J. R. "Paul's Great Doxology." *EvQ* 2 (1930) 150-61.

349. Maurer, C. "Der Hymnus von Epheser I als Schlüssel zum ganzen Briefe." *EvT* 11 (1951-52) 151-72.

350. McGough, M. E. "An Investigation of ἐπουράνιος in Ephesians." Th.D. thesis, New Orleans Baptist Theological Seminary, 1987.

Considers the implications of this term for the discussion of heaven.

351. McHugh, J. "A Reconsideration of Ephesians 1.10b in the Light of Irenaeus." In *Paul and Paulinism,* ed. M. D. Hooker and S. G. Wilson. London: S.P.C.K., 1982, 302-9.

Attempts to determine the precise meaning of the primary phrase of 1:10 after surveying with dissatisfaction the standard lexica. On the basis of Irenaeus' usage of ἀνακεφαλαιοῦσθαι and relevant partistic Latin material, McHugh moves away from "unification" to "recapitulation."

352. McNicol, J. "The Spiritual Blessings of the Epistle to the Ephesians." *EvQ* 9 (1937) 64-73.

353. Montagnini, F. "Christological Features in Eph 1:3-14." In *Paul de Tarse: Apôtre du nôtre Temps,* ed. L. de Lorenzi et al. Rome: Abbaye de Saint Paul, 1979, 529-39.

Traces the references to Christ.

354. Mussner, F. "The People of God According to Eph 1, 3-14." *Concilium* 10 (1965) 96-109.

355. O'Brien, P. T. "Ephesians 1: An Unusual Introduction to a New Testament Letter." *NTS* 25 (1979) 504-16.

An examination of the structure of Ephesians 1. The opening of this letter is unique because the more customary Pauline introductory thanksgiving (vv. 15-19a) follows the *berakah* (an intercessory prayer of thanksgiving to God) in vv. 3-14. O'Brien considers the didactic function of the opening chapter, briefly states its implications for authorship, and locates the nature of the prayer of vv. 3-19 in the Qumran form *Hodayoth*. A concentrated, well-documented study.

356. Odeberg, H. *The View of the Universe in the Epistle to the Ephesians.* Lund: Lund Universitets Arsskrift, 1934.

357. Perez, G. "El plan divino de la salvación." *CulB* 11 (1954) 149-160.

On 1:3-14

358. Piper, O. A. "Praise of God and Thanksgiving." *Int* 8/1 (1954) 3-20.

In an wide-ranging article on the doctrine of prayer, Piper cites Eph 1:3-14 to show Paul's stress on the need to praise God.

359. Poganski, D. "7th Sunday after Trinity: Eph 1:3-14." *CTQ* 46 (1982) 61-62.

A homiletical outline prefaced by a brief introduction to the structure and theme of the passage. Contains cross references and some sermonic helps. Immediately useful to preachers.

360. Potter, R. "The Expectation of the Creature." *SCR* 4 (1951) 256-262.

361. Pratt, F. V. "Ephesians 1:6." *ExpT* 23 (1910-11) 331.

362. Ramaroson, L. "`La grande benediction' (Eph 1:3-14)." *Science et Esprit* 33 (1981) 93-103.

The passage comprises a eulogy blessing God for his salvific plan that consists of two parts: election to holiness and predestination to adoption. A redactor at some stage inserted 1:6b-9a to direct attention on the theme of Col 1:13b-14, 20.

363. Rayburn, S. "Cosmic Transfiguration." *Church Quarterly Review* 168 (1967) 162-67.

Finds that God has transfigured the cosmos in Christ. While the Eastern church retained this truth it has only been recently rediscovered in the West, especially by Teilhard de Chardin.

364. Reumann, J. "OIKONOMIA-Terms in Paul in Comparison with Lucan *Heilsgeschichte.*" *NTS* 13 (1966-67) 147-67.

Investigates what in Luke's background led to his theology being described as *heilsgeschichtlich* and where in Paul's writings his views might also be considered as promoting "salvation history" as understood by modern scholars. To do so, Reumann follows the word study method, tracing *oikonomia* and related terms in Hebrew and Christian literature as well as in Luke and Paul. Two of the key passages for Paul occur in Ephesians: 1:10 and 3:2, 9. In the Ephesians texts *oikonomia* conveys the administration or "carrying out" of the mystery of God's plan. Indeed, for Paul *oikonomia* means "administration" more often than "plan of salvation."

365. Rimbault, L. "Éph. 1:3-6." *ETR* 30/4 (1955) 16-17.

366. Robbins, C. J. "The Composition of Eph 1:3-14." *JBL* 105 (1986) 677-87.

The author proposes that, in spite of common statements to the contrary, the length of the sentence, 1:3-14, and the manner of its composition are not unique but in accord with the principles of Greek rhetoric as understood by the ancient Greek rhetoricians. A similarly long sentence in Isocrates' *Panegyricus* (47-49) provides the basis for this comparative study, which is preceded by a discussion of "periodic" structures. An interesting and enterprising article providing a Greek diagram of the passage.

367. Robinson, J. M. "Die Hodajot-Formel in Gebet und Hymnus des Frühchristentums." In *Apophoreta,* FS E. Haenchen, ed. W. Eltester and F. H. Kettler, *BhZNW* 30. Berlin: Töpelmann, 1964, 194-235.

368. Rodd, C. S. "The Riches of God." *ExpT* 97 (1986) 207-8.

A short sermon designed for Trinity Sunday consisting, appropriately, of three points: God's Plan; Christ's Redemption; and The Holy Spirit, Guarantee of our Inheritance. Written in conversational style with illustrations.

369. Romaniuk, K. *L'amour du Pere et du Fils dans la sotériologie de saint Paul.* Analecta Biblica 15. Rome: Pontifical Biblical Institute, 1961, 153-183.

A discussion, in French, of the love of God and of Christ in the provision of redemption according to the teaching of Paul. On pp. 153-83 the author exegetes Eph 1:3-14 to understand the Father's initiative—the divine will—in salvation. Conducts extensive Greek word studies and reflects on the nature of divine election: it imposes on believers the obligation to imitate God. Wide-ranging in its consideration of other biblical texts and concepts. The biblical index shows that the author cites Ephesian texts extensively throughout this careful study.

370. Rongy, H. "La doxologie de l'Épître aux Éphésiens (Eph 1, 3-14)." *Revue Ecclesiastique de Liege* 31 (1940) 253-70.

371. Sanders, J. T. "Hymnic Elements in Ephesians 1-3." *ZNW* 56 (1965) 214-32.

Evaluates the various passages in Eph 1-3 that some have considered as hymns quoted by the author. Concludes that probably 1:3-14 and 1:20-23 and perhaps 2:4-10—texts with alleged hymnic elements—are not quotations but compositions of the author, possibly expansions of Col 2:10-13. On the other hand, the hymn in 2:14-18, because of differences in style and language from its context is a quotation. Includes an extensive exegesis of 1:3-14, deciding it is probably not a hymn.

372. Scharlemann, M. H. "The Secret of God's Plan: Studies in Ephesians." *CTM* 40 (1969) 532-44.

Following a brief introduction to the study of Ephesians and to two terms that unpack God's plan in Ephesians—"mystery" and "design" (*prothesis*)—the study investigates 1:3-14. The approach is descriptive and homiletic, not technical.

373. Schattenmann, J. *Studien zum neutestamentlichen Prosahymnus.* Munich: C. H. Beck, 1965, 1-10.

Shows that the hymns in the Gospels and Epistles for a Hellenistic, not a Semitic pattern. Compares the structures and rhythms of the NT hymns to Mithraic, Gnostic, and Philonic sources.

374. Schille, G. *Frühchristliche Hymnen.* Berlin: Evangelische Verlangsanstalt, 1965, 65-73.

Studies 1:3-12 and 2:4-10 among what he considers the genre of initiation-songs in the NT. He also considers "Redeemer-songs" (2:14-18).

375. Schlier, H. *Der Brief an die Epheser.* 2d ed. Düsseldorf: Patmos, 1958, 159-67.

Pages on wisdom in this text.

376. Schnackenburg, R. "Die grosse Eulogie Eph 1, 3-14: Analyse unter textlinguistischen Aspekten." *Biblische Zeitschrift* 21 (1977) 67-87.

Analyzes the formal aspects of the section which divide into six subsections of two verses each. The author seeks to elicit gratitude, humility, and joy in the readers and to move them to unity in their joint praise of God. The structure does not result from hymnic, poetic, or thematic factors.

377. Schweizer, E. "Aufnahme und Korrektur jüdischer Sophiatheologie im Neuen Testament." In *Neotestamentica.* Zürich: Zwingli, 1963, 110-21.

On the beginning and the correction of Jewish wisdom theology in the NT.

378. Staerck, W. "Anakephalaiosis." *RAC* I (1950) 411-14.

379. Stanley, D. M. "The Definitive Formulation of Pauline Soteriology. Eph, 1, 3-14." In *Christ's Resurrection in Pauline Soteriology. AnBib* 13. Rome: Pontifical Biblical Institute, 1961, 216-220.

In chapter 8 of this comprehensive study of the topic of Jesus' resurrection in Paul's writings, the author considers six Ephesian texts (1:3-14, 19b-23; 2:4-8, 14-18; 4:32 - 5:2; and 5:5-26). As the title for the first text indicates, the author considers 1:3-14 to be a solemn act of thanks in which Paul sums up "the various moments in God's loving plan of salvation in favour of `the people of his acquiring'" (217). Includes brief commentary on all these texts that provide insight into Paul's understanding of Christ's resurrection.

380. Strack, H. L., and P. Billerbeck. *Kommentar zum Neuen Testament aus Talmud und Midrasch.* 6 Vols. Munich: Beck, 1922-61, II: 353-58.

Discusses the Jewish background of wisdom behind John 1:1-6.

381. Sullivan, K. "Blessed be the God and Father of our Lord Jesus Christ." In *Liturgy for the People.* FS for G. Ellard, ed. W. J. Leonard. Milwaukee: Bruce Pub. Co, 1963, 29-37.

Samples the lack of scholarly consensus regarding the theme and structure of 1:3-14 and proposes that we have in this hymn one of two known types of liturgical prayer (or *eucharistia*) which consists of the blessing proper and the motive(s) for the blessing. Paul's opening exhortation to bless God is followed in the remainder of the passage by six specific gifts of God that provide the impetus for worship.

382. Summers, R. "One Message—Revelation." *RE* 60/4 (1963) 380-87.

An exegetical study of 1:3 - 2:10 to aid those intending to teach this section.

383. Suski, A. "Eulogia w liście do Efezjan (L'eulogie dans l'épitre aux Ephésiens)." *Studia theologica Varwaviensia* 16/1 (1978) 19-47.

Divides 1:3-14 into two parts: the first (vv. 3-10) a liturgical hymn akin to Qumran or the Psalms of Solomon, and the second (vv. 11-14) an editorial expansion. Similarities in terms, style, and theology argue that 1:3-10, along with 1:20-22 and 2:4-7, derive from a baptismal setting. The entire section of 1:2-14 serves as the thematic prologue to the letter.

384. Thomas, W. H. G. "Ephesians 1:6." *ExpT* 29 (1917-18) 561.

385. Trinidad, J. T. "The Mystery Hidden in God. A Study of Eph 1, 3-14." *Bib* 31 (1950) 1-26.

386. Van Imschoot, P. "'Recapitulare omnia in Christi' (Eph 1, 10)." *Collationes Gandavenses* 29 (1946) 3-7.

387. Wilson, R. A. "'We' and `You' in the Epistle to the Ephesians." *StEv* 2, ed. F. L. Cross. *TU* 87. Berlin: Akademie-Verlag, 1964, 676-80.

Studies "the inexplicable vacillation between `you' and `we'" throughout Ephesians (quoting Mitton's commentary, p. 225), concentrating mostly on the passages up through 2:10. Concludes that "we" always refers to all Christians, while "you" refers to a smaller group distinct from other Christians. Yet in the first half of the letter this smaller group has been joined to the rest of the church, and the remainder of the epistle consists of instructions to this smaller group, the newly baptized. Finds in this reconstruction evidence that Ephesians derives from Paul—perhaps his basic form of baptismal catechesis.

388. Zerwick, M. "'Benedictus Deus et Pater D. N. Jesus Christi qui
       benedixit nos ...' (Eph 1, 3)." *VD* 22 (1942)   3-7.

Ephesians 1:15-23

389. Allen, T. G. "Exaltation and Solidarity with Christ: Ephesians 1.20
       and 2.6." *JSNT* 28 (1986) 103-20.

Investigates the unity between Christ and believers in an attempt to
discern some overall pattern of thinking. The clear association
between Christ's exaltation in 1:20 and the believer's exaltation in
2:6 sheds light on how the author views the bond between Christ and
believers. Shows the parallelism in the thought and vocabulary in
the two texts. Investigates the nature of believers' exaltation with
Christ. Surveys explanations for the possible historical and religious
background of these verses. The correlation between 1:20 and 2:6
reflects the Semitic pattern of corporate solidarity/personality—the
One and Many. The church as Christ's body experiences corporate
unity with Christ and is the corporate expression of Christ's self-
giving love.

390. _____. "God the Namer. A Note on Ephesians 1.21b." *NTS* 32
       (1986) 470-75.

God is the subject of all the verbs in 1:20-22, and thus God is the
one who names the various names mentioned in v. 21b. This
conclusion accords best with the OT and ancient Near Eastern
thought and best fits the context of Eph 1.

391. Barr, R. R. "The Soteriological Value of Resurrection." *AER* 146
       (1962) 304-14.

Unpacks Van Roo's analysis of the resurrection in terms of

instrumental efficient causality by adding the quasi-formal cause, the Holy Spirit.

392. Barth, K. *Church Dogmatics,* IV: 1-3. Edinburgh: T. & T. Clark, 1956, 1958, 1961.

See especially 1: 660-68; 2: 621-27; 3: 752-62, 790-95 on the topics of head, body, fullness and their implications.

393. Bedale, S. "The Meaning of κεφαλή in the Pauline Epistles." *JTS* 5 (1954) 211-15.

Seeks in the Hebrew *rosh* the background for the Greek word translated "head." The Hebrew has two senses: the literal, anatomical head and hence "top" of something; and the meaning of "first" or beginning. Concludes that Paul typically employed the sense of "beginning" and we ought not construe his use at Col 1:18 or Eph 4:15 to mean "ruler." In view of the context of Eph 1:22, the sense there might well be "over-lord." In 5:23 "headship" refers to causal priority in the order of being.

394. Benoit, P. "Body, Head and Pleroma in the Epistles of the Captivity." In *Jesus and the Gospel,* Vol. 2. Tr. B. Weatherhead. New York: Seabury; London: Darton, Longman and Todd, 1974, 51-92. [French original in *RB* 63 (1956) 5-44; repr. in *Exégèse et théologie,* II. Paris: Du Cerf, 1961, 107-53.]

Investigates both the origin of the concept of the "Body of Christ" and whether that concept is used in Col and Eph differently than earlier in 1 Cor and Rom. Faith and baptism put believers physically and realistically—not mystically—within the body of Christ. Paul develops the concept in essentially the same ways in the early and later formulations in his letters. As "head" Christ has authority over all angelic powers. Provides an extensive analysis of the concept of *pleroma* (fullness) in Col and Eph as well.

395. _____. "The 'plérôma' in the Epistles to the Colossians and the Ephesians." *Svensk exegetisk årsbok* 49 (1984) 136-58.

In Ephesians, specifically, 1:23; 3:19; 4:13, Paul employed the concept of *plērōma* to speak of the fullness of divine life, or grace, a shift from its use in Colossians to describe the cosmic universe via Stoicism. Because of Christ's work the universe is no longer slave to cosmic powers; it is now regenerated and reunified and the location out of which the Creator shines.

396. Best, E. *One Body in Christ.* London: SPCK, 1955, 139-59.

Considers the main topic of the book within Ephesians, an epistle Paul probably wrote. Addresses the meaning of *pleroma* in Col and Eph: "Christ fills the church with his life; the Church is his *pleroma* even as he is the *pleroma* of God" (143). Eph 1:22-23 figure prominently in the discussion though Best moves on to 4:11-16 and 2:14-16 too. Concludes by comparing the teaching of the body of Christ in Eph to that of Col and the earlier epistles.

397. _____. "The Body of Christ." *EcuR* 9 (1957) 122-28.

398. Black, M. "πᾶσαι ἐξουσίαι αὐτῷ ὑποταγήσονται." In Paul and Paulinism. FS C. K. Barrett, ed. M. D. Hooker and S. G. Wilson. London: S.P.C.K., 1982, 74-82.

Notes the echoes of Psa 110:1 in 1 Cor 15:24-27; Eph 1:20-21; and 1 Pet 3:22 where Christ is viewed as destroying and superior to angelic "powers." Proceeds to trace the subservience of these powers in Jewish literature and the NT.

399. Bogdasovich, M. "The Idea of Pleroma in the Epistles to the Colossians and Ephesians." *Downside Review* 83 (1965) 118-30.

Investigates the larger background and Paul's uses of *pleroma* (including Eph 1:23) in the attempt to address its sources and literary origins, its place in the development of Judaeo-Christian thought, and its relevance to contemporary life and thought. Concludes that *pleroma* is an extremely expansive term for Paul, one hardly definable but one that can incorporate "almost all the truths of Christianity" (129).

400. Bonnard, P. "Mourir et vivre avec Jesus-Christ." *RHPR* 36 (1956)
      101-12.

      Classifies and evaluates the texts in Paul that employ expression
      "with Christ." Considers the various options for understanding
      believers' identification with Christ.

401. Caird, G. B. *Principalities and Powers.* Oxford: Clarendon, 1956.

      Distillation of lectures on the subject of the evil powers as they come
      to be reflected in the NT, but especially in Paul's writings. All these
      powers are vanquished in Christ.

402. Carr, W. *Angels and Principalities: The Background, Meaning and
      Development of the Pauline Phrase hai archai kai hai exousiai.*
      SNTSMS 42. Cambridge: Cambridge University Press, 1981,
      93-111.

      The entire study considers Paul's thoughts on the "powers" in the
      world. Pp. 93-111 focus on the references to the powers and the
      spiritual world in Ephesians, especially 1:21, 2:2, 3:10, and 6:12ff.

403. Colpe, C. "Zur Leib-Christi-Vorstellung im Epheserbrief." In
      Judentum, Urchristentum Kirche. FS J. Jeremias, ed. W.
      Eltester, *BhZNW* 26. Berlin: de Gruyter, 1960, 172-87.

404. Deichgräber, R. *Gotteshymnus und Christushymnus in der frühen
      Christenheit. Untersuchungen zu Form, Sprache und Stil der
      frühchristlichen Hymnen. SUNT* 5. Göttingen: Vandenhoeck
      & Ruprecht, 1967, 161-65.

      Seeks to isolate criteria for determining genuine hymnic material.
      See more on 1:3-14.

405. Delling, G. "πλήρης κτλ." *TDNT* 6 (1968) 283-311.

      Major article on fill, fulfill and cognates.

406. Dillistone, F. W. "How Is the Church Christ's Body?" *ThT* 2 (1945) 56-68.

Investigates whether the body-concept ought be interpreted: mystically, metaphorically, or realistically. In Rom and 1 Cor the body metaphor conveys the sense of the church's union with Christ in his suffering, death, and resurrection—an organism that employs the Spirit-given gifts with the messianic society. In Col and Eph the focus is on the head-body distinction where Christ is viewed as the head of the church which he fills (Eph 1:23).

407. Dubarle, A. M. "L'origine dans l'Ancient Testament de la notion paulinienne de l'église corps du Christ." *AnBib* 17-18, I (1963) 231-40.

408. Dupont, J. *Gnosis: La connaissance religieuse dans les Épîtres de Saint Paul.* Paris: J. Gabalda, 1949, 419-93.

409. Ernst, J. *Pleroma und Pleroma Christi. Geschichte und Deutung eines Begriffs der paulinischen Antilegomena.* Regensburg: F. Pustet, 1970.

Subjects five passages in Col and Eph to detailed exegesis in the attempt to understand the concept of *plērōma* and its relationship to Paul's presentation of "the body of Christ" and the description of God's nature. Studies the background of "fullness" in the pre-Socratics and the Stoics. Considers Eph 1:22-23; 3:19; and 4:8-13 (in addition to Col 1:19; 2:9-10). The study ends with the history of interpretation of *plērōma* from the time of the Fathers to the present.

410. Feuillet, A. "L'Église plérôme du Christ d'après Éphés. 1, 23." *NRT* 78 (1956) 446-72, 593-610.

Argues that alleged divergences between Col and Eph are needlessly exaggerated, demonstrating this by analyzing the word πλήρωμα. Divergences are better explained as material that comes from a master who has a great command of his words.

411. Fischer, K. M. *Tendenz und Absicht des Epheserbriefs.* Göttingen:

Vandenhoeck & Ruprecht, 1973, 118-20.

See on 1:3-14.

412. Flowers, H. J. "Paul's Prayer for the Ephesians: A Study of Eph. 1:15-23." *ExpT* 38 (1926-27) 227-33.

An explication of this passage against the backdrop of incipient Gnosticism against which Paul writes. In this passage Paul provides the full fruit of his thinking about the person of Christ, the creative work of Christ as *pleroma*, and his mystical understanding of the presence of Christ in the church.

413. Fowler, R. "Ephesians 1:23." *ExpT* 76/9 (1965) 294.

A brief note on the literary structure of 1:19b-23.

414. Gewiess, J. "Die Begriffe πληροῦν und πλήρωμα im Kolosser- und Epheserbrief." In *Vom Wort des Lebens*. FS M. Meinertz, ed. N. Adler. Münster: Aschendorff, 1951, 128-41.

Studies the concept conveyed by the verb "to fill" and the noun "fullness" in the letters of Col and Eph. After citing the key texts in the letters, he begins the study at Eph 4:10, moves to 3:19 and 1:23, and finally to Col 2:10. Christ enacts a double filling: he fills the universe in everything and fills the church which becomes his "fullness" (1:23). "To fill the universe" (4:10) probably means to make captive the rebellious powers.

415. Giblet, J. "Mysterium in Eph 1, 17 - 2, 10." *Collectanea Mechliniensia* 33 (1948) 552-56.

416. Goossens, W. *L'Église, corps du Christ, d'après S. Paul.* Paris: Gabalda, 1949.

417. Gourgues, M. *"Éphésiens 1:20."* Á la droite de Dieu. Paris, Gabalda, 1978, 63-73.

A study of Jesus' resurrection and its fulfillment of Psa 110:1 in the

NT. Pp. 63-73 focus on Eph 1:20. Fails to find in Eph 1:20 the citation of a hymn but rather it derives from diverse primitive Christian elements which the author put together.

418. Grossouw, W. *In Christ.* Westminster, Md.: Newman, 1952.

419. Gundry, R. H. *Sōma in Biblical Theology with Emphasis on Pauline Anthropology.* Cambridge: Cambridge University Press, 1976, 223-44.

On these pages Gundry considers the church as the body of Christ with special references to Eph 1:22-23, 2:16, 4:4, 11-16 and 5:23, 30. Interacts with numerous positions and scholars, especially J. A. T. Robinson.

420. Hanson, S. *The Unity of the Church in the New Testament, Colossians and Ephesians.* *ASNU* 14. Uppsala: Almqvist & Wiksells, 1946, 112-17.

Pursues the topic of unity in the OT and Judaism, the synoptic tradition, and Paul's writings before coming to the evidence in Col and Eph.   Especially addresses the unity of the Church in Ephesians—particularly 1:22-23; 2:20ff.; 4:25-16; and 5:23-32—from pp. 121-61. In Ephesians the church is viewed not as a local congregation, but as the church at large. Considers the concept of the church in 1:22-23 on pp. 126-29.

421. Hegermann, H. *Die Vorstellung vom Schöpfungsmittler im hellenistischen Judentum und Urchristentum.* *TU* 82. Berlin: Akademie-Verlag, 1961.

Provides background for the view of the cosmological Christus and salvation in Hellenistic Christianity and for the creation theme in Hellenistic Judaism. Special focus on the hymn in Col 1.

422. _____. "Zur Ableitung der Leib-Christi-Vorstellung." *TLZ* 85 (1960) 839-42.

Compares the concept of the body of Christ in 1 Cor 12 and Rom 12 with the concept in Col and Eph. On both sides, *sōma Christou* speaks of the Church as a unified, pneumatic totality animated by Christ. Finds parallels to this usage in Philo and Wisdom of Solomon putting it in the strain of a belief in a Creator and creation, not within pessimistic Gnosticism.

423. Hermans, R. and Geysels, L. "Efesiërs 1, 23: Het pleroma van Gods heilswerk" [Ephesians 1:23: The Pleroma of God's Salvific Work.] *Bijdragen* 28/3 (1967) 279-93.

Going against the majority of exegetes who take *plēroumenou* as a middle with an active sense, this study shows that the Church is the *pleroma* of what God is doing, viz, salvation. Salvation is being fulfilled and in turn has its fulfillment in Christ, and in the Church as it is united in him.

424. Hitchcock, A. E. N. "Ephesians 1:23." *ExpT* 22 (1910-11) 91.

Brief note on this verse in which he suggests that *plerounemou* (that which fills) is middle voice and refers to God.

425. Hitchcock, F. R. M. "The Pleroma as the Medium of the Self-realisation of Christ." *Exp* 48, series 8, 24 (1922) 135-50.

426. Holladay, J. M. "One of Paul's Prayers—Eph 1:15-23." *Union Seminary Review* 22 (1910-11) 181-87.

427. Howard, G. "Head/Body Metaphors of Ephesians." *NTS* 20 (1974) 350-56.

Examines the grammatical and syntactical usage of the head/body metaphors in Eph 1:22-23 and 4:15-16. "The primary thrust of the author lies in the correlative relationship between the metaphors 'head' and 'feet'" (356) expressing Christ's sovereignty over all things. Thus the "body" metaphor is subordinate to the other two.

428. Jewett, R. *Paul's Anthropological Terms.* Leiden: Brill, 1971.

In Chapter 5 Jewett considers the term *soma* (body), especially as it relates to the discussion of the body of Christ. Traces the history of interpretation of the concept leading to his list of the eight options that have won support (pp. 201-27).

429.   Käsemann, E. *Leib und Leib Christi.* Tübingen: Mohr, 1933.

430.   _____. "The Theological Problem Presented by the Motif of the Body of Christ." *Perspectives on Paul.* Tr. M. Kohl. London: SCM and Philadelphia: Fortress, 1971, 102-21.

Insists that three elements lay behind the body of Christ concept: the Stoic notion of organism; the Christological formulation that 'in Christ' the church is a body; and the Jewish idea of 'corporate personality.' This is not mere metaphor but a reality for Paul. Probably Paul did not invent the idea of the body of Christ. In fact, the thematic treatment of the church in the NT cannot be called Pauline. In that Eph and Col divide Christ the head from the body confirms they must be Deutero-Pauline, for Paul never divided Christ from his body: the church is the body of Christ.

431.   Kuhn, K. G. "Der Epheserbrief im Lichte der Qumrantexte." *NTS* 7 (1960-61) 335-46.

Attempts to discern whether Ephesians can be located within a similar world—of language, thought and presentation—as the documents from Qumran, as well as other late Palestinian literature like Jubilees, the Testaments of the twelve Patriarchs, and the Enoch literature. Ephesians exhibits language and style that is Semitic-Greek in nature. Ephesians and Qumran texts are not mutually dependent on the OT. Exhortations such as Eph 5:3-17 appear to derive from Essene paraenesis. The capital sins of immorality, all impurity and covetousness are all from the Essene tradition. The light-darkness contrasts, similar in Ephesians and Qumran, are different from that of Gnostic dualism.

432.   Lee, J. Y. "Interpreting the Demonic Powers in Pauline Thought." *NovT* 12 (1970) 54-69.

Asks whether we can completely dismiss Paul's concept of demonic powers from our NT study as only the product of apocalyptic imaginations. After identifying the key terms, Lee studies the Jewish background of cosmic powers and their presence in Gnostic astrological belief. He concludes that the ancients believed in the literal presence of invisible beings who stood behind the occurrences in the visible world. Christ as Redeemed descended from heaven and died in order to rescue the entire cosmos from the control of these powers. Lee concludes with a modern application of these concepts.

433. Lightfoot, J. B. *St. Paul's Epistles to the Colossians and to Philemon.* London: Macmillan, 1875, 223, 255-71, 323-39.

His discussion on key points in this passage.

434. Lindemann, A. *Die Aufhebung der Zeit: Geschichtsverständnis und Eschatologie im Epheserbrief.* Gütersloh: Gerd Mohn, 1975, 59-63, 204-17.

Argues that Ephesians reflects post-Pauline Christianity showing its theological assumptions, its *Weltbild* relating to space and time, and its essential perspectives toward past, present, and future. Decides that Eph does not distinguish between history and eschatology.

435. Lubac, H. de. "Corpus Mysticum." *RCR* 29 (1939) 257-302, 429-80; 30 (1940) 40-80, 191-225.

436. MacGregor, G. H. C. "Principalities and Powers: the Cosmic Background of Paul's Thought." *NTS* 1 (1954) 17-28.

Assesses Paul's cosmic and demonic terminology: *kosmos* (world) plus words translated as angels, principalities, powers, dominions, et al. Investigates the possible backgrounds for these ideas in Paul. What kind of reality and deity, if any, do they have? They are real but not divine. Christ's death redeemed the world from its servitude to these evil forces. Considers whether such notions can have any place in modern theology. Suggests we must "demythologize" them, interpreting existentially in terms of our own experience in the confidence of Christ's victory over the world's worst evils.

437. Malevez, L. "L'église, corps du Christ." *Recherches de Science Religieuse* 32 (1944) 27-94.

438. McGlashan, A. R. "Ephesians 1:23." *ExpT* 76/4 (1964-65) 132-33.

Addresses the difficult grammatical points of the terms behind "the fullness" and "that which fills" and what they mean. The "fullness" refers to Christ, and that which is filled is the church.

439. Merklinger, H. A. "Pleroma and Christianity." *CTM* 36 (1965) 739-43.

Paul found the basic roots and concept of the term, not in his Gnostic opponents, but in the OT (e.g., Jer 23:24; Isa 6:3; Psa 33:5; 72:19; 119:64; Num 14:21). What does "fullness" convey? Christ is the fullness of the divine Being, the temple of God; and the church as Christ's fullness is the temple of God because God indwells its members.

440. Meuzelaar, J. J. *Der Leib des Messias. Eine exegetische Studie über den Gedanken vom Leib Christi in den Paulusbriefen.* Assen: Van Gorcum, 1961.

Seeks to understand the meaning of the concept of "life of Christ" in Paul's epistles. He finds the idea to be a practical one, neither Gnostic nor "realist" nor mystical, but rooted in Judaism with a rabbinic flavor.

441. Meyer, R. P. *Kirche und Mission im Epheserbrief.* Stuttgart: Katholisches Bibelwerk, 1977.

Studies 1:22b-23 in context and then traces its significant themes: the mystery of all coming together in Christ, the church as the body of Christ, and the church as the *plērōma* of Christ. Proceeds to show how ideas in Eph can be used to develop a theology of mission concluding that the church functions as missionary.

442. Minear, P. *Images of the Church in the New Testament.* Philadelphia: Westminster, 1960.

Considers both minor and major images used for the church. On pp. 173-220 takes up "the Body of Christ" in the Pauline letters. The variety of Paul's uses preclude any single definition of the concept. Some attention to the evidence from Eph occurs on pp. 213-20, though without presumption of Pauline authorship.

443. Montague, G. T. "From Faith and Charity to Knowledge: Eph. 1:15-17." In *Growth in Christ*. Kirkwood: Maryhurst Press, 1961, 86-95.

The book provides subsequent chapters on many following sections of Ephesians as well.

444. Montgomery-Hitchcock, F. R. "The Pleroma of Christ." *Church Quarterly Review* 125 (1937-38) 1-18.

445. Moule, C. F. D. *The Epistles of Paul the Apostle to the Colossians and to Philemon*, Cambridge Greek Testament Commentary. Cambridge: Cambridge University Press, 1958, 164-69.

In an appendix to this short commentary Moule considers the term *pleroma* (fullness). He concludes, "Christ is thought of as containing, representing, all that God is; and the destiny of Christians, as the Body of Christ, is to enter, in him, into that wealth and completeness" (169).

446. _____. "'Fullness' and 'Fill' in the New Testament." *SJT* 4 (1951) 79-86.

Studies the Greek root *plēr-* (full, fill) with a view towards its bearing on the theology of the NT. Disagrees with the majority view articulated by J. A. Robinson that *pleroma* in Eph 1:23 refers to the church, but takes it to refer to Christ: "God gave Christ to be head over all things to the Church, which is his body, {and that Christ should be} the *fullness* of him {God} who fills all in all." The basic idea of the root is "filling." Its key teaching centers on Christology, ecclesiology, and prophecy.

447. _____. "A Note on Ephesians i, 22, 23." *ExpT* 60 (1948) 53.

First offers and briefly defends the view that the participle *pleroumenou* should be taken as middle voice referring to God, not the church. See previous article for a fuller study of the *pler-* roots and its implications.

448.   _____.   *The Origin of Christology.*   Cambridge: Cambridge University Press, 1977, 69-89.

After considering the major titles for Jesus, Moule discusses, in chapter 2 "the corporate Christ." He treats "the body" in this section considering the evidence in Eph 1:23; 2:15f.; 3:6; 4:4, 12-16; and chapter 5.

449.   _____.   "Pleroma." *IDB*, ed. G. A. Buttrick, et al. 5 Vols. New York: Abingdon, 1962, III: 826-28.

450.   Mouton, E.   "Preaching from the Lectionary: Ascension." *Journal of Theology for South Africa* 82 (1993) 78-87.

Discusses the intercessory prayers of Eph 1:15-21 and the confession in 1:22-23. The goal of the first is that the readers come to know God. The second exalts Christ's position and his gift of salvation. Ends with devotional thoughts.

451.   Mussner, F.   *Christus, das All und die Kirche.*   Trier: Paulus Verlag, 1955, rep. 1968, 29-64, 118-74.

After an investigation of the cosmic *ta panta* formula, the author explores the exaltation-of-Christ theme and the *plērōma*-language in Eph. The bulk of the study is devoted to the ecclesiology of Eph, especially in 2:11-22. He also compares the *sōma* terminology in Eph with that in 1 Cor and Col. Finally, Mussner considers the origins of the *kephalē-sōma* concept in Eph and compares the "cosmic" Christian language to that of Gnostic mythology.

452.   O'Brien, P. T.   "Ephesians 1: An Unusual Introduction to a New Testament Letter." *NTS* 25 (1979) 504-16.

Ephesians, alone among the Pauline corpus, begins with both a *berakah* (blessing) and an introductory thanksgiving. Unpacks the language, structure, purpose of 1:3-14, and concludes with an assessment of the place of the thanksgiving and intercessory prayer of 1:15ff. Vv. 3-19 have a clear didactic intent; the prayer reports claim to be accounts of actual prayers. Though there are parallels to Qumran texts, the content of the prayers is distinctively Christian.

453. _____. "Principalities and Powers and Their Relationship to Structures." *RThR* (1981); reprinted in EvRT 6 (1982) 50-61.

Traces and critiques the post-war view that when Paul spoke of "principalities and powers" he was actually referring to structures such as tradition, convention, law, authority and even religion, especially the state and its institutions, rather than literal and actual demons. Surveys the NT evidence in Eph and Col as well as the rest of the NT to conclude that "the powers of evil then are to be understood as personal, supernatural agencies" (60). Satan and his demons may work through people, not impersonal structures. "The powers" are not structures.

454. Overfield, P. D. "Pleroma: A Study in Content and Context." *NTS* 25 (1979) 384-96.

Attempts to demonstrate that "there is no integral relationship between the so-called technical or gnostic use of the word πλήρωμα as it is found in the second-century Christian heretical sects and the use of the word in the New Testament" (384). The normal meaning of the word is amply used in the ancient world, and this typical, secular use accords better with the uses in the NT.

455. Percy, E. *Der Leib Christi in den paulinischen Homologoumena und Antilegomena.* Lund: Gleerup; Leipzig: Harrassowitz. 1942.

Compares the concept of the body of Christ—the Christian community—in both the recognized Pauline writings, especially Rom 12:4-5 and 1 Cor 12:12-27, with that found in Col and Eph. Though the perspectives differ, both can be viewed as thoroughly Pauline, and Pauline authorship can be affirmed for Col and Eph.

456. Pierron, J. "Le triomphe du Christ (Ep 1, 17-23)." *AsSeign* ns 28 (1969) 14-22.

457. Pokorný, P. *Der Epheserbrief und die Gnosis. Die Bedeutung des Haput-Glieder-Gedankens in der entstehenden Kirche.* Berlin: Evangelische Verlagsanstalt, 1965.

Investigates how Eph employs the concept of body in light of how the concept is used in writings of the mystery religions. Finds that Eph goes against several Gnostic tendencies.

458. _____. "Σῶμα Χριστοῦ im Epheserbrief." *EvT* 20 (1960) 456-64.

Growing out of his understanding of Paul, the author of Eph transformed current Gnostic ideas of celestial body into the concrete Church and Christ himself by focusing on the OT notion of headship seen Christologically and eschatologically. Christian presuppositions, then, not some version of the "*Urmensch-Mythus,*" constituted the decisive influences in the formation of the "body of Christ" motif in Ephesians.

459. Potterie, I. de la. "Le Christ, Plérôme de l'Église (Ep 1,22-23)." *Bib* 58/4 (1977) 500-24.

Studies these verses along three lines: proceeds to show that the verb πληρουμένου (what is filled) is clearly passive, not middle; analyzes the various literary dimensions of the passage; and draws out their rich theology in parallel to other texts. Concludes that πλήρωμα (fullness) refers to Christ as the church's head and that "which is filled" points to his body, the church which partakes of the divine life dwelling completely in the heavenly Christ. This interpretation fits well with the epistle's overall presentation of Christ as head of the church and of the church's growth.

460. Ramaroson, L. "Une lecture de Éphésiens 1, 15 - 2, 10." *Bib* 58/3 (1977) 388-410.

Suggests a text critical reading of 2:4c (*eleesen* rather than *egapesen*) which sets the stage for a core sentence proceeding throughout the section 1:15 to 2:7. He sets out the structure of this section given this solution and describes the major concepts that proceed laterally as a result, especially our corporate salvation with and in Christ.

461. Rawlinson, E. J. "Corpus Christi." In *Mysterium Christi,* ed. G. K. A. Bell and A. Deissmann. London: Longmans, 1930, 225-44.

462. Read, D. H. C. "The Gospel in the Galaxies: What Message for Mars?" *ExpT* 89 (1978) 212-13.

Sermonette on 1:22-23 asserting, in these times of space ventures, that Paul's message of Christ's supremacy is as true now as when first written.

463. Ridderbos, H. Paul: *An Outline of His Theology.* Tr. J. R. de Witt. Grand Rapids: Eerdmans, 1975, 362-95.

In this chapter on "The Church as the Body of Christ," the author interacts with the key issues and perspectives on Paul's view of the church including body and head in Ephesians, the church as *pleroma,* and the church as the people of God.

464. Rigaux, B. "Ep 1,20-22." In *Dieu l'a ressuscité. Exégèse et théologie biblique.* Gembloux: Duculot, 1973, 158-160.

In this far-reaching study of many facets of Jesus' resurrection, the author considers the Christological hymns.

465. Rimbault, L. "Éph. 1:15-23." *ETR* 30/4 (1955) 68-69.

In his prayer Paul calls for faith, love, but mostly hope. Hope is not the capacity to have courage and confidence, nor a disposition of the spirit or heart. Rather, it is the fruit of revelation, of the knowledge that God gives, of illumination.

466. Robertson, A. C. "'Hope' in Ephesians 1:18: a contextual approach." *Journal of Theology for Southern Africa* 55 (1986) 62-63.

Concludes that *elpis* in 1:18 can refer to salvation as a present reality, hope of unity and reconciliation, and an expectation of future blessing in heaven.

467. Robinson, J. A. "The Church as the Fulfillment of the Christ: a Note on Ephesians 1:23." *Exp,* 5th series, 57 (1898) 241-59.

468. Robinson, J. A. T. *The Body.* SBT 5. London: SCM; Chicago: Henry Regnery, 1952, 49-83.

This third and final chapter of this is a classic study on "The Body of the Resurrection." Many citations of Ephesian texts throughout.

469. Roels, E. *God's Mission: The Epistle to the Ephesians in Mission Perspective.* Franeker: Wever, 1962, 84-139, 229-48.

470. Sanders, J. T. "Hymnic Elements in Ephesians 1-3." *ZNW* 56 (1965) 214-32.

See under 1:3-14

471. _____. "The Transition from Opening Epistolary Thanksgiving to Body in the Letters of the Pauline Corpus." *JBL* 81 (1962) 348-62.

Using P. Shubert's work (see below) as his point of departure, Sanders determines that a distinctive form introduces and signals various transitions in the body of the Pauline letters. He defines its form and function. This suggests that there were formal structures in letters far beyond the mere conventions of their opening and closing. This may suggest a kind of form criticism to study epistles.

472. Sawatzky, S. "Pleroma in Ephesians 1:23." *Taiwan Journal of Theology* 11 (1989) 107-115.

Lays out historically and contextually (1:23) possible meanings of *plērōma,* offering several interpretive options whose underlying fundamental issue is whether the Church somehow fulfills Christ or Christ fills the Church. Reviews scholarship on both sides and affirms the latter view, which accords with the OT meaning of "fullness" as God's unilateral act of making his presence known.

473. Scharlemann, M. H. "The Secret of God's Plan: Studies in Ephesians - Two." *CTM* 41 (1970) 155-64.

A kind of sermonic lecture that focuses on 1:20-23 and 4:1-16.

474. Schenke, H.-M. *Der Gott "Mensch" in der Gnosis: Ein religionsgeschichtlicher Beitrag zur Diskussion über die paulinische Anschauung von der Kirche als Leib Christi.* Göttingen: Vandenhoeck & Ruprecht, 1962.

Challenges the position of Schlier that the Gnostic myth of the Heavenly Man lay behind Paul's concept of the Church as the body of Christ. Suggests, instead, that a pantheistic view of God may be the origin.

475. Schlier, H. *Principalities and Powers in the New Testament.* New York: Herder, 1961.

A study that divides into three parts: the nature and operations of the principalities, Jesus Christ and the principalities, and the Christian and the principalities. There follows a section devoted to the Antichrist from Rev 13. These powers are personal beings with intellect and will and who are capable of purposeful activity. A serious study that interacts with the Greek text and a wide range of literature.

476. _____. *Christus und die Kirche im Epheserbrief.* BHTh 6. Tübingen: Mohr, 1930.

477. _____. "κεφαλή." *TDNT* 3 (1965) 673-82.

Observes that this term translated "head" takes on decisive theological significance when applied to Christ and the Church in Ephesians. Christ as the head of the Church emphasizes the unity between Christ and the Church. "The Church is the earthly body of the heavenly Head" (680).

478. Schmidt, K. L. "ἐκκλησία." *TDNT* 3 (1965), especially 509-13.

Discusses the uses of this lexeme in Colossians and Ephesians. The author believes that gnostic terminology and ideology are used in Ephesians to express the relationship between Christ and the Church. He says, "In this respect Eph. is wholly Pauline in substance, whether written by Paul himself or one of his disciples" (511).

479. Schnackenburg, R. "Gestalt und Wesen der Kirche nach dem Epheserbrief." *Catholica* 15 (1961) 104-20.

480. _____. "L'Idée de 'Corps du Christ' dans la lettre aux Éphésiens: Perspective pour nôtre temps." *Paul de Tarse: Apôtre du nôtre temps,* ed. L. de Lorenzi. Rome: Abbaye de St. Paul, 1979, 665-85.

481. Schubert, P. *Form and Function of the Pauline Thanksgivings.* *BhZNW* 20. Berlin: A. Topelmann, 1939.

482. Schweizer, E. *The Church as the Body of Christ.* Richmond: John Knox, 1964.

The substance of lectures that consider the background to the concept of the body of Christ, its meaning in the NT apart from Paul, in the undisputed letters of Paul, and in 1 Cor 12, Col and Eph. The institution of the Lord's Supper helped shape and bring into prominence the concept of Christ's body. Growing out of his OT background, Paul then gave it further development in the context of Hellenistic Corinth. From there the church came to be seen as the body of Christ, finally extended in Col and Eph in which the body of Christ is separate from but obedient to Christ its head.

483. _____. "The Church as the Missionary Body of Christ." *NTS* 8 (1961) 1-11. [Repr. in *Neotestamentica.* Zürich: Zwingli Verlag, 1963, 317-29.]

Paul's concept of the body of Christ developed from its roots in the Jewish patriarchal concept and the Stoic use of the term. For Paul it points to humans' responsibility toward God and others. Under the influence of Hellenistic groups, however, concerned as they were with Christ's lordship over the cosmos, the author of Colossians (Paul or a disciple) reinterpreted the body of Christ concept for this new environment. Heresy motivated a reinterpretation of orthodoxy: the repetition of old creeds for a new situation.

484. _____. "Die Kirche als Leib Christi in den paulinischen Homologoumena." *TLZ* 86 (1961) 161-74. [Repr. in *Neotestamentica*. Zurich: Zwingli Verlag, 1963, 272-92.]

A far-ranging article that traces the background of the Pauline image of the body to the documents of late Judaism (e.g., Qumran Wisdom literature and Philo), not a pre-Christian Redeemer-myth. Paul's concept of the eschatological Adam is parallel to the figure of the vine in John—the tradition that the head of a tribe is one with his descendants. Thus all mankind exists under its head, Adam, and the church exists as the body of Christ in which it must fulfill its Christian faith.

485. _____. "Die Kirche als Leib Christi in den paulinischen Antilegomena." *TLZ* 86 (1961) 241-56. [Repr. in *Neotestamentica*. Zurich: Zwingli Verlag, 1963, 293-316.]

Analyzes the hymn of Col 1:15-20 showing that it reflects a Christian answer to the loss of the cosmos' former unity. Due to the influence of Greek thought, Paul's ideas were recast such that Christ is conceived as the head of the body. The authors of Col and Eph brought these thoughts into some conformity with Paul's thought, though it clearly differs from what he taught in Rom and 1 Cor. Whereas in Jewish thought *kephale* identifies the leader, in Col and Eph it means lord over the powers and over the Church.

486. _____. "σῶμα." *TDNT* 7 (1971) 1024-94.

Major article on the term translated "body." The author evaluates the uses in Eph on pp. 1077-80. The author believes that the cosmic dimension of the term receives special emphasis in Eph in view of the situation now faced by the Christian community.

487. Stanley, D. M.   "The Christian's Comprehension of Christ's
     Resurrection. Eph 1:19b-23." In *Christ's Resurrection in
     Pauline Soteriology. AnBib* 13. Rome: Pontifical Biblical
     Institute, 1961, 220-21.

     Brief comments on this text as it instructs concerning Christ's
     resurrection.

488. Thornton, L. S. "The Body of Christ in the New Testament." In
     The Apostolic Ministry, ed. K. E. Kirk. 2d ed. New York:
     Morehouse, 1947, 53-111.

     A chapter in a collection of essays that trace the concept of "the
     ministry" from the apostolic age to the modern era. Thornton's study
     on the body of Christ includes a discussion of "The Head and the
     Body" that considers the evidence in 1 Cor, Rom, Col, and Eph.
     Believes that in Christ there is mystical union of Christ and his
     people.

489. Viard, A. "Ascension (Ep 1,17-23)." *EV* (prédication) 83 (1983)
     120-21.

490. Virgulin, S. "L'origine del concetto di πλήρομα in Ef 1, 23." In
     Studiorum Paulinorum Congressus 1961. Rome: Pontifical
     Biblical Institute, 1963, II: 39-43.

491. Wedderburn, A. J. M. "The Body of Christ and Related Concepts in
     I Corinthians." *SJT* 24 (1971) 74-96.

     Takes up certain questions raised by Käsemann's article, "The
     Theological Problem" noted above, but especially as they work out
     in Paul's earlier letters, and particularly 1 Cor. Includes a discussion
     of "in Christ" and Adam and Christ. Adopts the idea of corporate
     solidarity to explain the relation of Christ and his body.

492. Wikenhauser, A. *Die Kirche als der mystische Leib des Christus
     nach dem Apostel Paulus.* 2d ed. Münster: Aschendorff,
     1940.

493. Wink, W. *Naming the Powers.* Philadelphia: Fortress, 1984, 3-35, 60-64, 151-63.

In the study of the concept of power and power terminology in the NT, the author first considers the key terms (pp. 3-35). Then on pp. 60-64 he considers Eph 1:20-23 and the appendices on pp. 151-63 investigate the terms *archōn, archē, exousia,* and *dynamis.*

494. Yates, R. "A Re-examination of Ephesians 1:23." *ExpT* 83 (1972) 146-51.

Takes up the three grammatical/linguistic problems and a theological problem in the interpretation of this verse: the meaning of πλήρωμα (it could be active or passive); the voice of πληρουμένου; whether τὰ πάντα ἐν πᾶσιν should be adverbial or adjectival; and whether "fullness" is in apposition to "body" so that the Church is the completion of Christ or in apposition to "him" of v.22 and thus refer to Christ. Considers all the options and settles on conclusions.

495. Yorke, G. *The Church as the Body of Christ in the Pauline Corpus: A Re-examination.* Washington, D.C.: University Press of America, 1991.

The author argues that when used of the Church in the Pauline corpus, *soma* (body) designates the human body, not Christ's once-crucified and now risen body. The author analyzes the ecclesiological significance of *soma* within each of the Pauline letters. The book is technical, well-documented, and includes an excellent bibliography.

Chapter 4

TEXTS: Ephesians 2

Ephesians 2:1-10

496. Allen, T. G. "Exaltation and Solidarity with Christ: Ephesians 1.20 and 2.6." *JSNT* 28 (1986) 103-20.

See under 1:15-23.

497. Benoit, P. "Rapports littéraires entre les épîtres aux Colossiens et aux Éphésiens." In *Neutestamentliche Aufsätze.* FS J. Schmid, ed. J. Blinzler, O. Kuss, and F. Mussner. Regensburg: F. Pustet, 1963, 11-22. [Repr. in *Exégèse et théologie.* 4 vols. Paris: Du Cerf, 1961-82. III (1968): 318-334.]

A study of the literary relationships between Eph and Col with special attention to Eph 2:1-6 that makes use of Col 2:13 and 3:6-7, both of which serve again in the writing of Eph 5:6. Also, Col 3:5 has a parallel to Eph 4:17-24, and Col 1:21 presents a theme that is echoed in Eph 2:11-12. As a result of these studies of the literary form, the author doubts that Eph can be considered authentically Pauline.

498. Best, E. "Dead in Trespasses and Sins (Eph. 2.1)." *JSNT* 13 (1981) 9-25.

     After investigating the connection between Colossians and Ephesians at this point, the author concludes that "death" is a realized eschatological concept. Spiritual life, residing only within the sphere of the church, is contrasted with spiritual death—whatever is outside the church. Before entering the Christian community a person is dead. The lifestyle of the dead consists of sins and transgressions.

499. Bigare, C. "C'est par grâce que nous sommes sauvés!" *AsSeign* 17 (1970) 34-39.

500. Carr, W. *Angels and Principalities.* Cambridge: Cambridge University Press, 1981, 100-104.

     In dealing with powers and the spiritual world in Ephesians the author considers 2:2, especially "the prince of the power of the air."

501. Countess, R. H. "Thank God for the Genitive (Eph. 2:8-10)." *JETS* 12 (1969) 117-22.

     Seeks to thank God for the riches of His graces as portrayed in 2:8-10, especially illustrating God's free, sovereign grace. Argues that in spite of the feminine gender of the word *pistis* (faith) and the neuter *touto* (this), Paul is asserting that faith, not merely salvation, is a gift. A strong defense of Calvinism in opposition to the exegesis of H. J. Ockenga.

502. Crowther, C. "Works, Work and Good Works." *ExpT* 81 (1970) 166-71.

     Evaluates the text in which Paul speaks of works. The analysis includes Eph 2:8-10 which, though probably post-Pauline, is "in fact a brilliant summary of Paul's evangelical message," and "is probably the best brief summary in the whole of the Pauline Corpus of Paul's understanding of the Gospel." It is tragic that in many circles only the beginning of this text is affirmed; its truth shines forth in its entirety: grace and faith leading to salvation leads to good works.

This is Paul's understanding of the place of good works. They don't attain salvation, but they are the outworking of salvation.

503. Denbow, W. H. "A Note on Ephesians 2:1." *Congregational Quarterly* 35 (1957) 62-64.

The awkwardness of Eph 2:1 is due not to ellipsis (cf. A. V.), but the excursion of 1:20-23 which displaces the direct object "you" (2:1) from its verb "raised" (1:20). Paul's sense is: "He raised him from the dead and you, who were dead, . . ." Since this powerful juxtaposition is missed in the public reading of scripture, it requires pastoral explanation.

504. Fischer, K. M. *Tendenz und Absicht des Epheserbriefs.* Göttingen: Vandenhoeck & Ruprecht, 1973, 121-31.

See on texts, 1:3-14. Here the author considers 2:1-10.

505. Hagen, K., ed. *The Bible in the Churches. How Different Christians Interpret the Scriptures.* New York: Paulist, 1985.

A hermeneutical study illustrating how Catholics, Evangelicals and Lutherans interpret.

506. Halter, H. *Taufe und Ethos: Paulinische Kriterien für das Proprium christlicher Moral.* Freiburg: Herder, 1977, 233-42, 625-29.

See on texts, 1:3-14. Here is discussion of 2:1-10.

507. Hübner, H. "Glossen in Epheser 2." In *Vom Urchristentum zu Jesus.* FS J. Gnilka, ed H. Frankemölle and K. Kertelge. Freiburg/Basel/Wien: Herder, 1989, 392-406.

Article considers the glosses found in Eph 2.

508. Joüon, P. "Notes philologiques sur quelques versets de l'Épître aux Éphésiens (1,12; 2,1-3; 2,15; 3,13.15; 4,28; 5,18.19; 6,9.19-20)." *Recherches de Science Religieuse* 26 (1936) 454-64.

Philological insights on several texts in Eph 2, among others.

509. Larsson, E. *Christus als Vorbild.* Uppsala: Almqvist & Wiksells, 1960, 105-9.

Investigates the question of the imitation and following of Christ through historico-critical exegesis. Considers two types of Pauline texts: baptismal (including Eph 2:4-7) and the "icon" texts (including Eph 4:24).

510. Legido López, M. "La Iglesia entre la communión y la tentación. Analisis exégetico en torno a Ef. 2, 5-7." *Salmanticensis* 18/2-3 (1971) 205-32.

Argues that the enthroned Lord rules the church and the world. Because of the church's communion with the Lord (the church is in Christ and communion occurs in sacramental actions, especially in baptism), the church actively battles against the world.

511. Lincoln, A. T. "Ephesians 2:8-10—A Summary of Paul's Gospel?" *CBQ* 45 (1983) 617-30.

Investigates how this texts fits Paul's soteriology and whether, in fact, it can be understood to express the essence of Paul's concept of the gospel as people like Crowther (above) argue. Suggests that the author of Ephesians may have softened or removed the element of tension in Paul's presentation of the gospel that requires the human response of faith. The text, then, may exhibit a movement from Paul's covenantal nomism to the more predestinarian pattern of irresistible grace seen in later Augustinian and Calvinist theology.

512. Lindemann, A. *Die Aufhebung der Zeit: Geschichtsverständnis und Eschatologie im Epheserbrief.* Gütersloh: Gerd Mohn, 1975, 106-40.

See on texts, 1:15-23.

513. Lloyd-Jones, D. M. *God's Way of Reconciliation. Studies in Ephesians Chapter 2.* Grand Rapids: Baker, 1972.

Sermons on Eph 2 by the famous Welsh physician-turned-preacher at London's Westminster Chapel.

514. Luz, U. "Rechtfertigung bei den Paulusschülern." In *Rechtfertigung.* FS E. Käsemann, ed. J. Friedrich, W. Pöhlmann, and P. Stuhlmacher. Tübingen: Mohr-Siebeck, 1976, 365-83.

Investigates the major topic of the book, justification, in the deutero-Pauline writings.

515. Mehlmann, J. *Natura filii Irae: Historia interpretationis Eph 2, 3 ejusque cum doctrina de Peccato Originali nexus.* Rome: Pontifical Biblical Institute, 1957.

516. Merklein, H. "Paulinische Theologie in der Rezeption des Kolosser- und Epheserbriefes." In *Paulus in den neutestamentlichen Spätschriften. Zur Paulusrezeption im Neuen Testament,* ed. K. Kertelge. Freiburg: Herder, 1981, esp. 37-51.

In a volume dedicated to analyzing attitudes toward Paul found in the later writings of the NT, Merklein's contribution considers how Col and Eph responded to Pauline theology.

517. Mussner, F. *Christus, das All und die Kirche.* 2d ed. Trier: Paulinus, 1968, 16-20, 24-27, 91-94. See further on 1:15-23 and under 2:11-22 below.

518. _____. "Eph 2 als ökumenisches Modell." In *Neues Testament und Kirche.* FS R. Schnackenburg, ed. J. Gnilka. Freiburg: Herder, 1974, 325-336.

Isolates various themes in Eph 2—especially those that touch on evangelism and "catholicity"—showing how Eph 2 provides a stimulus and model for ecumenicity.

519. Priero, D. "Un perchè nella Redenzione . . . *Ut ne quis glorietur* (Efes. 2, 8)." *PaCl* 41 (1962) 809-23.

An explanation of this verse. God's original creative plan was for him to share his supernatural life with his human creatures through the Incarnation of his Son. In his foreknowledge of the fall of humanity, God made the provision of redemption through Christ's death. This displayed God's boundless goodness and removed any human basis for boasting.

520. Ramaroson, L. "Une lecture de Éphésiens 1. 15 - 2, 10." *Bib* 58 (1977) 388-410.

The article argues that Eph 1:15-2:7 constitutes a doctrinally rich single phrase of simple design, though it contains various lateral patterns and parentheses, followed by an observation in 2:8-10. The singularity of phrase emerges more clearly if with P[46] and other witnesses one reads ἣν ἠλέησεν ("with which he had mercy") in 2:4 in place of ἣν ἠγάπησεν ("with which he loved") that occurs in modern critical editions. This presents in clear terms the mystery of salvation in Christ. Extensive interaction with other literature.

521. Read, D. H. C. "What Makes an Evangelical?" *ExpT* 89 (1978) 309-10.

Loosely based on Eph 2:8-9, this sermon attempts to define the essence of what constitutes an evangelical and an evangelical church: salvation by grace through faith.

522. Riensche, R. H. "Exegesis of Ephesians 2:1-7." *Lutheran Quarterly* 2 (1950) 70-74.

Brief exegesis, employing Greek, of this text.

523. Romaniuk, K. *L'Amour du Père et du Fils dans la sotériologie de Saint Paul.* Rome: Pontifical Biblical Institute, 1961, 212-16, 247-49.

This book constitutes a full study, in French, of the doctrine of redemption in the NT, but especially of divine love in Paul's writings. The author considers the evidence of Eph 2:4ff. on pp. 212-16 and again, 2:4-7 on pp. 247-49. The index points to many other references to Eph 2.

524. Sanders, J. T. "Hymnic Elements in Ephesians 1-3." *ZNW* 56 (1965) 218-23, 232.

Comments on the first part of Eph 2. See more at 1:3-14.

525. Schille, G. *Frühchristliche Hymnen.* Berlin: Evangelische Verlangsanstalt, 1965, 53-60.

In the course of his study of the genre of "redeemer-songs" in the NT, this study also treats initiation-songs which includes 2:4-10. See also on 1:3-14.

526. Schweizer, E. "Die hellenistische Komponente im neutestamentlichen *sarx*-Begriff." *ZNTW* 48 (1957) 237-53.

Studies from Qumran confirm that Paul and John were influenced by OT Jewish concepts of flesh, but there seems, as well, to be definite Hellenistic influences. Among other texts, Eph 2:3 shows clear influence of Greek thought on the concept of *sarx*.

527. Schnackenburg, R. *Baptism in the Thought of St. Paul.* Tr. G. R. Beasley-Murray. Oxford: Basil Blackwell; New York: Herder and Herder, 1964, 73-78.

In the discussion of baptism as salvation-event σύν Χριστῷ (with Christ), the author considers Eph 2:4-6 noting its relationship to Col 2:13. What happened to Christ (Eph 1:20) is now applied to Christians in 2:6. In Eph the baptized are presently "raised with Christ and installed in heaven," though the final consummation of divine grace will come in the future.

528. Stanley, D. M. "Salvation the Act of God's Merciful Love. Eph 2, 4-8." In *Christ's Resurrection in Pauline Soteriology. AnBib* 13. Rome: Pontifical Biblical Institute, 1961, 222-24.

Brief comments on this text as it instructs concerning Christ's resurrection.

529. Steinmetz, F.-J. *Protologische Heils-Zuversicht. Die Strukturen des*

*soteriologischen und christologischen Denkens im Kolosser-
und Epheserbrief.* Frankfurt: Knecht, 1969, 37-44, 51-67.

Compares the eschatology of Col and Eph with that of the major
Pauline letters. Contrasts the futurist eschatology of the Paulines in
relation to Christology and soteriology with the "present" eschatology
of Col and Eph and their more spatial categories. Col and Eph shift
the Pauline future orientation to a "protological" Christology, and
reflect a conceptual background divergent from Paul's. It will only
mislead to attempt to harmonize these disparate viewpoints.

530. Steinmetz, F.-J. and Wulf, F.   "Mit Christus auferstanden.
      Auslegung und Meditation von 1 Kor 15, 20; Eph 2, 6 und 2
      Tim 2, 18." *GeistL* 42 (1969) 146-50.

Expositions and meditations on three texts. On Eph 2:6, we see that
God has raised us with Christ and seated us in the heavens in Christ
Jesus. Christians must live in view of these accomplished realities:
they are raised and seated with Christ.

531. Tachau, P. *"Einst" und "Jetzt" im Neuen Testament. FRLANT* 105.
      Göttingen: Vandenhoeck & Ruprecht, 1972.

Examines the "then" and "now" motif in the OT, NT, and extra-
biblical literature, though with special attention to Pauline and
deutero-Pauline texts. Eph 5:8 receives analysis, and an examination
of Eph 2 draws the study to its conclusion.

532. Turner, D. L. "Ephesians 2:3c and peccatum originale." *GTJ* 1/2
      (1980) 195-219.

Noting the use of Eph 2:3c to defend the doctrine of "original sin"
(hereditary moral corruption), this study investigates the exegetical
basis for that claim—including the semitic background and contextual
study of *tekna physei orges* and a word study of *physei*. Tables
display pertinent correlations. It concludes that the text does provide
some basis for the Christian doctrine, though it does not sustain all
its later developments. An appendix counters opposing positions.

533. Viard, A. "La vie nouvelle accordée par Dieu aux croyants dans le Christ (Ép 2, 4-10)." *EV* (prédication) 79 (1979) 86-88.

534. Wink, W. *Naming the Powers.* Philadelphia: Fortress, 1984.

Seeks to understand the concept and terminology of power and "the powers" in the NT. Considers Eph 2:1-2 on pp. 82-84.

Ephesians 2:11-22

535. Barclay, W. "The One, New Man." In *Unity and Diversity in New Testament Theology.* FS G. E. Ladd, ed. R. A. Guelich. Grand Rapids: Eerdmans. 1978, 73-81.

In his fresh, readable style, with word studies of the two Greek words for "new" (*kainos* and *neos*) and simple, everyday illustrations, Barclay explains 2:11-22. In saying that Christ makes a "new" man, Paul means that Christ makes "not just another man but a different kind of man." Barclay draws out some implications for ecumenicity.

536. Barth, M. *Israel und die Kirche im Brief des Paulus an die Epheser. Theologische Existenz Heute* 75. München: Kaiser, 1959.

Lecture that concludes that Ephesians supports the church's responsibility both to continue its mission to the Jews and to avoid anti-Semitism in any form.

537. _____. "Conversion and Conversation: Israel and The Church in Paul's Epistle to the Ephesians." *Int* 17 (1963) 3-24.

Argues that the internal evidence in the letter makes an impressive case for Pauline authorship. The major task of the essay is to show that the Gentiles' adoption into the household of God compares to the Prodigal Son's reception in his father's house. Key passages in the discussion are Eph 1:11-14, 2:11-20, and 3:5-6. The study includes an outline of the theological implications of the oneness of Jew and

Gentile in Christ and concludes with a discussion of the practical consequences of Ephesians' teaching on the church and Israel one of which is that the church has no business in engaging in a "mission to the Jews."

538.   Bartlett, R. E. "St. Paul on the Trinity—Ephesians 2:18." *Exp*, 2d series, 4 (1882) 321-31.

539.   Best, E. "The Body of Christ." *EcuR* 9 (1957) 122-28.

An adequate understanding of Paul's concept of the body of Christ must correlate with the rest of his theology. His use of a variety of figures cautions us from attempting to impose one figure as the definitive construct for understanding his view of the church. From Eph we learn that believers are "in Christ," a construct that applies to the "interior relationships" of Christ to believers and of believers to one another, not to the relationship of the church to the world—a popular understanding.   Shows how the phrase preserves the importance of the individual member while conveying (1) identity of the church and Christ, and (2) the supreme "otherness" of Christ.

540.   _____. "Ephesians 2.11-22: a Christian View of Judaism," in *Text as Pretext*. FS Robert Davidson, ed. R. P. Carroll. Sheffield, UK: JSOT Press, 1992, 47-60.

Examines the evidence to see how people in the ancient world viewed Jews, in order to shed light on how the author of Ephesians (probably not Paul) expresses the superiority of Christianity to Judaism. Eph 2:11-22 presents a picture of Judaism that is very different from what Gentiles generally held; it is also largely different from that of Judaism itself. He describes Judaism only in terms of those items he can use as a Christian.

541.   Betz, O. "The Eschatological Interpretation of the Sinai Tradition in Qumran and in the New Testament." *RQum* 6 (1967) 89-107.

Defends that the ancient Israelites considered the Sinai-event as the fundamental act of God's self-disclosure.   The Qumranians hoped again that God's grace might become a powerful reality for them as well: that God would come again and usher in the end times. Shows how this motif informs various NT passages. Believes that the author of Ephesians picks up a Qumran motif of the "breaking through the boundary of the Law" in Eph 2:14-16. Christ abolished the Law in his flesh by breaking down the wall of hostility dividing Jew and Gentile.

542. Bigare, C. "Le Christ, notre paix (Eph 2, 13-18)." *AsSeign* n.s. 47 (1970) 39-43.

543. Bony, P. "L'épître aux Éphésiens." In *Le Ministère et Les Ministères Selon Le Nouveau Testament,* ed. J. Delorme. Paris: Seuil, 1974, 74-92.

In the discussion of "ministry" in Ephesians, this section (pp. 75-79) is devoted to a consideration of the text of Eph 2:20, the foundational ministry of the apostles and prophets. The article continues the topic by discussing 3:1-13 and 4:1-16.

544. Bouwman, G. "Wachsende Einheit—Betrachtung über Eph 2:11-22." *Getuigenis* 11 (1966-67) 170-76.

Col and Eph are related while they also differ. The Colossian church's problem is alienation in a growing and changing world. Paul's answer centers in Christ's supremacy which should bring unity to the church. Ephesians concerns oneness within the church. The Law is a wall between Jews and Gentiles that Christ removed. People use the law to hide behind, and so the law is also a wall within an individual Christian. The Spirit is the foundation for unity. The Spirit provides the foundation for unity. The human spirit seeks unity and should do so in the community's differences. The final section of the paper discusses spiritual gifts—unity in the church involves all members having their own functions in Christ's body.

545. Burger, C. "Der Hymnus in Epheser 2, 14-18." In *Schöpfung und Versöhnung: Studien zum liturgischen Gut im Kolosser- und Epheserbrief.* Neukirchen-Vluyn: Neukirchener, 1975, 117-57.

The two parts of this volume provide detailed reconstructions and interpretations of two NT hymns: Col 1:15-20 and Eph 2:14-18. Closely reasoned and interacting with numerous writers, mostly German, the study shows how Eph 2:14-18 fits into its context and what it contributes to the meaning of the argument of the letter.

546. Chase, F. H. "Note on the Word ναός in Ephesians 2:21." *Exp,* 3d series, 6 (1887) 318-19.

547. Cleland, J. T. "Someone There Is Who Doesn't Love a Wall. From Text to Sermon on Ephesians 2, 11-22." *Int* 21 (1967) 147-57.

Explains his method for deriving a sermon on the basis of the "four P's": Primer, Purpose, Pattern and Proposition, demonstrating the technique on this passage. Presents the resulting sermon.

548. Coggan, F. D. "A Note on Ephesians 2:14: αὐτὸς γάρ ἐστιν ἡ εἰρήνη ἡμῶν." *ExpT* 53 (1941-42) 242.

Brief comment on the clause "for he is our peace" suggesting that its background is Semitic conveying the sense that Christ is a peace offering, an offering of value for Jew and Gentile.

549. Deichgräber, R. *Gotteshymnus und Christushymnus in der frühen Christenheit.* Göttingen: Vandenhoeck & Ruprecht, 1967, 165-67.

See on texts, 1:15-23.

550. Denton, D. R. "Inheritance in Paul and Ephesians." *EvQ* 54 (1982) 157-68.

Studies the concept of inheritance in Paul's *Hauptbriefe* and then in Ephesians. Challenges Hammer's findings in his article (see on 1:3-14 above). Concludes that the alleged differences between Paul's use of the inheritance concept and that in Ephesians cannot be sustained under examination and thus cannot be used to argue against the Pauline authorship of Ephesians.

551. Feine, P. "Eph 2, 14-16." *TSK* 72 (1899) 540-74.

552. Fischer, K. M. *Tendenz und Absicht des Epheserbriefs.* Göttingen: Vandenhoeck & Ruprecht, 1973, 79-94, 131-37.

See on texts, 1:3-14.

553. Gärtner, B. *The Temple and the Community in Qumran and the New Testament.* Cambridge: Cambridge University Press, 1965, 60-66.

A study of the concepts surrounding the priesthood and temple as understood in both the Qumran literature and several NT texts (2 Cor 6:14 - 7:1; 1 Cor 3:16-17; Eph 2:18-22; 1 Tim 3:15; 1 Pet 2:3-6; Heb 12:18-24; and in the Gospels). In the seven pages on the Ephesian text, the author seeks to understand the "holy temple" mentioned in Eph 2:21, drawing parallels to texts in the LXX, from Qumran, and Eph 4:12, 16. The Holy Spirit has moved residence from the Jerusalem temple to the Christian church, the new Temple which the Spirit has brought into existence. In fact, the temple is the one people who have been joined together in Christ.

554. Giavini, G. "La structure littéraire d'Eph 2:11-22." *NTS* 16/2 (1969-70) 209-11.

Sets out the literary structure of this passage with a short explanation and defense. Believes its structure was suggested by Col 1:12-20. Finds a kind of concentric symmetry or regression of the form: C B A X A' B' C', and within the central X element two series of parallel phrases of the form: a b c d a' b' c' d'.

555. Gill, A. "Note upon Ephesians 2:14." *ExpT* 2 (1890-91) 93.

556. Girgensohn, H. "Die Gestalt der Kirche aus der Sicht des Briefes an die Epheser." In *Heilende Kräfte der Seelsorge.* Göttingen: Vandenhoeck & Ruprecht, 1966, 198-205.

Three sections that address the state of the church as viewed in the Ephesian letter. The second part considers the topic in Eph 2:19-22. Through the picture of the church as the body of Christ its personal character can be seen. The institution is really an organism. The church works out its true nature only when, in faith, gives room or place to Christ's work through her.

557. Gnilka, J. "Christus unser Friede—ein Friedens-Erlöserlied in Eph 2, 14-17: Erwägungen zu einer neutestamentlichen Friedenstheologie." In *Die Zeit Jesu.* FS H. Schlier, ed. G. Bornkamm and K. Rahner. Freiburg: Herder, 1970, 190-207.

A careful consideration of the concept of peace and, especially, "Christ our peace" in what he considers to be a hymn—the peace-redeemer hymn of Eph 2:14-17—in the attempt to understand the NT theology of peace. In seeing the likelihood that this passage reflects a hymn, Gnilka follows G. Schille and J. T. Sanders (see under Literary Issues: Hymns, below).

558. Gonzáles Lamadrid, A. "Ipse est pax nostra. (Estudio exegético-teológico de Ef 2, 14-18)." *EstBi* 28 (1969) 209-62; 29 (1970) 101-36, 227-66.

Argues that Eph 2:11-22 treats salvation-history in three periods: before Christ (vv. 11-12), the time of his coming and work (13-18), and at the time of the epistle itself (19-22). God establishes peace with man, and as a consequence, peace between Jews and Gentiles. Comparisons with the rest of Paul's writings and the OT show that 2:14-18 was probably framed in a Gnostic *Sitz im Leben*, following H. Schlier.

559. Greeves, F. "One God." *ExpT* 87 (1976) 268-69.

Meditation on Trinity Sunday of the Christian Year based on Eph 2:18 that asks the key question: "Am I truly worshipping *one* God?"

560. Grob, F. "L'Image du Corps et de la Tête dans L'Épitre aux Éphésiens." *ETR* 58/4 (1983) 491-500.

In considering the images of body and head in Ephesians, the author discusses Eph 2:11-18 and 4:12-16. The "body" consists of a union or alliance of two inseparable parties. This body is also seen as an edifice. In Eph it is clear that the body is the body of Christ (Eph

4:12; cf. 5:28). Christ's headship is not one that stresses sovereignty in the universe but rather one that speaks of the eschatological horizon of the church over which Christ is head and of a humanity reconciled in Christ.

561. Hanson, S. *The Unity of the Church in the New Testament: Colossians and Ephesians. ASNU* 14. Uppsala: Almqvist & Wiksells, 1946, 141-48.

A comprehensive biblical analysis of the concept of unity: in the OT and Judaism, in Jesus in the synoptic tradition, in Paul, and in Col and Eph. The discussion in Eph goes from pp. 121-161, with special attention to Eph 2:11-19 on pp. 141-48. The atoning work of Christ abolished whatever barriers existed (especially the Law) between Jews and Gentiles so that Gentiles and the Jews merge into one another in Christ.

562. Howard, J. E. "The Wall Broken: An Interpretation of Ephesians 2:11-22." In *Biblical Interpretation: Principles and Practices.* FS J. P. Lewis, ed. F. F. Kearley, E. P. Myers, and T. D. Hadley. Grand Rapids: Baker, 1986, 296-306.

Considers the literary background, the context of chapters 1-3, and engages in a short analysis that breaks down 2:11-22 into three sections. Helpful despite its brevity.

563. Hull, W. E. *Beyond the Barriers.* Nashville, TN: Broadman, 1981.

Investigates the concept of reconciliation in Christ in 2:11-22, especially in v. 14, as it relates to the temple metaphor on one hand and hostilities between groups in society on the other. Breaking down walls, Christ helps people to move beyond social, sexual, sacral, and spiritual divisions. Indeed, Christ brings people together in peace and unity with equal access to the Father in one Spirit.

564. Jacob, J. "Christian Unity and the Jewish People." *Wor* 33 (1959) 574-580.

Drawing upon numerous Catholic sources and several NT texts, the author defends Pope John XXIII's deletion of the word "perfidious" from the prayer for the Jews in the Good Friday liturgy. This supports the theological truth of this passage that all humans are one in Christ.

565. Jeremias, J. "Der Eckstein." *Angelos* 1 (1925) 65-70.

566. _____. "Eckstein-Schlussstein." *ZNW* 36 (1937) 154-57.

On the cornerstone-keystone meanings growing out of Psa 118:22 and Isa 28:16. Early Christian literature understood the cornerstone as the Head of the Temple.

567. _____. "γωνία." *TDNT* 1 (1964) 791-93.

Suggests the idea of "final stone" in a building as the sense intended for Jesus here. He is the cornerstone who binds the spiritual temple together.

568. _____. "κεφαλὴ γωνίας—᾽Ακρογωνιαῖος." *ZNW* 29 (1930) 264-80.

569. _____. "λίθος." *TDNT* 4 (1967) 119-59.

Major article on "stone."

570. Käsemann, E. "Epheser 2, 17-22." *Exegetische Versuche und Besinnungen,* Vol. 1. Göttingen: Vandenhoeck & Ruprecht, 1960, 280-83.

571. Kirchschläger, W. "Christus, unser Friede - Gedanken zu Eph 2, 14-18." *BiLit* 48 (1975) 173-179.

572. Kirschner, W. F. "Ele e a nossa paz: uma exegese de Efesios 2:13-18." *Vox Script* 1 (1991) 11-18.

In Portuguese on the theology of reconciliation taught in these verses.

573. Klein, G. "Der Epheserbrief." In *Die zwölf Apostel, FRLANT,* N.F.

59. Göttingen: Vandenhoeck & Ruprecht, 1961.

The book investigates the origin and significance of the Twelve as apostles as found in the post-apostolic and NT materials. Pages 66-75 focus on Eph 2:20.

574. Klinzing, G. *Die Umdeutung des Kultus in der Qumrangemeinde und im Neuen Testament.* Göttingen: Vandenhoeck & Ruprecht, 1971.

Traces the reinterpretation of the Temple cult and the priesthood in the Qumran community. The third part of the study pursues various parallels to this reinterpretation of the Temple in the NT, among which he considers Eph 2:19ff. on pp. 184-91. Eph 2:22 stands in the tradition of 2 Cor 6:16; 1 Cor 3:16; and 1 Cor 6:19.

575. Kolbe, A. "Auslegung der Stelle Eph. 2, 19-22." *TSK* 51 (1878) 135-50.

576. Lincoln, A. T. "The Church and Israel in Ephesians 2." *CBQ* 49 (1987) 605-24. [Repr. in *The Best in Theology,* Vol. 3, ed. J. I. Packer. Carol Stream, IL: CTi, 1989, 61-79.]

577. _____. "The Use of the OT in Ephesians." *JSNT* 14 (1982) 16-57.

Seeks to redress the neglect of scholarly study of the overall use of the NT in Ephesians. The focus is on actual quotations from the OT, not merely allusions such as the "cornerstone" imagery in 2:20, etc. The texts studied are 4:8-10 (Psa 68:18); 2:17 (Isa 57:19); 5:31-32 (Gen 2:24); 6:2-3 (Exo 20:12); 1:20, 22 (Psa 110:1); plus shorter studies of uses of the OT in 4:25, 26; 5:18; and 6:14-17. He concludes by noting the conspicuous absence of introductory formulae to the citations. He suggests that this is due to the later author's attempt to update Paul's message and uses the OT in that same way that he employs liturgical and catechetical traditions. The OT does not have the same role for him as it does for Paul. Again, as in the prior study, Lincoln disputes the conclusions of M. Barth on this point (see Barth's commentary, p. 30).

578. Lindemann, A. *Die Aufhebung der Zeit: Geschichtsverständnis und
      Eschatologie im Epheserbrief.* Gütersloh: Gerd Mohn, 1975,
      152-81.

      See on texts, 1:15-23.

579. Long, W. R. "Ephesians 2:11-22." *Int* 45 (1991) 281-83.

      An expository article, including references to reconciliation of
      Christianity and Judaism.

580. Lyall, F. "Roman Law in the Writings of Paul—Aliens and
      Citizens." *EvQ* 48 (1976) 3-14.

      Seeks to shed light on the use of legal concepts (e.g., citizenship,
      aliens and alienage, sojourners and citizens) in the Pauline epistles,
      1 Peter, and Hebrews by studying these concepts in the Roman legal
      system.   Considers the use in Eph 2:19 of the citizen versus
      stranger/foreigner metaphor.

581. Lyonnet, S. "De Christo summo angulari lapide secundum Eph 2,
      20." *VD* 27 (1949) 74-83.

582. Martin, R. P. *Reconciliation: A Study of Paul's Theology.* London:
      Marshall; Atlanta: John Knox, 1981. [Repr. Grand Rapids:
      Zondervan, 1990, 157-98.]

      Traces the theme of reconciliation in Paul and his followers. The
      section on Ephesians sets the letter in its context, showing how the
      author put a new slant on Paul's teaching for his new situation. Eph
      2:11-22 receives special attention where, now, "Jewish Christianity
      has passed into history as a once-posed threat to Paul's Gentile
      converts, but it has no continuing relevance to the audience of
      Ephesians."   The destruction of the "dividing wall of hostility"
      probably referred to the destruction of the Jerusalem Temple in A.D.
      70. Rejects H. Schlier's appeal to a gnostic myth as the background
      for 2:11-22. Proceeds to outline and defend the literary structure of
      2:12-19, suggesting that vv. 14-16 may be a Christ-hymn. Provides
      an extensive exegesis of 2:11-22 showing how it asserts both

personal and ethnic reconciliation.

583. McEleney, N. J. "Conversion, Circumcision, and the Law." *NTS* 20 (1974) 319-41.

Under the larger concern of the relationship of Christianity to Judaism, studies the practice of proselytism as it developed through the centuries up to the first century and the role of circumcision in proselytism. This sets the stage for a consideration of Paul's attitudes toward circumcision, and especially his teaching in Eph 2:11-22. Paul seems to reflect the more liberal wing of Judaism of the day that was willing to dispense with circumcision, rather stressing the importance of ethical activity over the letter of casuistry. Later, the strict school won out in Judaism, once again requiring circumcision of all proselytes and hardening the rift between Judaism and Christianity.

584. McKelvey, R. J. "Christ the Cornerstone." *NTS* 8/4 (1962) 352-59.

A short study to determine whether Christ as *akrogōniaios* in Eph 2:20 ought be understood in the traditional way meaning "cornerstone," or as recently suggested "topstone"—the head of the body, or even "keystone." Decides on the traditional understanding of a stone located at one of the corners that bound together the walls and the foundation.

585. _____. *The New Temple.* London: Oxford University Press, 1969.

Convinced that the metaphor of the church as temple has suffered neglect, the author makes a thorough study of "temple" in the OT, in Jewish and Greek literature and in various NT texts, including Eph 2:20-22. Appendix C also considers "Christ the Cornerstone" (195-204). Seeks to explain the features of the text, drawing implications for the theme of the book. The temple-building has a foundation and a cornerstone upon which the superstructure (Jews and Gentiles together) rises. God himself dwells within the edifice. This teaching on the new temple is more developed than what is found in the Corinthian letters. At the same time, it stands in continuity with the earlier epistles and reflects the same Jewish milieu.

586. Meeks, W. A. "In One Body: The Unity of Humankind in Colossians and Ephesians." In *God's Christ and His People.* FS N. A. Dahl, ed. J. Jervell and W. A. Meeks. Oslo: Universitetsforlaget, 1977, 209-21.

The encyclical letter of Ephesians employs elements from the baptismal liturgy and catechism of the Pauline churches of Asia. Takes the structure of Eph 2:11-22 to be a midrash on Isa 57:19 where Jew and Gentile are united and reconciled to God in the central saving act. Yet the language employed reflects a mythical and cosmic notion of reconciliation.

587. Merklein, H. *Christus und die kirche. Die theologische Grundstruktur des Epheserbriefes nach Eph 2, 11-18.* Stuttgart: Katholisches Bibelwerk, 1973.

Detailed exegetical study of this passage followed by an appraisal of the theological perspective of Eph and its relation to the Pauline tradition. This study grows out of a chapter in the following book (# 588).

588. _____. *Das kirchliche Amt nach dem Epheserbrief.* Munich: Kösel, 1973, 118-58.

After a consideration of Ephesians' authenticity (composed by one officially involved in theology in the post-apostolic era), conducts detailed exegeses of 2:19-22 (as well as 3:1-7 and 4:7-16). Shows the importance of these texts for the offices of the church. Considers the pre-Pauline offices of apostle, prophet, and teacher, Paul's understanding of them, and how the author Eph understands apostle, prophet, evangelist, shepherd, and teacher.

589. _____. "Zur Tradition und Komposition von Eph 2, 14-18." *BZ* 17/1 (1973) 79-102.

Acknowledges that Eph 2:14-18 is some kind of excursus, though it is probably not a hymn, as some have suggested. Rather, it is the author's own ecclesiastical commentary on the cosmic Christological hymn of Col 1:15-20.

590. _____. "Paulinische Theologie in der Rezeption des Kolosser- und Epheserbriefes." In *Paulus in den neutestamentlichen Spätschriften*, ed. K. Kertelge. Freiburg: Herder, 1981, 25-69.

See on texts, 2:1-10.

591. Meuzelaar, J. J. *Der Leib des Messias. Eine exegetische Studie über den Gedanken vom Leib Christi in den Paulusbriefen.* Assen: van Gorcum, 1961, 59-101.

See on texts, 1:15-23 for further discussion of this study of the meaning of the concept of "life of Christ" in Paul's epistles.

592. Michel, O. "οἶκος κτλ." *TDNT* 5 (1967) 119-59.

Discusses the term "house, dwelling" and its various cognates.

593. Moore, M. S. "Ephesians 2:14-16: A History of Recent Interpretation." *EvQ* 54 (1982) 163-68.

The study questions the current and popular viewpoint concerning the background to Eph 2:14-16—that author/editor quotes pre-Pauline hymnic material to elaborate Isa 52:7. Though possible, this is certainly not the only explanation for the background of this text. The reason for the popularity of this current consensus lies in the recent tendency to focus on alleged hymnic forms rather than upon the theological content of the letter.

594. Morton, H. O. "No Walls in Heaven." *ExpT* 89 (1977-78) 109-11.

A sermon on the text "No longer strangers" from Eph 2:19. A call for ecumenism.

595. Mussner, F. *Christus, das All und die Kirche. Studien zur Theologie des Epheserbriefes.* 2d ed. Trier: Paulinus, 1955, 1968, 76-118.

After an investigation of the cosmic *ta panta* (all things) formula, the author explores the exaltation-of-Christ theme and the *plērōma* (fullness)-language in Eph. The bulk of the study is devoted to the ecclesiology of Eph, especially in 2:11-22. He also compares the *sōma* (body) terminology in Eph with that in 1 Cor and Col. Finally, Mussner considers the origins of the *kephalē-sōma* (head-body) concept in Eph and compares the "cosmic" Christian language to that of gnostic mythology.

596. _____. "Eph 2 als ökumenisches Modell." In *Neues Testament und Kirche*. FS R. Schnackenburg, ed. J. Gnilka. Freiburg: Herder, 1974, 325-36.

See on texts, 2:1-10 (# 517).

597. Nauck, W. "Eph 2, 19-22—ein Tauflied?" *EvT* 13 (1953) 362-71.

598. Pfammatter, J. *Die Kirche als Bau. Eine exegetisch-theologische Studie zur Ekklesiologie der Paulusbriefe*. Rome: Libreria Editrice dell'Università Gregoriana, 1960.

This dissertation exegetes Paul's allusions to the metaphor of building as a way of understanding the nature of the church. Excurses on *themelios* (foundation), *akrogōniaios* (cornerstone), and the origin on the building theme.

599. Rader, W. *The Church and Racial Hostility. A History of the Interpretation of Eph 2, 11-22. Beitrage zur Geschichte der biblische Exegese*, 20. Tübingen: Mohr-Siebeck, 1978.

In view of the contemporary problem of racial hostility, this study catalogues the interpretation of Eph 2:11-22 throughout the history of the church. He concludes that the majority of contemporary interpreters see the passage as relevant to concrete fellowship between Jews and Gentiles in the church. Consequently this passage speaks a crucial message for race relations within the church today, e.g., between blacks and whites.

600. Ramaroson, L. "'Le Christ, nôtre paix' (Ep. 2, 14-18)." *Science et Esprit* 31 (1979) 373-82.

The study compares Eph 2:14-18 with the apocryphal Letter of Aristeas, the short ending of Mark and selected Pauline passages (Eph 2:14b-15a is compared to Rom 6:6; Col 2:14, and Eph 2:15b is compared to Rom 6:4; Col 2:12-13; 3:1; Eph 2:6). Baptism, in Eph 2:14-18, stands as the crucial rite in mediating Christ "our peace" by reconciling pagans and Jews to each other and to God. As well, through their death in baptism Christ destroys the Law that divided pagans and Jews and the sin that kept them from God. And in their baptism Christ raises them from death to build of them a single church united to him and pleasing to God. Christ still proclaims this good news of peace through his representatives today.

601. Rese, M. "Die Vorzüge Israels in Röm 9, 4f. und Eph 2, 12: exegetische Anmerkungen zum Thema Kirche und Israel." *ThZ* 31 (1975) 211-22.

Examines the concept of the preference given to Israel in Rom 9:4-5 and Eph 2:12 in order to shed light on the relationship between the Church and Israel, Christianity and Judaism. The texts show Israel's preference in different ways, and this colors the conclusions about the church's relationship to Israel. Eph 2:12 provides a picture of the time before Christ. But what Israel was, the church now is in Christ. Christ now bridges the gap between God and people, and in the church both Jews and Gentiles find unity in Christ.

602. _____. "Church and Israel in the Deuteropauline Letters." *SJT* 43/1 (1990) 19-32.

Discussing the meaning of "Deuteropauline" plus the historical and theological background of the relation of the church and Israel, the study examines the view of Israel portrayed in Rom 9-11 and Eph 2:12 and follows that with a study of Judaism in the other Deutero--Paulines.

603. Rey, B. "Le Christ, homme nouveau (Ep 2,15)." In *Crées dons le Christ Jésus. La création nouvelle selon saint Paul.* Paris: Cerf, 1966, 131-143.

Studies the concept of the new creation in several key Pauline texts

(Gal 6:15; 2 Cor 5:17), the New Adam (1 Cor 15 and Rom 5), Paul's concept of "putting on the new man," and last, conforming to Christ, the image of God.

604.   _____. "L'homme nouveau d'après S. Paul. *RSPT* 48 (1964) 603-629; 49 (1965) 161-195.

Anticipated in Rom 6 in a baptismal context where Christians *put on* the new man, the contrast between old and new man finds fullest expression in Eph 2 where Christ *is* the new man. Christ unites all humanity and gradually leads them to fullness (Eph 4:13).

605.   Richardson, P. "Colossians and Ephesians: the relaxation of hope." In *Israel in the Apostolic Church.* London: Cambridge University Press, 1969, 147-158.

Investigates whether Eph 2:11-22—the relationship of Jew and Gentile—represents a live or a dead situation at the time of the letter's writing (and how parallels or differences in Col shed light on the question). After tracing the "we/you" shifts in the language of chapters 1-2, the author analyzes the passage, including a consideration of proposed textual emendations. Eph represents a milestone in the church's self-identification as the new Temple and separation from historical Israel.

606.   Roetzel, C. J. "Jewish Christian—Gentile Christian Relations: A Discussion of Ephesians 2, 15a." *ZNW* 74/1-2 (1983) 81-89.

The study finds that an initial writer of Ephesians modified a hymn dealing with cosmic reconciliation to encourage Jewish and Gentile Christians to be reconciled. Finding support in Paul's convictions about provisional nature of the Law, the writer, in keeping with Hellenistic beliefs, asserted that Christ demolished the commandments for Christians who were now "perfect," "wise," or "spiritual." Then a later redaction qualified Eph 2:14a, implying that Christ's eradication of the law applied not to the holy, just, and good Law that Paul affirmed, but only to human ordinances and ascetic teachings. This resulted in the confusing text we have today.

607. Sahlin, H. "'Omskärelsen i Kristus.' En interpretation av Ef. 2:11-22." *SvTk* 1 (1947) 11-24.

608. _____. "'Die Beschneidung Christi': Eine Interpretation von Eph 2, 11-22." *Symbolae Biblicae Upsalienses* 12 (1950) 5-22.

609. Sanders, J. T. "Hymnic Elements in Ephesians 1-3." *ZNW* 56 (1965) 21-18.

See discussion on texts, 1:3-14.

610. _____. *The New Testament Christological Hymns.* SNTSMS 15. Cambridge: Cambridge University Press, 1971, 14-15, 88-92.

A formal analysis of the alleged hymn of Eph 2:14-16 occurs on pp. 14-15. Evaluates the positions of H. Schlier and P. Pokorný on pp. 88-92.

611. Schafer, K. T. "Zur Deutung von ἀκρογωνιαῖος Eph 2,20." In *Neutestamentliche Aufsätze.* FS J. Schmid, ed. J. Blinzler, O. Kuss, and F. Mussner. Regensburg: F. Pustet, 1963, 218-24.

612. Schille, G. *Frühchristliche Hymnen.* Berlin: Evangelische Verlangsanstalt, 1965, 24-31.

An investigation of the genre "Redeemer-songs" in the NT: Eph 2:14-18 and Col 2:9-15. An excursus considers the eschatology of Ephesians.

613. Schnackenburg, R. "Die Kirche als Bau: Epheser 2:19-22 unter ökumenischem Aspekt." In *Paul and Paulinism.* FS C. K. Barrett, ed. M. D. Hooker and S. G. Wilson. London: SPCK, 1982, 258-70.

Considers the picture of the church as a building through a careful exegesis of the elements of Eph 2:19-22. Draws out implications for ecumenism today.

614. _____. "Die Politeia Israels in Eph 2, 12." In *De la Tôrah au*

Messie. FS H. Cazelles, ed. M. Carrez et al. Paris: Desclée,
1981, 467-74.

Seeks to shed light on the phrase "the commonwealth of Israel" in
view of the comparison provided in Rom 9:4f. It stands for the
assembly (*Versammlung*) of the people of God, God's own
community of people which he has constituted. The best overall
translation of *politeia* is "the community of Israel."

615. _____. "Zur Exegese von Eph 2, 11-22: im Hinblick auf der
Verhältnis von Kirche und Israel." In *The New Testament Age.*
FS B. Reicke. Vol. 2, ed. W. C. Weinrich. Macon, GA:
Mercer University Press, 1984, 467-91.

Investigates the relationship between the church and Israel and
between Christianity and Judaism through a study of Eph 2:11-22.
Interacts with several key authors along the way: M. Barth, H.
Merklein, K. M. Fischer, P. Tachau, and A. Lindemann before
engaging in his own exegesis of the passage. Provides conclusions
on the intention of the writer as over against his readers, the
contemporary background, and the theological perspective.

616. Schweitzer, W. "Überlegungen zum Verhältnis von Christen und
Jeden nach Epheser 2, 11-22." *Wort und Dienst* 20 (1989)
237-64.

Studies the various aspects of Christ's reconciling and peace-making
work in bringing Gentiles and Israelites together in the church.

617. Scott, R. "Ephesians 2:14." *ExpT* 2 (1890-91) 106.

618. Smith, D. C. "The Two Made One: Some Observations on Eph 2:1-
18." *Ohio Journal of Religious Studies* 1/1 (1973) 34-54.

Finds the background for the unity of duality in a mixture of sources,
mostly classical and Hellenistic Greek philosophical traditions.
These ideas were taken up in turn by Hellenistic Judaism, early
Christianity, and later gnosticism. The Jewish idea of the new
creation through the forgiveness of sins or through conversion to

Judaism probably underlies the motif of new creation in Eph 2:15, and the author of Eph adroitly combines ideas from both Greek and Jewish sources.

619. _____. "The Ephesian Heresy." In *Biblical Literature: 1974 Proceedings,* ed. F. Francis. Tallahassee, FL: American Academy of Religion, 1974, 45-54.

Arguing against the prevailing thinking, this study suggests that some of the language used in Ephesians was determined by the language the author seeks to refute. Considers such concepts as "peace to the far and to the near" (2:13, 17), "blood of circumcision" (2:13), and spiritual circumcision and heavenly ascension (refuted in 2:14-18).

620. _____. "Cultic language in Ephesians 2:19-22: a test case." *RestQ* 31/4 (1989) 207-17.

Though NT writers may interpret the temple language differently from that at Qumran, the close convergence of concepts in Eph 2:19-22 (e.g., spiritual temple, house, foundation, building) and the Qumran documents suggests some dependency.

621. Snaith, N. "Further Note on Ephesians 2:14." *ExpT* 53 (1941-42) 325-26.

Objects to Coggan's view that behind Paul's use of εἰρήνη (peace) was שָׁלֵם (peace offering). Finds the origin, rather, in Isa 53:5 where the LXX reads εἰρήνης ἡμῶν.

622. Spreer, L. Über Ephes. 2, 19-22." *TSK* 52 (1879) 128-30.

623. Stanley, D. M. "Christ our Peace: New Variation on Reconciliation Theme. Eph 2, 14-18." In *Christ's Resurrection in Pauline Soteriology. AnBib* 13. Rome: Pontifical Biblical Institute, 1961, 224-228.

Brief comments on this text as it instructs concerning Christ's resurrection.

624. Stegemann, E. "Alt und Neu bei Paulus und in den Deuteropaulinen
      (Kol-Eph)." *EvT* 37 (1977) 508-36.

      First establishes Paul's understanding of the place of Christ's death
      as the most radical turning point in history. The Deutero-Pauline
      letters of Col and Eph, replace that temporal disjunction of old versus
      new with spatial categories, fundamentally altering how major
      categories were understood.

625. Steinmetz, F.-J. "Beyond Walls and Fences: Somatic Unity in
      Ephesians." *TDig* 35/3 (1988) 227-32.

      The writer asks, if it were possible according to Eph 2:16 that Jews
      and Gentiles were united in one body, why not that peoples who are
      separated today find "somatic" unity with Christ?

626. Story, C. I. K. "Bible Study on Peace: Ephesians 2:11-3:21."
      Princeton Seminary Bulletin, n.s. 5/1 (1984) 59-66. [Repr. in
      EvRT 9/1 (1985) 8-17.]

      The study divides the section into two parts: Peace—the provision of
      Christ for the world (2:11-22) and Peace—the purpose of God in
      Christ for the world, to be channeled to the world through the church
      (3:1-21).

627. Stuhlmacher, P. "'Er ist unser Friede' (Eph 2,14): Zur Exegese und
      Bedeutung von Eph 2,14-18." In *Neues Testament und Kirche.*
      FS R. Schnackenburg, ed. J. Gnilka. Freiburg: Herder, 1974,
      337-58. ET "'He is our Peace' (Eph. 2:14). On the Exegesis
      and Significance of Ephesians 2:14-18." In *Reconciliation,
      Law, and Righteousness.* Philadelphia: Fortress, 1986,
      182-200.

      In dialogue with Gnilka (Ephesian commentary), the author seeks to
      pursue three questions: on what traditions and concepts does Eph
      2:14-18 depend? what is its literary form? and what is the intention
      of the statements in the context of Ephesians and its original
      historical situation? Rejects both a Gnostic background and a
      hymnic explanation for the origin of the text. Instead, he defends the

thesis that in 2:13-18 the author of Ephesians offers a Christological exegesis of Isa 9:5-6; 52:7; and 57:19.

628. Sudbrack, J. " ... er ist unser Friede und unsere Versöhnung (Eph. 2,14)." *GeistL* 56 (1983) 143-44.

629. Tachau, P. *"Einst" und "Jetzt" im Neuen Testament.* Göttingen: Vandenhoeck & Ruprecht, 1972, 134-43.

See on texts, 2:1-10 (# 531).

630. Thexton, S. C. "The Communion of Saints." *ExpT* 88 (1976) 25-26.

A short meditation based on Eph 2:19 and Rom 1:7 that stresses the fellowship of Christian believers.

631. Toews, J. E. "Biblical Foundations for Interdependence." In *Mission Focus,* ed. W. Shenk. Scottdale, PA: Herald Press, 1980, 129-36.

Finds in Eph 2:11-22 an anchor for a theology of interdependence in mission—one of mutuality and reciprocity that involves the legitimate inculturation of the gospel. The passage suggest two foundations for interdependence: the Christ event and Christ's creation of a single new man, the church.

632. Vielhauer, P. *Oikodome. Augsätze zum Neuen Testament,* Vol. 2. Munich: Kaiser, 1979.

In one of the essays of this volume, Vielhauer traces the image of *oikodomē* (building) in Christian literature from the NT to Clement of Alexandria.

633. Watson, P. S. "The Blessed Trinity." *ExpT* 90 (1979) 242-43.

A meditation on the nature of the trinity loosely referenced to Eph 2:11-22.

634. Wengst, K. "Das Versöhnungslied." In *Christologische Formeln und Lieder des Urchristentums.* Gütersloh: G. Mohn, 1972, 181-94.

Discusses formulaic expressions of the earliest Aramaic-speaking Christians, and the catechetical formulas and then liturgical acclamations and hymns of the Hellenistic Jewish-Christian and Gentile-Christian churches, one of which is the "reconciliation-hymn" of Eph 2.

635. Whitaker, G. H. "The Chief Cornerstone." *Exp* 47, 8th series, 22 (1921) 470-72.

636. _____. "The Building and the Body (Eph. 2, 21f.; 4, 16; Col. 2, 19)." *Theology* 13 (1926) 335f.

Argues against the common view that these passages refer to the interrelation of the different parts of the Body of Christ. He believes they speak, rather, to the relation of the whole Body to its Head. Shows his objections to the usual view and then presents his case in both the structure and the context of the passages that they speak of adaptation to and harmony with Christ—agreeing with the main thought of the letters. Union comes, then, with Christians seeking to grow closer to Christ, to a more complete understanding of and harmony with His will.

637. White, R. F. "Gaffin and Grudem on Eph 2:20: In Defense of Gaffin's Cessationist Exegesis." *WTJ* 54/2 (1992) 303-20.

Tackles the question of whether prophecy as a biblical gift continues in the church today by assessing what two contemporary writers say about Eph 2:20. For Gaffin, prophecy was a temporary gift; for Grudem only the apostolic gift ceased, and so prophecy continues today as it was practiced in NT times. White's thorough analysis of the various issues—and especially Grudem's exegesis which he finds faulty—leads White to side with Gaffin.

638. Wilhelmi, G. "Der Versöhner-Hymnus in Eph. 2:14 ff." *ZNW* 78 (1987) 145-52.

In dialogue with major recent German studies, he engages in a literary-structural analysis and reconstruction of what he considers the hymn of Eph 2:14-18.

639. Williams, R. "Resurrection and Peace." *Theology* 92/750 (1989) 481-90.

Tries to jar readers from too facile or comfortable an understanding of reconciliation by means of a discussion of the implications of Eph 2:14-18.

640. Wittschier, S. "'Denn Er ist unser Friede' (Eph 2, 14)." *Renovatio* 38 (1982) 129-44.

641. Wulf, F. "Er selbst ist unser Friede." *GeistL* 30 (1957).

Discussion of the "peace to you" citation, referencing Eph 2:14.

642. Zerwick, M. "He is our Peace (Eph 2:11-18)." *Biblebhashyam* 1/4 (1975) 302-11.

Following Gnilka, Zerwick believes that the author is refashioning an existing hymn that contained some potentially dangerous cosmic elements. The result underscores that Christ has abolished the Law that separated Jews and Gentiles, transforming them into a new humanity reconciled to himself through his death on the cross.

Chapter 5

TEXTS: Ephesians 3

Ephesians 3:1-13

643. Barth, M. "Gnade für die Anderen (Eph 3:2-3a; 5-6)." In *Parola e spirito.* FS S. Cipriani, 2 vols., ed. C. C. Marcheselli. Brescia: Paideia, 1982, 679-87.

A short study on the grace for others in these verses of chapter 3.

644. Best, E. "The Revelation to Evangelize the Gentiles." *JTS* 35 (1984) 1-31.

Starts with the conclusion to each of the Gospels and then the Acts to investigate the revelation that the gospel must be proclaimed to Gentiles. Next Best evaluates Paul's statements in Gal and other places before moving to the post-Pauline tradition found in Col and Eph 3:1-13 before moving on to the Pastoral Epistles. The tradition seems clearly two-fold: the Apostles received a commission and Paul received a commission; both converge that the Gospel must be preached to Gentiles.

645. _____. "A Damascus Road Experience?" *Irish Bible Studies* 7/1 (1985) 2-7.

Investigates various accounts of Paul's Damascus road experience in both Acts and the epistles, including Eph 3:1-13.

646. Bony, P. "L'épître aux Éphésiens." In *Le Ministère et Les Ministères Selon Le Nouveau Testament,* ed. J. Delorme. Paris: Seuil, 1974, 74-92.

In the discussion of "ministry" in Ephesians, this section (pp. 79-82) investigates Paul's own view of his ministry in Eph 3:1-13. His personal mission derived from his specific understanding of the mystery of Christ specially revealed to him. Paul considered his ministry as a "grace" from God consisting in his call to proclaim the mystery of the church's cosmic dimension. See also on 2:11-22 and 4:1-16.

647. Borucki, B. "Paulus vinctus Iesu Christi." *VD* 6 (1926) 342-48; 7 (1927) 20-23.

648. Brown, R. E. *The Semitic Background of the Term "Mystery" in the New Testament.* Philadelphia: Fortress, 1968, 56-66.

Adapted from three articles originally appearing in *CBQ* 20 (1958) 417-43 and *Bib* 39 (1958) 426-48; 40 (1959) 70-87, this short study traces the concept of mystery in semitic and NT usage. On pp. 55-66 Brown treats mystery in Ephesians, concentrating on chapter 3. Finds the most likely background for mystery in the semitic world rather than the Greek.

649. Caragounis, C. C. *The Ephesian Mysterion.* Lund: Gleerup, 1977, 52-56, 72-74, 96-112.

Within the project's analysis of mystery in Ephesians, these pages focus the discussion on 3:1-13. Goes against a common interpretation that the central component of meaning of "mystery" is "secret." Confirms the conclusions of Brown (above) that the background for mystery in Jewish and Semitic, not the mystery religions. It speaks of God's unified eschatological purpose that has cosmic dimensions to sum up all things in Christ.

650. Coppens, J. "Le 'mystère' dans la théologie paulinienne et ses parallèles Qumraniens." In *Litterature et Theologie Pauliniennes,* ed. A. Descamps. *RechBib* 5. Bruges: Desclee de Brouwer, 1960, 142-65. ET "'Mystery' in the Theology of St. Paul and Its Parallels at Qumran." In *Paul and Qumran,* ed. J. Murphy-O'Connor. Chicago: Priory Press, 1968, 132-58.

After summarizing common conclusions about Paul's uses of the concept of "mystery," he traces the use at Qumran with a view to interpreting Paul in the light of these findings. Discussions concerning Eph 3 occur on pp. 149-53.

651. Dahl, N. A. "Das Geheimnis der Kirche nach Eph 3:8-10." In *Zur Auferbauung des Leibes Christi.* FS P. Brunner, ed. E. Schlink and A. Peters. Kassel: Johannes Stauda, 1965, 63-75.

A study of the mystery of the church according to Eph 3:8-10. This section makes clear to Gentile Christians the revelation of the Christ-mystery and their existence as the church and body of Christ and successor to the promises made to Israel. One may not unilaterally interpret the terminology in Ephesians in terms of Gnostic texts. Better parallels occur in Qumran, rabbinic texts, synagogue liturgies, Hellenistic Jewish literature or other early church texts. Nearly all the specific terms for the major thought of Ephesians are Pauline in character.

652. Davies, L. "'I Wrote Afore in Few Words' (Eph 3, 3)." *ExpT* 46 (1934-35) 568.

Suggests that the mention of a prior "few words" may well be, not to a previous letter nor even to Eph 1:9ff. or 2:11-22, but to Rom 16:25-27 where Paul mentions mystery, presuming that Rom 16 may have originally been a part of a letter to Ephesus.

653. Fischer, K. M. *Tendenz und Absicht des Epheserbriefs.* Göttingen: Vandenhoeck & Ruprecht, 1973, 95-108.

See 1:3-14.

654. Flowers, H. J.   "The Grace of God Given to Paul—A Study of Ephesians 3:1-13." *RE* 25 (1928) 155-72.

Addresses a number of features of this passage that scholars sometimes cite to argue that Paul did not write Ephesians. Engages in various word studies and grammatical argumentation to defend authenticity. Then Flowers proceeds to elaborate his understanding of the passage.

655. Gewiess, J.   "Die Begriffe πληροῦν und πλήρωμα im Kolosser- und Epheserbrief." In *Vom Wort des Lebens.* FS M. Meinertz, ed. N. Adler. Münster: Aschendorff, 1951, 128-41.

Considers 3:19; see on 1:15-23.

656. Girgensohn, H.   "Die Gestalt der Kirche aus der Sicht des Briefes an die Epheser." In *Heilende Kräfte der Seelsorge.* Göttingen, Vandenhoeck & Ruprecht, 1966, 206-10.

The third section of an essay on the state of the church from the viewpoint of the Ephesian letter considers the recognition of the majesty of God in 3:14-21. The outworking of God's program for the church attains glory for God. It entails power in the inner person through the Holy Spirit, and a strengthening that occurs in two directions: in our relationship to Christ and to other people.

657. Gnilka, J.   "Das Paulusbild im Kolosser- und Epheserbrief." In *Kontinuität und Einheit.* FS F. Mussner, ed. P. G. Müller and W. Stenger.   Freiburg: Herder, 1981, 179-93.

A study of the image of Paul as found in the letters of Col and Eph.

658. Hoyt, H. A.   "The Purpose and Program of the Prophetic Word." *GTJ* 4 (1983) 163-71.

The stated issue is suggested by three texts: Rev 4:11, Eph 1:11, and Eph 3:11.

659. Jones, C. P. M. "The Calling of the Gentiles." In *Studies in Ephesians,* ed. F. L. Cross. London: Mowbray, 1956, 76-88.

Elaborates Paul's thinking on Eph 3:8-9, speaking, as they do, of Paul's apostolic commission, his message, and its mystery.

660. Joüon, P. "Notes philologiques sur quelques versets de l'Épître aux Éphésiens (1,12; 2,1-3; 2,15; 3,13.15; 4,28; 5,18.19; 6,9.19-20)." *Recherches de Science Religieuse* 26 (1936) 454-64.

Comments on words. See on 1:3-14.

661. Kim, S. *The Origin of Paul's Gospel, WUNT* 2/4. Tübingen: Mohr, 1981, 20-25.

Considers Eph 3:1-13 as a context where Paul speaks of his call.

662. Klein, G. *Die Zwölf Apostel.* Göttingen: Vandenhoeck & Ruprecht, 1961, 69-72.

See on 2:11-22.

663. Lincoln, A. T. *Paradise Now and Not Yet.* Cambridge: Cambridge University Press, 1981; Grand Rapids: Baker, 1992, 154-55.

Considers the church and the powers in the heavenlies (3:9-10).

664. Lindemann, A. Die *Aufhebung der Zeit: Geschichtsverständnis und Eschatologie im Epheserbrief.* Gütersloh: Gerd Mohn, 1975, 221-30.

See on 1:15-23.

665. Lloyd-Jones, D. M. *The Unsearchable Riches of Christ. An exposition of Ephesians 3:1-21.* Grand Rapids: Baker, 1979.

A collection of twenty-four sermons on the texts in Eph 3.

666. Lührrnann, D. *Das Offenbarungsverständnis bei Paulus und in den*

paulinischen Gemeinden. Neukirchen-Vluyn: Neukirchener Verlag, 1965, 119-33.

Part of an exegetical study of all the locations in the Pauline letters where the words conveying ideas of revelation occur. Words studied: *apokalyptein, apokalypsis, phaneroun,* and *phanerōsis.*

667. Mare, W. H. "Paul's Mystery in Ephesians 3." *BETS* 8/2 (1965) 77-84.

Surveys the meaning of the word *mysterion* in secular and Jewish literature and in Paul and seeks to relate and apply the *mysterion* teaching in Eph 3:5, 6 to the teaching of the OT, NT and Paul's teaching.

668. Mehlmann, I. "Ἀνεξιχνίαστος—investigabilis." *Bib* 40 (1959) 902-14.

In Latin, a study of the adjective translated "unfathomable" or "inscrutable" used both in Rom 11:33 and to describe the Messiah's riches in Eph 3:8.

669. Merklein, H. *Das kirchliche Amt nach dem Epheserbrief.* Munich: Kosel, 1973, 159-224.

See on 2:11-22.

670. _____. "Paulinische Theologie in der Rezeption des Kolosser- und Epheserbriefes." In *Paulus in den neutestamentlichen Spätschriften,* ed. K. Kertelge. Freiburg: Herder, 1981, 27-31.

See on 2:1-10.

671. Meyer, R. P. *Kirche und Mission im Epheserbrief.* Stuttgart: Katholisches Bibelwerk, 1977, 58-60, 64-65.

See on 1:15-23.

672. Minear, P. S. "The Vocation to Invisible Powers: Ephesians 3:8-10."

In *To Die and to Live.* New York: Seabury, 1977, 89-106.

One of the five texts chosen that elucidate the thinking of NT writers on the theme of Christ's resurrection and the vocation of the Christian.

673. Mussner, F. *Christus, das All und die Kirche.* 2nd ed. Trier: Paulinus, 1968, 144-47.

See on 1:15-23.

674. Orbe, A. "Una variante heterodoxa de Eph 3, 5a." *Greg* 37 (1956) 201-19.

675. Percy, E. *Die Probleme der Kolosser- und Epheserbriefe.* 2d rev. ed. Lund: Gleerup, 1964, 342-53.

See on 1:1-2.

676. Pesch, R. "Lesung (Eph 3, 8-12, 14-19): Das Mysterium Christi." *Herz-Jesu-Fest,* ed. E. Beuron. *Am Tisch des Wortes* 18. Stuttgart: Katholisches Bibelwerk, 1967, 11-17.

A reading of these texts that focuses on the key points that grow out of each: the announcement of the mystery of Christ and the understanding of the mystery of Christ. The outcome should be a celebration of the body of Christ.

677. Pierron, J. "L'épiphanie du mystère (Ep 3, 2-3a, 5-6)." *AsSeign* n.s. 12 (1969) 11-18.

678. Preuschen, E. "Σύνσωμος." *ZNW* 1 (1900) 85-86.

679. Purton, J. S. "Note on Ephesians III, 3-4." *Exp,* 2d series, 7 (1884) 237-38.

680. Ryrie, C. C. "The Mystery in Ephesians 3." *BSac* 123 (1966) 24-31.

Set against what Ryrie considers the errors of amillennialism and covenant premillennialism, this study seeks to show that the mystery in Eph 3 argues for recognizing the distinctiveness of the church as over against Israel and, hence, the unique place of the church in God's program—a dispensational hallmark. The mystery Paul reveals in Eph 3 is the equality of Jews and Gentiles in the body of Christ.

681.   Sullivan, K. "The Mystery Revealed to Paul—Eph. 3:1-13." *BiTod* 1/4 (1963) 246-55.

Popular-level, verse-by-verse analysis of this passage.

682.   Thomas, R. E. "Ephesians 3, 8." *ExpT* 39 (1927-28) 283.

Seeks to illustrate Paul's use of the adjective "unsearchable" from the Greek play *Agamemnon* by Aeschylus. Mortals cannot trace out God's riches.

683.   Thompson, G. H. P. "Eph iii, 13 and 2 Tim ii, 10 in the Light of Col i, 24." *ExpT* 71 (1959-60) 187-89.

Paul's sufferings for the sake of founding churches are part of the Messianic woes and thus help bring about the final manifestation of Christ in glory with the Ephesians.

684.   Ubieta, J. A. "La maturité chrétienne vécue dans le Mystère du Christ (Eph 3, 8-21)." *AsSeign* 56 (1967) 13-31.

685.   Viard, A. "La revelation du mystère du Christ (Ep 3,2.6)." *EV* (prédication) 82 (1982) 359-61.

686.   Wink, W. *Naming the Powers.* Philadelphia: Fortress, 1984, 89-96.

Ephesians 3:14-21

687. Arnold, C. E. *Ephesians: Power and Magic.* Cambridge: Cambridge University Press, 1989, 85-102.

In this study of "power" in Ephesians in light of its historical setting, the author analyzes power terminology in the prayer of Eph 3:14-19. Concludes that the magical papyri provide an informative background for the four dimensions of the prayer, providing a rhetorical expression for the vastness of God's power. The section concludes with a short study of the praise of divine power in 3:20-21.

688. Caragounis, C. C. *The Ephesian Mysterion.* Lund: Gleerup, 1977, 74-77.

See on 1:3-14.

689. Cerfaux, L. "A genoux en présence de Dieu (la priere d'Eph III, 14-19)." *Bible et Vie chrétienne* 10 (1955) 87-90. [Repr. in *Recueil Lucien Cerfaux,* vol. 3, ed. F. Neirynck. Leuven: Leuven University Press, 1985, 309-12.]

A short devotional study on the prayer of Eph 3:14-19 that calls forth worship.

690. Dahl, N. A. "Cosmic Dimensions and Religious Knowledge (Eph 3:18)." In *Jesus und Paulus.* FS W. G. Kümmel, ed. E. E. Ellis and E. Grässer. Göttingen: Vandenhoeck & Ruprecht, 1975, 57-75.

Pursues the meaning of 3:18, part of a prayer recorded in 3:14-19, where the aim of Paul's intercession is that his readers grasp the magnitude of four *dimensions.* The study asks especially the question, the dimensions of what? Seeks the answer, not in an alleged Gnostic background of Ephesians, but by tracing "trajectories" that lead to Ephesians and from Ephesians to Christian Gnosticism and Early Catholicism. Concludes that the dimensions of 5:18 refer to revealed knowledge of the immeasurable dimensions

of the universe, and that the phrase σὺν πᾶσιν τοῖς ἁγίοις as
a reference to the angels whose fellow citizens the baptized
Christians have become and whose comprehension of cosmic
mysteries they are to share.

691. Deichgräber, R. *Gotteshymnus und Christushymnus in der frühen
     Christenheit.* Göttingen: Vandenhoeck & Ruprecht, 1967, 25-
     40.

     See on 1:3-14.

692. Düsberg, H. "Le Mystère de l'infinie sagesse." *AsSeign* 70 (1965)
     42-53.

693. Dupont, J. *Gnosis. La Connaissance religieuse dans les Épîtres de
     Saint Paul.* Paris: J. Gabalda 1949, 476-528.

694. Ernst, J. *Pleroma und Pleroma Christi.* Regensburg: F. Pustet,
     1970, 120-35.

     See on 1:15-23.

695. Feuillet, A. *Le Christ, Sagesse de Dieu.* Paris: J. Gabalda. 1966,
     307-19.

     See on 1:3-14.

696. _____. "L'Église plérôme du Christ d'après Éphés., I, 23." *NRT* 78
     (1956) 593-610.

     See on 1:15-23.

697. Giblet, J. "Ut impleamini in omnem plenitudiem Dei (Eph. III, 14-
     21)." *Collectanea Mechliniensia* 29/5 (1959) 519-21.

698. Hull, W. E, *Love in Four Dimensions.* Nashville: Broadman, 1982.

     Six sermons growing out of the four dimensions of love outlined in
     the prayer of Eph 3:14-19.

699. Jarvis, C. A. "Ephesians 3:14-21." *Int* 45 (1991) 283-88.

An expository article covering the themes of reconciliation and Gentiles in the NT.

700. Joüon, P. "Notes philologiques sur quelques versets de l'Épître aux Éphésiens (1,12; 2,1-3; 2,15; 3,13.15; 4,28; 5,18.19; 6,9.19-20)." *Recherches des Science religieuse* 26 (1936) 454-64.

See on 1:3-14.

701. Lloyd-Jones, D. M. *The Unsearchable Riches of Christ. An exposition of Ephesians 3:1-21.* Grand Rapids: Baker, 1979.

See on 3:1-13.

702. Liese, H. "De interiore homine (Eph 3, 13-21)." *VD* 12 (1932) 257-63.

703. Mackay, J. R. "Paul's Great Doxology." *EvQ* 2 (1930) 150-61.

704. M'Kenzie, F. "Exposition of Ephesians 3:15." *ExpT* 2 (1890-91) 93-94.

705. Montague, G. T. "Deeper Indwelling and Rooting in Love Leads to Knowledge and `God's Fullness': Eph. 3:16-19." In *Growth in Christ.* Kirkwood: Maryhurst Press, 1961, 96-112.

Part of a study that focuses on the Christian's growth to perfection by a study of key Pauline texts. Most pertinent are texts on Paul's prayers (the present passage), plus those on spiritual combat and Eph 4:10-16.

706. Montgomery-Hitchcock, F. R. "The Pleroma of Christ." *Church Quarterly Review* 125 (1937-38) 1-18.

707. Mussner, F. *Christus, das All und die Kirche.* 2nd ed. Trier: Paulinus, 1968, 71-75.

See on 1:15-23.

708. Pesch, R. "Das Mysterium Christi (Eph 3, 8-12, 14-19)." *Am Tisch des Wortes* 18 (1967) 11-17.

709. Rees, E. E. "The Cosmic Christ." *ExpT* 41 (1929-30) 335-336.

A praise-evoking meditation on the glory of God from Eph 3:21.

710. Söhngen, G. "Christi Gegenwart in uns durch den Glauben (Eph 3, 17)." In *Die Einheit in der Theologie.* Munich: K. Zink, 1952, 324-41.

A study of "Christ's presence in believers through faith" (found in Eph 3:17) that begins with the biblical foundation for the concept. Considers such formulae as "Christ in us" (Rom 8:10; 2 Cor 13: 3, 5; Gal 4:19; Col 1:27), "Christ in me" (Gal 2:20), "to be in Christ," as well as texts in Paul that present the concept of the indwelling Spirit. Proceeds to study the concept as it appears in the church's theology of the sacrament: in what sense is Christ present in the bread and wine? Finally, draws out some practical implications for actual ministry of the meaning of Christ's presence in us through the sacrament.

711. Spurrier, E. "Note on Ephesians 3:18." *ExpT* 2 (1890-91) 164.

712. Thompson, G. "The Fulness of God." *ExpT* 3 (1891-92) 225-26.

713. Whitaker, G. H. "The Address of the Prayer in Eph. 3, 14ff." *Theology* 13 (1926) 220-23.

Chapter 6

TEXTS: Ephesians 4:1 - 5:20

Ephesians 4:1-16

714. Ausejo, S. de. "La 'unidad de fe' en Eph 4, 5-13." In *El movimiento ecumenista.* Madrid: Liberia Cientifica Medinaceli, 1953, 155-194.

715. Barth, M. "Die Parusie im Epheserbrief, Eph 4, 13." In *Neues Testament und Geschichte.* FS 0. Cullmann, ed. H. Baltensweiler and B. Reicke. Zurich: Zwingli, 1972, 239-50.

Expands the eschatological implications of Eph 4:13—the church triumphant.

716. Basevi, C. "La missiione di Cristo e dei cristiani nella Lettera agli Efesini: una lettura di Ef 4:1-25." *RivB* 38 (1990) 27-55.

Comments on the Paul's teaching on the mission of the church and the theology of missions.

717. Baules, R. "Vivre l'unité (Ep 4)." *AsSeign* n.s. 48 (1972) 33-38.

718. Benoit, P. "Eph 4,1-24: Exhortation à l'unité." *AsSeign* 71 (1963)
      14-26.

719. _____. "L'unité de l'Eglise selon l'Épître aux Éphésiens." In
      Studiorum Paulinorum Congressus Internationalis Catholicus
      1961. An Bib 17. Rome: Pontifical Biblical Institute, 1963, I:
      66-75.

      Study on the unity of the church in Ephesians.

720. Best, E. *One Body in Christ.* London: S.P.C.K., 1955, 148-52.

      Considers Eph 4:10, particularly the clause, "that he might fill all
      things," and vv. 11-16 on the body of Christ.

721. Bieder, W. *Die Vorstellung von der Höllenfahrt Jesu Christi.*
      Zürich: Zwingli, 1949, 81-90.

722. Bjerkelund, C. J. *Parakalô. Form, Funktion und Sinn der parakalô-*
      Sätze in den paulinischen Briefen. Oslo: Universitetsforlaget,
      1967.

      A study of three stylistically related sentence-types in the Pauline
      literature, one of which comprises those instances where *parakalō* ("I
      urge") introduces the sentence. Eph 4:1-3 provides an example of
      this type. Concludes that *parakalō* may be an epistolary form and
      not only a paraenetic introduction.

723. Bony, P. "L'épître aux Éphésiens." In *Le ministère et les ministères*
      selon le Nouveau Testament, ed. J. Delorme. Paris: Seuil,
      1974, 74-92.

      On pp. 82-90 of this article devoted to the concept of "ministry" in
      Ephesians, the author considers 4:1-16: the church community, unity,
      and ministries. Ministry becomes the responsibility of all members
      of the body of Christ. Ministries are given by Christ; gifts are given
      for the equipment of the saints for ministry so that the faith and unity

may be attained. See also on 2:11-22 and 3:1-13.

724. Bover, J. "In aedificationem corporis Christi (Eph 4, 12)." *EstBi* 3
      (1944) 313-42.

725. Bröse. E. "Der descensus ad infernos, Eph. 4, 8-10." *Neue
      Kirchliche Zeitschrift* 9 (1898) 447-55.

726. Caird, G. B. "The Descent of Christ in Ephesians 4:7-11." *StEv* 2,
      ed. F. L. Cross, *TU* 87. Berlin: Akademie, 1964, 535-45.

An exegesis of these verses and the author's employment of Psa 68.
Argues that the "descent" of Christ refers neither to his incarnation
nor any descent into Hades—two interpretations with strong
supporters. Sees the reference, rather, to Christ's return at Pentecost
to bestow spiritual gifts upon the church. Defends this thesis with
textual, grammatical, and liturgical arguments.   Appends his
conclusion that the author of Ephesians had a mind that used rabbinic
arguments in a way uncommonly like Paul's.

727. Cambier, J. "La Signification Christologique d'Éph. iv. 7-10." *NTS*
      9/3 (1963) 262-75.

Investigates the intentional alteration of Psa 68:19a in Eph 4:8 and
the discussion of Christ's ascension in vv. 7-10. Sets the passage in
its doctrinal context in Ephesians. Views vv. 9-10 along the lines of
rabbinic commentaries or a midrash on the text of the Psalm. It
serves to underscore the celestial situation of the resurrected Christ.

728. Coppin, E. M. "The Relevance of the Ascension Gifts in the Life of
      the Church." Ph.D. thesis, California Graduate School of
      Theology, 1986.

Considers the implications of Eph 4 for pastoral and evangelistic
work.

729. Dalmer, J. "Bemerkungen zu I Kor. 10.3-4 und Eph. 4.8-10." *TSK*
      63 (1890) 569-92.

730. Dockery, D. S. "Ephesians 4:1-6." *RE* 88 (1991) 79-82.

An explication of 4:1-6 that underscores the "seven" *ones*, grounded in the "three" members of the Trinity, all in "one" God and Father of us all. On the basis of the message, calls for unity in the church.

731. Dögler, F. J. "Hadesfahrt Jesu im Epheserbrief 4, 9." *Antike und Christentum* 2 (1930) 316f.

732. Dubois, J.-D. "Ephesians IV, 15: ἀληθεύοντες δὲ or ἀλήθειαν δὲ ποιοῦντες. On the Use of Coptic Versions for Testament Textual Criticism." *NovT* 16/1 (1974) 30-34.

Insists that uses of the Sahidic and Bohairic Coptic versions must be considered for the light they shed on this textual problem.

733. Engelhardt, E. "Der Gedankengang des Abschnittes Eph 4, 7-16." *TSK* 44 (1871) 107-45.

734. Ernst, J. *Pleroma und Pleroma Christi.* Regensburg: F. Pustet, 1970, 135-49.

See on 1:15-23.

735. Everding, H. E., Snelling, C. H., Jr., and Wilcox, M. M. "A Shaping Vision of Community for Teaching in an Individualistic World: Ephesians 4:1-16 and developmental interpretation." *Religious Education* 83 (1988) 423-37.

These authors, all Christian educators, exegete 4:1-16 for their universalistic view of Christianity—a view that provides a corrective to the pervasive individualism of our age. Considers four dimensions of unity in the passage. Shows implications of the text for "the role of the teacher in building community in the classroom."

736. Fischer, K. M. *Tendenz und Absicht des Epheserbriefs.* Göttingen: Vandenhoeck & Ruprecht, 1973, 21-78, 137-39.

See on 1:3-14.

737. Fung, R. "The Nature of the Ministry According to Paul." *EvQ* 54 (1982) 129-46.

Considers Paul's concept of ministry in Eph 4:7-16 on pp. 139-44. Christ has instituted ministers to equip individual believers to exercise their gifts in Christian service so that the church will be built up. The article concludes with implications for the nature of the church that grow out of the study of the passages studied.

738. Gewiess, J. "Die Begriffe πληροῦν und πλήρωμα im Kolosser- und Epheserbrief." In *Vom Wort des Lebens*. FS M. Meinertz, ed. N. Adler. Münster: Aschendorff, 1951, 128-41.

Considers 4:10; see on 1:15-23.

739. Gonzales Ruiz, J. M. "'Los Logos' de unidad en Ef 4, 1-16." *Semana Biblica Española* 15 (1955) 267-83.

740. Grosheide, F. W. "Ef. 4:9, κατέβη εἰς τὰ κατώτερα (μέρη) τῆς γῆς." *TS* 28 (1910) 201-202.

741. Hadidian, D. Y. "Tous de euangelistas in Eph. 4:11." *CBQ* 28 (1966) 317-21.

From a survey of the period during which the NT was written, suggests that "evangelist" here refers to the "office" of gospel writer and not just the function of evangelization.

742. Hall, W. N. "Fatherhood and Sonship." *ExpT* 6 (1894-95) 190.

Argues that Eph 4:6 teach the universal fatherhood of God and, if Fatherhood is universal, the universal sonship of Christ.

743. Halter, H. "Eph 4, 1-6. Wandelt würdig der Berufung zur Einheit!" In *Taufe und Ethos: Paulinische Kriterien fur das Proprium christlicher Moral*. Freiburg: Herder, 1977, 242-48.

See on 1:3-14.

744. Hamann, H. P. "Church and ministry: an exegesis of Ephesians 4:1-
      16." *Lutheran Theological Journal* 16 (1982) 121-28.

      Analyzing Eph 4:1-16 to investigate what this passage says about the
      church and the function of ministry within it, this study takes issue
      with the common understanding of 4:12 and M. Barth's comments
      concerning this verse in his Anchor Bible commentary.

745. _____. "The Translation of Ephesians 4:12—A Necessary
      Revision." *Concordia Journal* 14 (1988) 42-49.

      Argues that solid exegetical support for the universal translation of
      Eph 4:11-12 is virtually non-existent.

746. Hanson, A. T. *The New Testament Interpretation of Scripture.*
      London: S.P.C.K., 1980, 135-50.

      Within a study of the NT interpretation of the OT, considers the
      scriptural background for the doctrine of Christ's descent into Hades
      in the NT, including Eph 4:7-10.

747. Hanson, S. *The Unity of the Church in the New Testament:
      Colossians and Ephesians. ASNU* 14. Uppsala: Almqvist &
      Wiksells, 1946, 148-61.

      Considers the motives and symbols of the unity of the church and the
      nature of ministry in Eph 4.

748. Harris, W. H. "The Descent of Christ in Ephesians 4:7-11: An
      Exegetical Investigation with Special Reference to the
      Influence of Traditions about Moses Associated with Psalm
      68:19." Ph.D. dissertation, University of Sheffield, 1988.

749. Hemphill, K. S. *Spiritual Gifts. Empowering the New Testament
      Church.* Nashville: Broadman, 1988, 152-96.

      Considers the Pauline texts that discuss spiritual gifts, especially 1

Thes 5:12-22; 1 Cor 12-14; Rom 12; and Eph 4:1-16. Finds the material in Ephesians to fall within the continuum of Pauline thought as represented in the other passage on spiritual gifts. Draws conclusions about the nature and use of spiritual gifts in Ephesians and correlates them with his findings from the other passages.

750. Howard, G. "The Head - Body Metaphors of Ephesians." *NTS* 20 (1974) 350-56.

On pp. 354-56 Howard considers how Christ fills according to Eph 4:15-16. Concludes that this text goes beyond merely asserting the Christ fills the church and that the act of filling emphasizes quantity rather than quality: he fills *all* things. As a result, Christ unifies all dissident elements within the cosmos, drawing ever closer to the goal of cosmic unity.

751. Käsemann, E. "Epheser 4, 1-6." In *Exegetische Versuche und Besinnungen,* vol. 1. Göttingen: Vandenhoeck & Ruprecht, 1970, 284-87.

Short meditation/sermon delivered in 1951 on these verses that begin the paraenesis of the Ephesian letter.

752. _____. "Epheser 4, 11-16." In *Exegetische Versuche und Besinnungen,* vol. 1. Göttingen: Vandenhoeck & Ruprecht, 1970, 288-92.

Short meditation/sermon on these verses from Ephesians delivered in 1949.

753. Kirby, J. C. *Ephesians. Baptism and Pentecost. An Inquiry into the Structure and Purpose of the Epistle to the Ephesians.* London: SPCK, 1968, 61-69, 90-100, 138-46.

This study argues that the pseudonymous Jewish author of Ephesians based the first part of the epistle on a Eucharistic prayer and the second part on a discourse tied to the feast of Pentecost. Applies his study of Jewish liturgy to an analysis of Ephesians.

754.   Klauck, H.-J.   "Das Amt in der Kirche nach Eph 4, 1-16."
       Wissenschaft und Weisheit 36/2-3 (1973) 81-110.

       A study focused on the question of the authorship of Ephesians. As
       a result of an analysis of 4:1-16 (especially its grammatical features,
       theology, and use of the OT) as compared with similar passages from
       acknowledged Pauline material—especially Rom 12 and 1 Cor 12—
       the study concludes that Ephesians is pseudepigraphic, an authentic
       reinterpretation of the Pauline tradition. Specific divergences of Eph
       from authentic Pauline writings include: different uses of *ekklēsia* and
       sōma; reverses Paul's order of the importance of unity and church
       structures; the apostles and prophets are figures from the past; and
       Eph adds evangelists and shepherds whereas Paul mentions only
       teachers. In Eph, concern for stability has replaced the Pauline
       spontaneity.

755.   Kroon, J. "Ephesians 4, 8." *VD* 1 (1921) 54-56.

756.   Lavender, E. *A Biblical Pattern for Church Growth. A Study of
       Ephesians 4:1-16.* Winoan, MS: J. C. Choate, 1990.

757.   Liese, H. "`In vinculo pacis' (Eph. 4:1-6)." *VD* 13 (1933) 289-94.

758.   Lincoln, A. T. *Paradise Now and Not Yet.* Cambridge: Cambridge
       University Press, 1981; Grand Rapids: Baker, 1992, 155-63.

       Discusses Eph 4:7ff. and particularly the uses of Psa 68, the descent
       of Christ, the exalted Christ, the Spirit, and the Church. Considers
       the thorny problems involved in this section.

759.   _____. "The Use of the OT in Ephesians." *JSNT* 14 (1982) 16-57.

       Provides an analysis of the author's use of Psa 68:18 in Eph 4:8-10
       (pp. 18-25). Prefers the interpretation that views the descent of
       Christ as the descent of the Spirit at Pentecost where he gave gifts.
       Thus the author uses Psa 68:18 in the manner of a pesher quotation
       which then undergoes a midrash in order to argue Christologically.

760.   Lindars, B. *New Testament Apologetic. The Doctrinal Significance*

of the Old Testament Quotations. London: SCM, 1961, 51-59.

Argues that Psa 68:19, quoted only in Eph 4:8 in the NT (but also alluded to in Acts 2:33 and 1 Cor 12) has an important role in the early history of Christian doctrine and lies behind the concept of the Gift of the Spirit.

761. Lloyd-Jones, D. M. *Christian Unity. An Exposition of Ephesians 4:1-16.* Reprint. Grand Rapids: Baker, 1980.

Twenty-two sermons growing out of Eph 4:1-16.

762. Lyons, G. *Holiness in Everyday Life.* Kansas City, MO: Beacon Hill, 1992.

Considers the biblical teaching about sanctification with special focus on Rom 12:1-2 and Eph 4:1-6.

763. MacArthur, Jr. J. *Walk Worthy.* Chicago: Moody, 1989.

Part of his Bible study series, the author considers Eph 4:1-6.

764. MacKay, J. A. "Church Order: Its Meaning and Implications. A Study in the Epistle to the Ephesians." *ThT* 9 (1953) 450-66.

On the basis of Eph 4:7-10 the author argues for the unity of the Church based on Christ the Head of the Church and the gifted people he has given to the Church which qualifies and empowers them for their several ministries. The ministers then equip the saints for ministry—the priesthood of all believers.

765. Maier, W. A. *Instruction Concerning the Pastoral Office from Ephesians.* Fort Wayne, IN: Concordia Theological Seminary, 1987.

A short study on the office of the clergy growing out of Eph 4:1-16.

766. Martin, F. "Pauline Trinitarian Formulas and Christian Unity." *CBQ* 30 (1968) 199-219.

A study of the Trinitarian formulas of 1 Cor 12:4-6 and Eph 4:4-6 to shed light on Paul's understanding of the relation between the unity of God and the unity of the church. Considers their literary parallels, other relevant Pauline formulations, Paul's uses of *plērōma*, and what he says about the Spirit. Paul bases the unity of the new people of God on the fact that "God is one" while asserting that Christ is primarily responsible for the unity as Christians are baptized into his Body.

767. Matthews, S. W. "Developing a Biblical Leadership Model Based on the Ministry Gifts of Ephesians 4:11." D.Min. thesis, Southwestern Baptist Theological Seminary, 1992.

768. Menoud, P. "Éphésiens 4:11-16." *ETR* 30/4 (1955) 75-76.

769. Merklein, H. *Das kirchliche Amt nach dem Epheserbrief.* Munich: Kosel, 1973, 57-117, 332-401.

See on 2:11-22.

770. _____. "Eph 4:1 - 5:20 als Rezeption von Kol 3: 1-17." In *Kontinuität und Einheit,* ed. P. G. Müller and W. Stenger. Freiburg: Herder, 1981, 194-210.

Argues that Eph 4:1 - 5:20 constitutes the "reception" of Col 3:1-17.

771. Meyer, R. P. *Kirche und Mission im Epheserbrief.* Stuttgart: Katholisches Bibelwerk, 1977, 65-77.

See on 1:15-23.

772. Montague, G. T. "Deeper Indwelling and Rooting in Love Leads to Knowledge and `God's Fullness': Eph. 3:16-19." In *Growth in Christ.* Kirkwood: Maryhurst Press, 1961, 96-112.

Also addresses 4:10-16. See further on 3:14-21.

773. Moore, W. E. "One Baptism." *NTS* 10/4 (1963) 504-16.

Examines J. A. T. Robinson's study (see below) and considers Eph 4:5 in its context to detect the unity denoted by "one baptism." He revisits all sixteen texts that Robinson surveyed and faults Robinson's methodology for reading his biblical theology into the texts rather than exegeting them in their own context. As a result (and after considering Eph 5:4 itself), Moore believes Robinson neglected the crucial role of and plain emphasis on faith as the requisite for sharing in the salvation in Christ.

774.   Nestle, E.   "Zum Zitat in Eph. 4:8."   *ZNW* 4 (1903) 344-45.

775.   Peri, I.   "Gelangen zur Vollkommenheit.   Zur lateinischen Interpretation von καταντάω in Eph 4,13."   *BZ* 23 (1979) 269-78.

Traces the uses of this verb (meaning "attain" or "come") in the LXX and its Latin equivalents in the *Vetus Latina,* and evaluates its translations into Latin in 1 Cor 10:11; 14:36; Phil 3:11; and Acts 26:7. Studies how the verb used in Eph 4:13 is rendered in the *Vetus Latina* and patristic sources. Notes the special concerns to avoid Pelagian concepts that good intentions or human works may enable one to attain the fullness of Christ.

776.   Porter, C. H. "The Descent of Christ: An Exegetical Study of Eph. 4:7-11."   In *One Faith: Its Biblical, Historical, and Ecumenical Dimensions.* FS S. J. England, ed. R. L. Simpson. Oklahoma: Phillips University Press, 1966, 45-55.

Undertakes to illuminate this obscure passage by addressing the interpretive problem of Christ's descent in v. 9. Rejects the view that it refers to Jesus' death (F. Büchsel), a visit to Hades (Origen, F. W. Beare), or the incarnation (R. Bultmann). Rather, cogently argues on the basis of the appositional genitive τῆς γῆς and the Targum of Psalm 68 for understanding here Christ's post-ascension return to earth in order to give gifts to the church.

777.   Robinson, J. A. T.   "The One Baptism."   *SJT* 6 (1953) 257-74. [Repr. in *Twelve New Testament Studies. SBT* 34. London: SCM; Naperville, IL: Allenson, 1962, 158-75.]

An investigation of the significance of *one* in the assertion that there is "one baptism" (Eph 4:4f.). Taking up Cullmann's suggestion and growing out of his study of all the relevant NT texts, concludes that this one baptism was a sovereign act of God that baptized the entire world without human cooperation or our faith.

778. Rogers, E. R. "Yet Once More—`One Baptism'." *RThR* 50 (1991) 41-49.
Addresses the issue of the baptism of the Holy Spirit.

779. Rubinkiewicz, R. "PS LXVIII 19 (=EPH IV 8): Another Textual Tradition or Targum?" *NovT* 17/3 (1975) 219-24.

In synoptic fashion lays out the various readings of the Hebrew text, LXX, Eph 4:8, and the Targum in order to study the nature of the author of Ephesians' use of Psa 68:19. Then considers parallels in the Apocryphal writings, Latin texts, and the Church Fathers. Concludes that the origin of this use of Psa 68 came first from a Targum which Paul then adapted and was spread among the Fathers.

780. Schelkle, K. H. "Christi Himmelfahrt." *GeistL* 41 (1968) 81-85.

Studies Eph 4:7-15 reflecting on Christ's ascension. It shows Christ's work as Savior at a specific moment of time and the glory of the Lord today and forever.

781. Scharlemann, M. "The Secret of God's Plan. Studies in Ephesians - Two." *CTM* 41 (1970) 155-64.

A sequel to the study on 1:3-14 (see above), this homiletical and devotional study focuses attention on 1:20-23 and 4:1-16.

782. Schnackenburg, R. "Christus, Geist und Gemeinde (Eph. 4:1-16)." In *Christ and Spirit in the New Testament,* ed. B. Lindars and S. Smalley. Cambridge: Cambridge University Press, 1973, 279-96.

Seeks to redress the neglect given to the importance of the Spirit in Ephesians through a study of 4:1-16. The far-ranging usage given to the Spirit suggests that the author stands at the conclusion of a process of theologizing. Just as there is only one Spirit, the Spirit is the operative factor in promoting the unity of the Church. As Christ is ascended, he has given gifts—really gifted persons who hold office in the church.

783. _____. "Er hat uns mitauferweckt." *Liturgisches Jahrbuch* 2 (1952) 159-82.

784. Scippa, V. "I carismi per la vitalita della Chiesa. Studio esegetico su 1 Cor 12-14; Rm 12, 6-8; Ef 4, 11-13; 1Pt4, 10-11." *Asprenas* [Naples] 38/1 (1991) 5-25.

Evaluates these key texts that discuss spiritual gifts. The Ephesian passage stresses the use of the gifts for building up the church.

785. Smith, G. V. "Paul's Use of Ps. 68:18 in Eph. 4:8." *JETS* 18/3 (1975) 181-89.

Discusses the various problems that Paul's use of Psa 68:18 raises. After interpreting Psa 68:18 itself the author pursues the exegetical principles Paul appeared to use in Eph 4:8. Rejecting midrash or pesher as explanations, he concludes that Paul remolded the thought of Psa 68:18 in light of other OT texts, especially Num 8:6-19; 18:6.

786. Smith, J. H. "Exegetical Note. Ephesians iv, 11-12." *Union Seminary Magazine* 1 (1889-90) 181-83.

787. Steinmetz, F. J. Protologische Heils-Zuversicht: Die Strukturen des soteriologischen und christologischen Denkens in Kolosser- und Epheserbrief. Frankfurt: Josef Knecht, 1969, 117-21.

See on 2:1-10.

788. _____. "'Bewahrt die Einheit des Geistes' (Eph 4, 3). Eine paulinische Gewissenserforschung zum Thema 'Kritik an der Kirche.'" *GeistL* 54 (1981) 201-12.

Surveys a variety of issues facing today's church that paralleled the church in Paul's time.

789. Strauss, R. L. "Like Christ: an exposition of Ephesians 4:13." *BSac*
      143 (1986) 260-65.

      Argues that Eph 4:13 presents God's ultimate goal in the body of
      Christ and in the lives of its members: unity. This entails: unity of
      faith and of knowledge of the Son of God and maturity—spiritual
      adulthood. The standard for measuring maturity is the "fullness of
      Christ."

790. Sweetman, L. "Gifts of the Spirit: A Study of Calvin's comments on
      1 Cor 12:8-10, 28; Rom 12:6-8; Ephesians 4:11." In *Exploring
      the Heritage of J. Calvin,* ed. D. E. Holwerda. Grand Rapids:
      Baker, 1976, 273-303.

      Surveys Calvin's comments on these passages in light of
      contemporary discussions about the role and gifts of the Holy Spirit.
      Spiritual gifts equip and qualify members of the church to function
      in the church's "offices."

791. Taylor, R. A. "The Use of Psalm 68:18 in Ephesians 4:8 in Light of
      the ancient versions." *BSac* 148 (1991) 319-36.

      Uses the study of this example to raise many larger questions
      including those related to text-criticism, hermeneutics, exegesis, and
      canon. Suggests a variety of possible solutions to the problem at
      hand: how Paul employs Psa 68:18 in Eph 4:8. Seeks to shed light
      through an analysis of the evidence coming from early Greek, Latin,
      Coptic, Aramaic, and Syriac versions. Paul may well have used a
      variant textual reading of the Psalm. He used an analogical
      patterning of OT teaching to make his point.

792. Theron, F. T.   "Christus, die Gees, Kerk en Kosmos volgens
      Efesiërs, 4:7-10." *Nederduitse Gereformeerde Teologiese
      Tydskrif* 14/3 (1973) 214-23.

      The writer of Eph 4:1-16 applies Psa 68:19 where Yahweh is subject,
      to Christ to intensify the Christological focus to emphasize the

outcome of the resurrection—victory. God's eschatological purpose is the unity of all creation (1:10), but the church functions to fulfill that goal in the present. So Eph 4:1-16 describes the church's unity as both its gift and goal.

793. Tromp, S. "'Caput influit sensum et motum.' Col. 2, 19 et Eph. 4, 16 in luce traditionis." *Greg* 39/2 (1958) 353-66.

Consults medical terminology in Hippocrates and Galen to clarify the obscure Vulgate renditions of Col 2:19 and Eph 4:16 where Paul compares Christ's role in the church to that of the head to the body. Jerome saw the point of the connection *not* in the nervous system (as the Greeks), but the circulatory system and, hence, the difficulty even impossibility of the Latin translation.

794. Vooys, J. "No Clergy or Laity: All Christians Are Ministers in the Body of Christ, Ephesians 4:11-13." *Direction* 20/1 (1991) 87-95.

Conducts a verse by verse discussion of the text showing that Christ has gifted his body so that all may minister and grow.

795. Warnach, P. V. "Taufwirklichkeit und Taufbewusstsein nach dem Epheserbrief." *Liturgie und Mönchtum* 33/34 (1963/64) 36-51.

A study of baptismal reality and baptismal consciousness according to Ephesians. Finds that specific sections of Ephesians corresponds to rather fixed Hellenistic Christian baptismal liturgies (e.g., 1:3-14; 2:4-10, 14-18, 19-22). Finds already in Paul a sense that baptism is an "inner" or "spiritual" act, though it cannot be restricted to a merely cognitive function. Rather its function is eminently *"heilsgeschichtliche."*

796. Wengst, K. *Christologische Formeln und Lieder des Urchristentums.* Gütersloh: Mohn, 1972, 131-43.

See on 2:11-22.

797. Whitaker, G. H. "The Building and the Body." *Theology* 13 (1926) 335f.

798. _____. "συναρμολογούμενον καὶ συνβιβαζόμενον. Eph. iv 16." *JTS* 31 (1929-30) 48-49.

799. White, L. M. "Social Authority in the House Church Setting and Ephesians 4:1-16." *RestQ* 29/4 (1987) 209-28.

Finds that the house church context implies notions of social authority and obligation, and these are raised to new levels in Eph in two ways: first, apologetically the social structure of the church emulates and legitimates the society at large through bringing more stringent ethics into place; second, it implements more developed institutional patterns of organization for the church. Leadership and ethics are spirit-endowed gifts that stand with those of the apostles for building up the body of Christ.

800. Wilcox, M. *The Semitisms of Acts.* Oxford: Clarendon Press, 1965.

Believes that the Ephesian writer's quotation of Psa 68:19 in Eph 4:8 was from a textual tradition that resembled the Targum but disagreed with traditions preserved in the LXX and Hebrew texts at that point.

801. Williams, R. R. "Logic *Versus* Experience in the Order of Credal Formulae." *NTS* 1 (1954-55) 42-44.

Notes the correlation between the principal items in Eph 4:4-6 and those mentioned in the Nicene Creed—though the items occur in *reverse* order. Perhaps the order of the creed (cf. 1 Cor 8 as well) is more logical or apologetic, whereas the order in Eph 4 (and 1 Cor 12:4-6) is based on experience. Notes, as well, the probably strong influence that the items in Eph 4:4-6 had in the actual formalizing of the typical Eastern Creed.

802. Zehr, P. M. "The Gifts of the Spirit: Ephesians 4:7-16." In *Encounter with the Holy Spirit,* ed. G. R. Brunk, II. Scottdale, PA: Herald Press, 1972, 46-62.

A wide-ranging study of spiritual gifts that studies Eph 4:7-16, among the other key texts. Concludes with four gifts-lists classified in various ways: the lists themselves, according to location, function, and importance.

Ephesians 4:17 - 5:20

803. Adai, J. *Der Heilige Geist als Gegenwart Gottes in den einzelnen Christen, in der Kirche und in der Welt. Studien zur Pneumatologie des Epheserbriefes.* Frankfurt: Peter Lang, 1985, 217-31.

In this investigation of the theme of the Holy Spirit in Ephesians, the author considers the pertinent terms and key Spirit-texts in the letter, among with are 4:23-24; 4:30; and 5:18.

804. Agrell, G. *Work, Toil and Sustenance.* Verbum: Hakan Ohlssons, 1976, 126-32.

An important and far-ranging study of the relation of human work to serving God, obtaining sustenance, toil, and suffering. Considers the OT, Apocrypha and Pseudepigrapha, early rabbinic Judaism, and the NT. Among the NT texts studied is Eph 4:28.

805. Anderson, C. "Rethinking 'be filled with the spirit.' Ephesians 5:18 and the Purpose of Ephesians." *EvJ* 7 (1989) 57-67.

Paul's command, "Let yourselves be filled with all the working of the Spirit," (πληροῦσθε taken passively, πνεύματι understood as a dative of sphere) must be understood in light of the two dominant themes of Ephesians: (1) God's redemptive activity in Christ, and (2) the church's solidarity with this activity. Anderson examines five phrases in the immediate context of the imperative (5:15-21) that provide links to the epistle as a whole. Concludes that the command exhorts believers to allow themselves to be immersed in God's activity in Christ, especially the spread of the gospel.

806. Arp, W. E. "An Interpretation of "be filled in spirit" in Ephesians
      5:18." Th.D. thesis, Grace Theological Seminary, 1983.

      Considers the teaching of this text on the subject of the Holy Spirit.

807. Benoit, P. "Eph 4,1-24: Exhortation a l'unite." *AsSeign* 71 (1963)
      14-26.

808. Berghe, van den P. "Oui, cherchez à imiter Dieu! Ep 4, 30 - 5, 2."
      AsSeign n.s. 50 (1974) 37-41.

809. Betz, H. D. Nachfolge und Nachahmung Jesu Christi im Neuen
      Testament. *BHTh* 37. Tübingen: Mohr, 1967.

      A study of the imitation language in the NT in light of the problem
      of the historical Jesus and the use of such concepts in the Gnostic
      movements. Studies Paul's usage in contrast to the Gospels and the
      theological implications for Paul's uses.

810. Bigaré, C. "Le chrétien se conduit comme un sage, il cherche sa
      plénitude dans l'Ésprit (Eph 5, 15-21)." *AsSeign* 75 (1965)
      14-25.

811. _____. "Sagesse chrétienne pour le temps présent (Ép 5)." *AsSeign*
      n.s. 51 (1972) 38-43.

812. Briggs, F. J. "Ephesians iv, 20, 21." *ExpT* 39 (1927-28) 526.

      The fact that Jesus is a "truth" is the basis for Paul's admonition to
      "learn Christ."

813. Bultmann, R. "Das Problem der Ethik bei Paulus," *ZNW* 23 (1924)
      123-40. ET "The Problem of Ethics in the Writings of Paul."
      In *The Old and the New Man.* Richmond: Knox, 1956, 7-32.

814. Casel, O. "Εὐχαριστια—εὐχαριτία (Eph. 5, 3 f)." *BZ* 18
      (1929) 84-85.

815. Coune, M. "Revêtir l'homme nouveau (Ep 4,23-28)." *AsSeign* 74

(1963) 16-32.

816. _____. "L'homme nouveau (Ep 4)." *AsSeign* n.s. 49 (1971) 41-47.

817. Dacquino, P. "Filii lucis in Eph. 5, 8-14." *VD* 36/4 (1958) 221-24.

818. Dahl, N. A. "Der Epheserbrief und der verlorene erste Brief des Paulus an die Korinther." In *Abraham unser Vater.* FS O. Michel, ed. O. Betz, M. Hengel, and P. Schmidt. Leiden: E. J. Brill, 1963, 65-77.

819. Dieterlé, C. "Statuts des textes bibliques et théologies du couple." *Lumiere et vie* 34, 174 (1985) 61-72.

Investigates what 5:21-33 teaches about wives' submission and the headship of Christ (vv. 22-24), the picture of Christ and the church (vv. 25-29), and the picture of the man and the woman (vv. 30-32). Concludes by exploring a theology of the human couple and how human love celebrates Christ's love for the church.

820. Dodd, C. H. "Blind or Hard of Heart?" *Theology* 69 (1966) 223-24.

Defends the NEB's translation of *pōrōsis* to have its proper sense of petrification, and, hence, "hard as stone."

821. Dolger, F. J. *Sol Salutis: Gebet und Gesang im christlichen Altertum.* Münster: Aschendorff, 1925, 364-410.

822. Engberg-Pedersen, T. "Ephesians 5, 12-13: ἐλέγχειν and Conversion in the New Testament." *ZNW* 80/1-2 (1989) 89-110.

Attempts to shed light on these enigmatic verses and, particularly, to understand better the meaning of ἐλέγχειν and the notion of conversion as presented in the NT. Goes against Bauer's understanding of the key word, concluding it involves confronting someone with the aim of showing him/her to be at fault. Thus the readers must not only not have anything to do with the works of darkness, but they must confront them directly to show their errors.

When so exposed, these errors lose their attraction or "power."

823.   Findlay, J. A. "Ephesians iv. 29." *ExpT* 46 (1934-35) 429.

Suggests the translation, "Let no unclean speech issue from your lips, but such witty talk as is useful for edification."

824.   Fischer, K. M. *Tendenz und Absicht des Epheserbriefs.* Göttingen: Vandenhoeck & Ruprecht, 1973, 140-50, 152-61.

See on 1:3-14.

825.   Flowers, H. J. "The Old Life and the New — A Study of Ephesians 4:17-24." *RE* 26 (1929) 272-85.

826.   Foston, H. "Wrath's Quiet Curfew: An Expository Note on Eph. iv. 26." *ExpT* 18 (1906-07) 480.

Let reverent wrath have its due, and when its brief working day is over, let it be done.

827.   Furnish, V. P. *Theology and Ethics in Paul.* Nashville: Abingdon, 1968.

An attempt to apply the critical exegesis of Pauline texts to an understanding of Christian ethics. Surveys the sources of Paul's thinking in the OT, Judaism, the Hellenistic world, and the Jesus tradition. Proceeds to evaluate Paul's exhortations, the key themes of his preaching, and, finally, the character of the Pauline ethic. Considers Ephesians among the Deutero-Pauline writings.

828.   Giblet, J. "Les fruits de la lumière (Eph 5, 1-9)." *AsSeign* 30 (1964) 18-25.

829.   Gill, A. "Ephesians 5:19: Psalms and Hymns of Spiritual Praise." *ExpT* 2 (1890-91) 165.

Short note.

830. Gnilka, J. "Paränetische Traditionen im Epheser brief." In *Mélanges Bibliques*. FS B. Rigaux, ed. A. Descamps and A. de Halleux. Gembloux: Duculot, 1970, 397-410.

831. Gosnell, P. W. "Eph 5:18-20 and Mealtime Propriety." *TynB* 44 (1993) 363-71.

   Rather than seeing the filling of the Spirit as a contrast to excessive drunkenness that may have existed within Christian gatherings, the author finds the contrast in behavioral patterns of various Greco-Roman mealtime, convivial gatherings. On these occasions some people regularly chose stimulating—even religious—discussion rather than drunkenness. The writer of Ephesians draws upon this practice in his exhortation to Christians to prefer godly speech to drunkenness.

832. Goston, H. "Wrath's Quiet Curfew: An Expository Note on Eph. 4:26." *ExpT* 18 (1906-07) 480.

833. Grosart, A. B. "Psalms and Hymns of Spiritual Praise." *ExpT* 2 (1890-91) 180.

834. Halter, H. *Taufe und Ethos: Paulinische Kriterien fur das Proprium christlicher Moral.* Freiburg: Herder, 1977, 248-69.

   See on 1:3-14.

835. Hengel, M. "Hymns and Christology." In *Between Jesus and Paul. Studies in the Earliest History of Christianity.* London: SCM, 1983, 78-96.

   Considers the mention of hymns in Eph 5:18c-20 in this chapter about the "riddle of early Christian worship."

836. Horst, P. W. van der. "Is Wittiness Unchristian? A Note on εὐτραπελία in Eph. v. 4." In *Miscellanea Neotestamentica. NovT Supp.* 47, vol. 2, ed. T. Baarda, A. F. J. Klijn, and W. C. van Unnik. Leiden: E. J. Brill, 1978, 163-77.

A chronological cataloging of texts (with English translations for Greek texts) containing words of the εὐτραπελ- group forms the basis of this word study. Several biblical translations suggest εὐτραπελία refers to dirty jokes, a seeming incongruity given its etymology and virtuous, even witty, sense in Greek literature (esp. Aristotle). While the survey turns up "no clear indication" that this word denotes the former, the latter, positive sense has been exaggerated. Included in its semantic range are negative aspects— e.g., it is often at another's expense—that sufficiently preclude its inclusion as a Christian virtue.

837. Haulotte, E. "La formule paulinienne `revêtir le Christ.'" In *Symbolique du vêtement selon la Bible.* Paris: Aubier, 1966, 210-233.

A study of garments and vestments, both literally and as used metaphorically, in the Bible. Clothes picture spiritual realities as, e.g., Paul's armor of God.

838. Jervell, J. *Imago Dei.* Göttingen: Vandenhoeck & Ruprecht, 1960, 236-56, 288-92.

The overall study investigates the concept of the image of God from Gen 1:26-27, studying late Judaism and Gnosticism as a background for its use in the Pauline epistles. Clearly advances our study of this concept in Paul, though he is on less than solid ground in connecting the Pauline texts about the "image" with a baptismal liturgy. Interpreting Paul against a Gnostic background may also involve fundamental problems.

839. Joüon, P. "Notes philologiques sur quelques versets de l'Épître aux Éphésiens (1,12; 2,1-3; 2,15; 3,13.15; 4,28; 5,18.19; 6,9.19-20)." *Recherches Science religieuse* 26 (1936) 454-64.

See on 1:3-14.

840. Keener, C. S. *Paul, Women & Wives. Marriage and Women's Ministry in the Letters of Paul.* Peabody, MA: Hendrickson, 1992.

Appendixes to this study concerning women's roles include a discussion of Eph 5:18-21 and the threat of subversive religions. See next section for more.

841. Klug, E. F. "Will of God in the Life of a Christian." *CTM* 33 (1962) 453-68.

Through an exegesis of Eph 4:17-32, explicates "justification by works," that is, how Christians, growing out of their love for God, seek and do God's will.

842. Kuhn K. G. "The Epistle to the Ephesians in the Light of the Qumran Texts." In *Paul and Qumran,* ed. J. Murphy-O'Connor. London: Chapman, 1968, 115-31.

Seeks to display the ways in which Ephesians shows a particular affinity to the Qumran texts in terms of their language, terminology, thought, and ideas. Believes that 5:3-17 exhibits specific evidences of the Essene paraenesis found in Qumran texts and late-Jewish texts. Alleges that even the structure of the "light-darkness" antithesis found in Eph parallels that of the Qumran texts.

843. Lang, M. B. "A Comparison: Isaiah I. 18 and Ephesians IV. 25-29." *ExpT* 8 (1896-97) 405-06.

Explains the Isaiah text that sins, once scarlet, shall be snow-white through a comparison with the Eph verses that speak of replacing sins with virtues. "The sin is made white."

844. Larsson, E. *Christus als Vorbild: Eine Untersuchung zu den paulinischen Tauf- und Eikontexten.* Uppsala: Almqvist & Wiksells, 1962, 223-30.

Research into the motif of imitating and following Christ in two types of Pauline texts: baptismal and "icon." Considers Eph 4:24 among the second group.

845. Leggett, D. "Be filled with the Spirit: Ephesians 5:18." *Paraclete* 23 (1989) 9-12.

Popular but sound exegesis of 5:18 that gives context, expounds on the imperatives, and shows how the positive command is applied in the coordinate participles in vv. 19-20. The Spirit-filled life is not an optional benefit for those wanting a more vibrant Christian life, but is the means of godliness that the church is called to.

846. Liese, H. "Filii lucis, non iam tenebrarum (Eph. 5, 1-9)." *VD* 12 (1932) 33-38.

847. Lindemann, A. *Die Aufhebung der Zeit: Geschichtsverständnis und Eschatologie im Epheserbrief.* Gütersloh: Gerd Mohn, 1975, 232-34.

   See on 1:15-23.

848. Lloyd-Jones, D. M. *Darkness and Light. An Exposition of Ephesians 4:17 - 5:17.* Edinburgh: Banner of Truth; Grand Rapids: Baker, 1982.

   As in the other volumes in the series, a compilation of sermons (thirty-six here) on this section.

849. Lopez, U. "Caridad fraterna en las parenesis de Ef. 4, 25 - 5, 2 y Col. 3, 8." *Cuadernos Pont. Colegio Español* 2 (1955) 63-95.

850. Martin, R. P. "Hymns and Spiritual Songs." In *Worship in the Early Church.* London: Marshall, Morgan and Scott, 1964, 39-52.

   This chapter devoted to early Christian hymnody considers Eph 5:14 as a cogent example of the phenomenon.

851. Merklein, H. "Eph 4:1 - 5:20 als Rezeption von Kol 3:1-17." In *Kontinuität und Einheit,* ed. P. G. Müller and W. Stenger. Freiburg: Herder, 1981, 194-210.

   See 4:1-16.

852. Morris, W. D. "Ephesians iv. 28." *ExpT* 41 (1929-30) 237.

Takes the participle *ergazomenos* to mean "earning" along with the variant "bread." The former bandit is to earn his own bread.

853. Noack, B. "Das Zitat in Ephes. 5, 14." *StTh* 5 (1951-52) 52-64.

A study of the quotation located in Eph 5:14. Assuming an Old Testament *Vorlage* (earlier draft, basis), he backtranslates the quotation into Hebrew in an attempt to discern possible correspondences to other OT writings including Psa 43:24 and Isa 26:19 as well as smaller fragments. Finds that the quotation represents a hymn that celebrates the parousia or resurrection. Its context is baptismal—to be buried and raised with Christ.

854. Ogara, F. "`Imitatores Dei ... lux in Domino' (Eph. 5, 1-9)." *VD* 17 (1937) 33-38, 70-74.

855. Orlett, R. "Awake, Sleeper." *Wor* 35 (1961) 102-105.

A short meditation on 5:14-19. The quotation is from a hymn that was used at baptismal ceremonies. Asks what prompted early Christians to think of baptism in terms of life and light.

856. Peters, E. "`Nec nominetur in Vobis...' (Ep 5, 3)." *RCB* 3 (1959) 39-43.

857. Porter, S. E. "ἴστε γινώσκοντες in Ephesians 5, 5: Does Chiasm Solve a Problem?" *ZNW* 81 (1990) 270-76.

Surveys four issues surrounding the verse: the textual variant, the translation, the possible Semitic origin of the construction [answer is "no"], and the question of whether the finite verb ought to be indicative or imperative [decides for indicative]. Discerns a clear chiastic structure in 5:3-5 with these two verbs of knowing forming the central points.

858. Potterie, I. de la. "Jésus et la verité d'après Eph 4.21." *Studiorum Paulinorum Congressus Internationalis Catholicus 1961. AnBib* 18 (1963) 45-57.

859. Rey, B. "L'homme nouveau selon S. Paul," *RSPT* 48 (1964)
      603-29, esp. 615ff.; 49 (1965) 161-95, esp. 173-84.

      See on 2:11-22.

860. Rogers, C. L. "The Dionysian Background of Ephesians 5:18."
      BSac 136 (1979) 249-57.

      Argues that, rather than an issue of control contrasting wine versus
      the Spirit, the meaning of Paul's two commands in Eph 5:18 grows
      out of cultural background of the wild, drunken practices associated
      with the worship of Dionysus or Bacchus (the god of wine). Thus
      the prohibition against drunkenness is against a manner of life and is
      to be contrasted with a manner of life lived in the Spirit.

861. Sampley, J. P. "Scripture and Tradition in the Community as Seen
      in Eph 4:25ff." *StTh* 26 (1972) 101-9.

      Suggests that scholarship has unwittingly neglected the significance
      of Ephesians' indebtedness to OT and later Jewish traditions. Shows
      the pervasive influences of these Jewish sources on 4:25ff. Avers
      that both the specific points as well as the overall form of the
      passages derives from the OT.

862. Schille, G. *Frühchristliche Hymnen.*   Berlin: Evangelische
      Verlangsanstalt, 1965, 94-101.

      See on 1:13-14.

863. Schmitt, J. "Un fragment de la prière baptismale, Eph., V, 14b." In
      Jésus ressuscité dans la prédication apostolique.   Paris:
      Gabalda, 1949, 86-93.

864. Schnackenburg, R. "'Er hat uns mitauferweckt.' Zur Tauflehre des
      Epheserbriefes." *Liturgisches Jahrbuch* 2 (1952) 160-66.

865. Schulte, R. "Se conduire en enfant de lumière." *AsSeign* n.s. 17
      (1970) 11-16.

866. Schweizer E. "Gottesgerechtigkeit und Lasterkataloge bei Paulus (inkl. Kol und Eph)." In *Rechtfertigung*. FS E. Käsemann, ed. J. Friedrich, W. Pohlmann, and P. Stuhlmacher. Tübingen, Mohr, 1976. 461-77.

Studies the righteousness of God in connection with the various vice lists in the Pauline literature.

867. Scott, C. A. "Ephesians 4:21: As the Truth is in Jesus." *Exp,* 8th series, 3 (1912) 178-85.

868. Siber, P. *Mit Christus leben.* Zürich: Theologischer Verlag, 1971, 200-205.

Studies both resurrection or being with Christ and glorification with Christ through suffering.

869. Trowitzsch, M. "Eph 5, 14; Predigt und Fortführungen; zugleich die Vorstellung einer homiletischen Übergangsform." *EvT* 45 (1985) 546-60.

870. Vamarasi, J. "Wine or Spirit? Rotuman Understanding of a Controversial Text." *BT* 40 (1989) 241-43.

A discussion based on field notes of the Rotuman understanding of the translation of Eph 5:18 in their native language. Reactions to the text by those having no access to other Bible translations are given phrase by phrase.

871. Wallace, D. B. "'Οργίζεσθε in Ephesians 4:26: command or condition?" *Criswell Theological Review* 3 (1989) 353-72.

Sets out the various options for understanding the imperative "be angry," evaluates the strengths for each, analyzes the context, and concludes that the text places a moral obligation on believers to be angry as the occasion requires. The anger commanded is probably a righteous indignation that culminates in church discipline.

872. Wegenast, K. *Das Verständnis der Tradition bei Paulus und in den*

Deuteropaulinen. Neukirchen: Neukirchener Verlag, 1961,
131-32.

A study of Paul's understanding of tradition and how it is used in
Deutero-Pauline writings, and, thus, the early Christian period. Seeks
the connection between revelation and tradition.

873. Wild, R. A. "'Be Imitators of God': Discipleship in the Letter to the
Ephesians." In *Discipleship in the New Testament,* ed. F. F.
Segovia. Philadelphia: Fortress, 1985, 127-43.

Assuming that Ephesians, a pseudepigraphal, late first-century,
Christian writing, presents some sort of "Hellenistic Christianity," the
article seeks to understand how the author calls his readers to be
imitators of God (Eph 5:1-2; 4:24). Seeks to show the relevance of
Philo's formulation of the "imitation of God" to interpreting
Ephesians. Considers evidence of the imitation theme elsewhere in
Ephesians as well, concluding that discipleship in Ephesians stands
in a clear Platonic tradition mediated through Hellenistic Judaism.
Yet it is distinctively Christian because the writer is not primarily a
philosopher but a follower of Jesus and a believer in revelation.

874. Wilson, W. "Ephesians iv. 32." *ExpT* 33 (1921-22) 279.

Seeks an answer to why the AV rendered the *en Christō* as "for
Christ's sake" instead of the obvious and correct "in Christ." Why
also did this occur in the Tyndale version and in Calvin?

875. Wulf, F. "Wach auf, der du schläfst (Eph 5,14). Weckruf zum
Advent." *GeistL* 51 (1978) 401-406.

876. Zyro, F. "Ephes. 4, 26, ὀργίζεσθε, καὶ μὴ ἁμαρτάνετε."
TSK 14 (1841) 681-90.

Chapter 7

TEXTS: Ephesians 5:21 - 6:20

Ephesians 5:21-33

877. Allmen, D. von. "Les noces du Christ et de l'Église." In *La Famille de Die.* Orbis Biblicus et Orientalis, 41. Fribourg: Editions Universitaires; Göttingen: Vandenhoeck & Ruprecht, 1981, 238-256.

Raises the problems of studying images in Paul's writings before focusing on images of the family. Among the various themes surveyed include the marriage of Christ and the church.

878. Allmen, J. -J. von. *The Pauline Teaching on Marriage.* New York: Harper, 1952.

Assess a wide variety of issues concerning marriage in this eighty-page study. Directs attention to Eph 5:22-33 when he considers the typological implications of the couple in chapter 3, esp. pp. 35-39, 44f.

879. Baltensweiler, H. "Epheserbrief (Kap 5, 22-32)." In *Die Ehe im*

Neuen Testament. ATANT 52. Zurich: Zwingli, 1967, 218-35.

Researches the essence and function of marriage through an extensive analysis of NT texts set against their OT, Jewish, and Hellenistic backgrounds. Among the texts from the epistles is Eph 5:22-33.

880. Balthasar, H. U. von. "Ephesians 5:21-33 and humanae vitae: a meditation." In *Christian Married Love,* ed. R. Dennehy. San Francisco: Ignatius Press, 1981, 54-73.

Expands on, but "makes no pretense at an exact exegesis" of, a text that *Humanae Vitae* cites to enhance appreciation of the encyclical's central truths. "Mystery," whatever its precise referent, means that conjugal relationships must exist in the context of the union of Christ and the church, which is "by its nature a fruitful one." References the Virgin Mary, characteristics of male and female biology, and pertinent theological (Latin) terminology.

881. Batey, R. A. "'Jewish Gnosticism' and the 'Hieros Gamos' of Eph. v: 21-33." *NTS* 10 (1963) 121-27.

Locates the nuptial imagery neither in the OT nor from Hellenistic and Gnostic sources. Seeks to show that it arose in a milieu influenced by a Jewish Gnosticism similar to that found in Justin the Gnostic's book, *Baruch.* Shows various parallels between *Baruch* and Ephesians, but also notes differences, e.g., Ephesians' emphasis on Christ's historical sacrifice and the church as a corporate salvific community. Yet Ephesians draws upon the same kinds of mythical presuppositions as other Gnostic writings.

882. _____. "Paul's Bride Image." *Int* 7 (1963) 176-82.

Contends that this imagery in Paul, seen, e.g., in 2 Cor 11:2-3, is best explained in terms of realized eschatology—the bride image clearly implies that the End has begun and will be consummated by a historical divine intervention.

883. _____. "The "The μία σάρξ Union of Christ and the Church." *NTS* 13/3 (1966-67) 270-81.

Evaluates the Jewish, Hellenistic, and Gnostic background to the "one flesh" concept before studying its use in the New Testament. Drawing conclusions about its meaning in the NT (ideally effecting the perfect blending of two separate lives into one), the author lists implications for understanding the NT doctrine of the church. The church as a corporate society is united to Christ, this union being the fulfillment of God's eternal purpose for creation.

884. _____. *New Testament Nuptial Imagery.* Leiden: Brill, 1971, 20-37.

Considers the nuptial imagery of Eph 5:21-33 an expansion in the interest of ecclesiology of the initial exhortation of a *Haustafel* similar to Col 3:18 - 4:6. Performs an exegesis of the passage including analyses of key terms like "image," "head" (means the authority grounded in priority of being), and "one flesh" (referring readers to his previous article noted above). Overall, considers the passage to reflect mythological categories similar to the Jewish Gnosticism in Justin's *Baruch.* Borrows extensively from his article above on "Jewish Gnosticism."

885. Baules, R. "L'époux et l'épouse dan le Christ. Ep 5, 21-32." *AsSeign* 52 (1974) 37-42.

886. Beck, J. R. "Is There a Head of the House in the Home? Reflections on Ephesians 5." *Journal of Biblical Equality* 1 (1989) 61-70.

On Eph 5:21-33, a popular defense of mutual submission as the key concept in the entire passage. Redefines the husband's headship as self-sacrificing love.

887. Best, E. *One Body in Christ.* London: SPCK, 1955, 169-83.

A discussion of the nuptial metaphor—and specifically, the bride of Christ—in the NT. Shows how Eph 5:22-33 provides the fullest development of this metaphor in the NT. Draws conclusions for the theme of the book, an understanding of the body of Christ.

888. Bouwman, G.   "Eph V 28—Versuch einer Übersetzung."   In
      Miscellanea Neotestamentica. Vol. 2, ed. T. Baarda, A. F. J.
      Klijn, and W. C. van Unnik. Leiden: Brill, 1978, 179-90.

      Addresses the proper translation of this verse.

889. Bowman, J. W.   "The Gospel and the Christian Family. An
      Exposition of Ephesians 5:22 to 6:9." *Int* 1 (1947) 436-449.

      Contending that the structure of Ephesians argues for its Pauline
      origin, the author posits that in 5:22-6:9 Paul uses the family as an
      example of the gospel's social ethic. Indeed the family functions as
      an allegory of the corporate life of the church.

890. Burkill, T. A. "Two into One: The Notion of Carnal Union in Mark
      10,8, I Kor 6,16, Eph 5,31." *ZNW* 62 (1971) 115-120.

      Responds and reacts to ten major points in R. A. Batey's article noted
      above, "The "The μία σάρξ Union."   Finds Batey's analysis
      unsatisfactory, and, beyond that, that the explanations of the marriage
      union in these biblical texts are ultimately imprecise and incoherent.
      Perhaps that is why Eph 5:32 speaks of this as a "great mystery."
      The writer must confess a relative ignorance that will only be
      dispelled at the eschaton.

891. Cambier, J. "Le Grand Mystère concernant le Christ et son Église:
      Eph. 5:22-33." *Bib* 47 (1966) 43-90, 223-42.

      An extensive exegesis of the great mystery of Christ and his church,
      including the larger section of Eph 5:22-33. Sets out the principal
      options for understanding the concept of the mystery: the ancient and
      now abandoned understanding of marriage as a sacrament; a hidden
      sense growing out of Paul's own reading of Gen 2:24; and the
      profound sense that expresses the relation and the reality of Christ
      and the church. Concludes that the mystery consists of four pieces:
      the importance of Christ's role, Christ's lordship over his church, the
      historic death of Christ showing that Christ is the savior of his body,
      and God's insertion of believers into the church upon their acceptance
      of God's renewal and baptism. The author draws conclusions for

marital relations and for a theology of marriage.

892.   _____. "Doctrine paulinienne du marriage chrétien: Étude critique
de I Cor 7 et d'Eph 5:21-33 et essai de leur tradition actuelle."
Église et théologie (Ottawa) 10 (1979) 13-59.

Studies these two passages with a view to constructing the theology
of marriage they present. The Eph passage emphasizes the mutuality
of husband and wife—mutuality of support, service, and submission.
Institutions like marriage are renewed in Christ.

893. Campbell, P. E. "This Is a Great Sacrament." *HPR* 50 (1949) 462-
72.

894. Carre, A. M. "Comme le Christ et l'Église." *L'Anneau d'Or* 6
(1945) 5-7; 7 (1946) 5-9.

895. Chavasse, C. *The Bride of Christ.* London: Faber, 1940.

896. Clark, S. B. *Man and Woman in Christ.* Ann Arbor: Servant
Books, 1980, 71-87.

In a work that considers the roles of men and women in light of
Scripture and the social sciences, this section examines in depth Eph
5:22-33. Sees Paul directing his instructions to the ones who are the
subordinates in their relationships—wives, children, slaves—and then
to those who are the "heads" so that they treat their subordinates in
appropriate ways. Rejects the conclusion that "mutual submission"
is a valid understanding of Eph 5:21. The marriage of Adam and
Eve is a type of Christ and the church, and so the marriage of
Christians should imitate Christ and the church.

897. Cothenet, E. "L'Église, épouse du Christ (Eph 5; Apoc 19 et 21)."
In *L'Église Dan La Liturgie,* ed. A. M. Triacca and A. Pistoia.
Rome: Edizioni Liturgiche, 1980, 81-106.

After listing the variety of the images used to describe the church,
focuses especially on the Church as the spouse of Christ as found in
the Ephesian *Haustafel* of 5:21-33, and then in Revelation 19 and 21.

Christ enters into a conjugal alliance with his church, the consequence of which is the church's loving submission to her Lord.

898.   Dacquino, P. "Note su Ef. 5, 22-31." *ScuolC* 86/5 (1958) 321-31.

A careful exegesis of the passage and its parallels in the NT with the view of formulating an understanding of Christian marriage, and the question of marriage as a sacrament. Beyond that expressed in Gen 2:24, Christian marriage expresses an elevated reality of love and union since it participates in the union and love Christ has for his church.

899.   Dawes, G. W. "Analogies, Metaphors and Women as Priests." *Pacifica* 7 (1994) 47-58.

The metaphors of "head" and "body" allow the author to draw the parallel between Christ/Church and husband/wife. Denies that the passage argues against women priests. The prohibition only works if "headship" is a priori defined as a male trait women cannot possess.

900.   Dieterle, C. "Status des textes bibliques et theologies du couple." *LumVie* 34/174 (1985) 61-72.

On Eph 5:21-33, the study evaluates the passage's teaching on wives' submission and Christ's headship, the picture of Christ and the Church and the man and the woman, finally exploring how a theology of a human couple may be constructed.

901.   Dougherty, J. "The Confraternity Version of Eph. 5:32." *CBQ* 8 (1946) 97.

Gives a four-fold reason why the Catholic Confraternity version adopted the translation "This is a great mystery," replacing the older "This is a great sacrament."

902   Fennema, D. "Unity in Marriage: Ephesians 5:21-33." *Reformed Review* 25 (1971) 62-71.

Understands the passage under the rubric of mutual self-giving concern of one Christian for another, not the superiority of one person over another. Prefers to see the wife's role as devotion rather than submission. In devotion a marriage finds unity. This husband's love for his wife does not differ qualitatively from the wife's submission. In fact, his love demands the same kind of devotion that the wife gives to him.

903.   Feuillet, A.   "La dignité et le rôle de la femme d'après quelques textes pauliniens." *NTS* 21 (1975) 157-91.

Compares what several Pauline texts say about the role of women with what is found in the OT. Studies the woman as the glory of the man (1 Cor 11:7); women's silence in the church (1 Cor 14:33b-35); and the union of man and woman and the union of Christ and the church (Eph 5:22-33) before tracing OT precedents to these Pauline conceptions.

904.   Fischer, K. M.   *Tendenz und Absicht des Epheserbriefs.* Göttingen: Vandenhoeck & Ruprecht, 1973, 176-200.

See on 1:3-14.

905.   Fuchs, E.   "De la soumission des femmes. Une lecture d'Ephesiens 5, 21-33." *Supplement* 161 (1987) 73-81.

The author finds the focus on the idea of mutual submission finding no contradiction between submission and reciprocity.

906.   Gächter, P.   "Die Ehe nach Eph. 5, 21-33."   *Katholische Kirchenzeitung* 71 (1931) 122-25.

907.   Greeven, H.   "Der Mann ist des Weibes Haupt." *Die neue Furche* 6 (1952) 99-109.

908.   _____.   "Zu den Aussagen des Neuen Testaments über die Ehe." *ZEE* 1 (1957) 109-25.

909.   Grob, F.   "L'image du corps et de la tête dans l'Épître aux

Éphésiens." *ETR* 58/4 (1983) 491-500.

910. Guillemette, N. "Saint Paul and Women." *East Asian Pastoral Review* [Manila] 26/ 2 (1989) 121-33.

The author discusses Paul's various statements on women, including Eph 5:21-32. These texts reflect the tension between his claim of egalitarianism on the one hand and his patriarchal and anti-feminist background on the other.

911. Hahn, F. "Die christologische Begründung urchristlicher Paränese." *ZNW* 72 (1981) 88-99.

Pursues the Christological bases behind early Christian paraenesis, including the *Haustafel* to be found in Eph 5:22 - 6:9. The bases may differ, but no early Christian paraenesis lacked a connection to Christology or to the preaching of the gospel.

912. Hall, B. "Church in the World. Paul and Women." *ThT* 31 (1974) 50-55.

Seeks to retain Paul's teachings in a day of women's liberation by removing obstacles: our careless and superficial way of reading him. She observes that some of the offending texts (those in Col Eph 1 Tim, and Titus) were not actually written by Paul, and she believes that in texts such as Eph 5:21-33 the early church got such "household rules" from its surroundings, not via revelation. She proceeds to consider Pauline texts: Gal 3:28; 2 Cor 11:3; 1 Cor 7:1-40; 1 Cor 11:2-16; and 14:33-36. In the end, the author avers, we may agree or disagree with some of Paul's convictions, but we must remain in dialogue with him.

913. Halter, H. *Taufe und Ethos: Paulinische Kriterien fur das Proprium christlicher Moral.* Freiburg: Herder, 1977, 281-86.

See on 1:3-14.

914. Howard, G. E. "The Head/Body Metaphors of Ephesians." *NTS* 20 (1975) 350-56.

See 1:15-23.

915. Johnston, L. "The Mystery of Marriage." *Scripture* 11/13 (1959) 1-6.

Studies the relationship between the Mystical Body of Christ and marriage which interpret each other. "Mystery" in Paul's usage is connected with progressive revelation which reaches its fullness in the union of Christ and his church. Marriage is a part of the mystery of Christ and the Church and so the use of "mystery" in 5:32 suggests that marriage represents the Mystical Body and recreates and reenacts the union of Christ and the Church; it does not merely symbolize it.

916. Joüon, P. "Notes philologiques sur quelques versets de l'Épître aux Éphésiens (1,12; 2,1-3; 2,15; 3,13.15; 4,28; 5,18.19; 6,9.19-20)." *Recherches Science Religieuse* 26 (1936) 454-64.

See on 1:3-14.

917. Kahlefeld, H. "Wie wird in der Perikope Eph 5, 22-33 über des eheliche Leben gesprochen?" *Katechetische Blätter* 91 (1966) 185-92.

918. Kähler, E. "Die Aussagen über die Frau in Eph 5, 21ff." In *Die Frau in den paulinischen Briefen unter besonderer Berücksichtingung des Begriffes der Unterordnung.* Zürich/Frankfurt: Gotthelf, 1960, 88-140.

The entire volume studies the place of women and the concept of subordination in Paul's letters. Besides Eph 5:12ff., exegetes the topic in 1 Cor, 1 Tim 2, and Tit 2. Considers, as well, the concept of submission in other contexts in the ancient world.

919. Kamlah, E. "Ὑποτάσσεσθαι in den neutestamentlichen `Haustafeln.'" In *Verborum Veritas.* FS G. Stählin, ed. O. Böcher and K. Haacker. Wuppertal: Brockhaus, 1970, 237-43.

A study of how the concept of "submission" fits into the various household code lists in the NT.

920. Keener, C. S. *Paul, Women & Wives. Marriage and Women's Ministry in the Letters of Paul.* Peabody, MA: Hendrickson, 1992.

Examines four key passages traditionally interpreted to require women's submission: 1 Cor 11:1-16 (on head coverings), 1 Cor 14:34-35 (silence in the assembly and asking questions), 1 Tim 2:9-15 (learning in silence), and Eph 5:18-33. Concerning the Eph 5 text, he examines the social situation in Ephesus and the theme of mutual submission, incorporating insights from Eph 6:5-9 (the submission of slaves). Concludes that much of Paul's teaching concerns specific situations, and that mutual submission is Paul's underlying principle for both husbands and wives. Appendixes include discussion about women's ministry elsewhere in Paul and Eph 5:18-21 and the threat of subversive religions.

921. Kostenberger, A. J. "The Mystery of Christ as the Church: Head and Body, 'One Flesh.'" *TrinJ* 12/1 (1991) 79-94.

On 5:32: discusses the various ways of understanding *mysterion* in 5:32, concluding the analogical interpretation fits best exegetically and with Paul's theology elsewhere. Touches also on the mystical body of Christ and biblical teaching about marriage.

922. Kraus, G. "Subjection: a New Testament Study in Obedience and Servanthood." *Concordia Journal* 8 (1982) 19-23.

Considers the NT uses of *hypotassō* (submit) and *hypotagē* (submission) concluding that the concepts of subjection and obedience guide all relationships, not only marriage. Responds to three objections that wives submit to husbands applying Eph 5:21 - 6:9 to the issue.

923. La Bonnardiere, A.-M. "L'interprétation augustinienne du magnum sacramentum de Éphés. 5,32." In *Recherches Augustiniennes,* Volume XII. Paris: Études Augustiniennes, 1977, 3-45.

A study of Augustine's view of the great sacrament of Eph 5:32.

924. Leipoldt, J. *Die Frau in der antiken Welt und im Urchristentum.* 3d ed. Leipzig: Koehler & Arnelang, 1965.

A study of women in the ancient world and early Christianity. The historical background considers women and wives in ancient Egypt, Rome, Greece, and in Judaism. Studies Jesus' relationship to women and how the early Christians viewed women as reflected in Jewish Christianity, in Gentile Christianity, in Paul's writings and the community. Discusses young women and married women in special sections.

925. Lincoln, A. T. "The Use of the OT in Ephesians." *JSNT* 14 (1982) 16-57.

See on 4:1-16.

926. Lloyd-Jones, D. M. *Life in The Spirit. An Exposition of Ephesians 5:18-6:9.* Grand Rapids: Baker, 1973.

As with prior volumes, sermons covering this section.

927. Lochet, L. "Autorité et amour dans la vie conjugale." *L'Anneau d'Or* 68 (1956) 108-21.

928. Maillet, H. "Alla-plen: metaphore et pedagogie de al soumission dans les rapports conjugaux, familiaux, sociaux et autres selon Éphésiens 5:21 - 6:9." *ETR* 55 (1980) 566-75.

929. Marco, di A. "'Misterium hoc magnum est ...' (Ef 5, 32)." *Laurentianum* 14/1 (1973) 43-80.

930. McGlone, L. "Genesis 2:18-24; Ephesians 5:21 - 6:9." *RE* 86 (1989) 243-47.

Considers the implications of both texts as a resource for preaching on the family. Stresses an intimacy that recognizes individuality plus a reciprocal respect based on mutual submission.

931. Meeks, W. A. "The Image of the Androgyne: Some Uses of a
      Symbol in Earliest Christianity." *History of Religions* 13
      (1974) 165-208.

      A study of the place of women in the Roman world and how Paul's
      elevation of their status would set the church apart from the society
      as a whole and from contemporary Judaism in particular.

932. Messenger, E. C. *Two in One Flesh.* 3 vols. London: Sands,
      1948-49.

933. Miletic, S. F. *"One Flesh": Eph. 5.22-24, 5.31: Marriage and the
      New Creation. AnBib* 115. Rome: Pontifical Biblical Institute,
      1988.

      After introducing the nature of the problem to be studied, common
      interpretive approaches and solutions, and the problematic nature of
      the letter of Ephesians more basically, the author pursues his own
      analysis of the texts. He defends the thesis that the injunction to
      subordination (5:22-24) is rooted in Pauline and Jewish theological
      reflections about Adam's role in the redemptive process. He argues
      that the author of Ephesians retains an androcentric conceptual
      structure but rejects its potential for domination. A wife's submission
      entails her acceptance of her husband's love as a gift from God. At
      the same time the husband must love his wife completely, even to
      the point of death.

934. Muirhead, I. A. "The Bride of Christ." *SJT* 5 (1952) 175-87.

      After briefly tracing "bridal theology" through Christian literature,
      pursues its OT background and its source in the epistles and gospels.
      Pays attention to Eph 5:22-33 which highlights the special place the
      church enjoys among all the communities of the world. And as the
      church is the extension of the incarnation, Christ's body, so husband
      and wife are one body and the husband is to love his wife as his own
      body.

935. Munro, W. "Col. iii.18 - iv.1 and Eph. v.21 - vi.9: Evidence of a
      Late Literary Stratum?" *NTS* 18 (1972) 434-47.

Concludes that both passages are interpolations into their respective books. But although Eph generally depends upon Col, in this case the Col passage presupposes Eph 5:21ff. which, in turn, presupposes both letters. The Ephesian *Haustafel* was written to imitate the style of Ephesians.

936. Mussner, F. *Christus, das All und die Kirche.* 2d ed. Trier: Paulinus, 1968, 147-60.

See on 1:15-23.

937. Neuhäusler, E. "Das Geheimnis ist gross: Einführung in die Grundbegriffe der Eheperikope Eph 5, 22-29." *BibLeb* 4/3 (1963) 155-67.

Christian marriage depends upon the principle established in the ontological reality of Christ's union with the church, his body (an idea which 1 Cor 6 amplifies). Paul adopts this concept in using Gen 2:24 as a reference to Christ and his church.

938. Nygren, A. *Agape and Eros.* 2 parts in 3 vols. London: SPCK, 1932, 1938, 1939. [Rev. and pub. in one vol., London: SPCK; Philadelphia: Westminster, 1953.]

Investigates the problem and fundamental motifs suggested by the terms *agape* and *eros*, tracing the discussion growing out of the NT and right on through the Reformation period.

939. O'Hagan, A. P. "The Wife According to Eph. 5:22-33." *Australasian Catholic Record* 53/1 (1976) 17-26.

All Christians are called to mutual submission. So Christian wives are called to manifest that attitude and replicate the unifying mystery of salvation and the church's response to Christ.

940. Pagels, E. H. "Adam and Eve: Christ and the Church." In *The New Testament and Gnosis.* FS R. McL. Wilson, ed. A. H. B. Logan and A. J. M. Wedderburn. Edinburgh: T. & T. Clark, 1983, 146-75.

Surveys the Apostolic Fathers and Apologists noting their ascetic tendencies, especially regarding that sexual purity that they believed the gospel required. Believes that the "Paul" of Ephesians corrects or challenges radically ascetic interpretations of Paul returning to a view more in keeping with the Jewish concepts and the OT. At various points the author shows how the Ephesian 5 texts were used.

941.   Park, D. M.   "The Structure Of Authority in Marriage: an Examination of ὑποτάσσω and κεφαλή in Ephesians 5:21-33." *EvQ* 59 (1987) 117-24.

Though Paul seems to mirror the Greek and Jewish cultures' views of authority in marriage, in fact he redefines the key concepts of `love' and `respect' through the analogy of Christ's relation to the Church. So `headship' means servanthood, sacrifice, and love, not a structure in which one person dominates another.  A patriarchal model may work for some couples, but it is not normative for all; what is universal are the Christocentric principles of `love' and `respect.'

942.   Perkins, P. "Marriage in the New Testament and Its World." In *Commitment to Partnership,* ed. W. Roberts. New York: Paulist, 1987, 5-30.

A survey of the papyri provides the legal and social context of marriage and divorce in the world of the NT. Expansions and challenges to these cultural presuppositions are then demonstrated (through the Dead Sea Scrolls, heterodox Jewish interpretation of Genesis, and Cynic/Stoic philosophy), informing the differences also evident in Christian marriage. Treats three dimensions of NT teaching on marriage: asceticism, permanence, and sacralization.

943.   Pierron, J. "Come le Christ a aimé l'Église (Ep 5, 22-33)." *AsSeign* 97 (1967) 16-30.

944.   Pokorný, P. "Σῶμα Χριστοῦ im Epheserbrief." *EvT* 20 (1960) 456-64.

See a Gnostic origin to the Pauline notion of the mystical body of

Christ. Through his ties to Paul, the author adapted Gnostic ideas of celestial body both ecclesiologically and Christologically via the OT idea of headship. No mere adoption of Gnostic ideas, the body-motif in Ephesians has been thoroughly Christianized.

945. Rémy P. "Le mariage, signe de l'union du Christ et de l'église; les ambiguités d'une référence symbolique." *RSPT* 66 (1982) 397-414.

946. Rengstorf, K. H. "Die neutestamentlichen Mahnungen an die Frau, sich dem Manne unterzuordnen." In *Verbum Dei manet in aeternum.* FS O. Schmitz. Witten: Luther Verlag, 1953, 131-45.

947. Revira, E. "Wives, Be Subjected to Your Husbands." *Phillippiniana Sacra* 3 (1968) 231-47.

948. Rios, de los, M. "La prueba del sacramento del matrimonio en Ef. 5, 22-23." *EstBi* 7 (1935) 14-19.

949. Robilliard, J. A. "Le symbolisme du mariage selon S. Paul." *RSPT* 21 (1932) 242-48.

950. Rodgers, P. R. "The allusion to Genesis 2:23 at Ephesians 5:30." *JTS* n.s. 41 (1990) 92-94.

Argues for the longer reading of Eph 5:30 that adds "from his flesh and from his bones," a phrase that was omitted intentionally by a later editor caught up in the second century Gnostic controversy, or, perhaps, even unintentionally as the scribe's eye skipped from one word to another. The longer reading buttresses that claim that the allusion to Gen 2:23 grows out of the author's rich meditation on the OT. The inclusion of the phrase makes the verse run much more smoothly.

951. Sampley, J. P. *"And the Two Shall Become One Flesh": A Study of Traditions in Eph 5.21-33.* Cambridge: Cambridge University Press, 1971.

Builds on Käsemann's view of Ephesians as a mosaic of early
Christian traditions and conventions. Subjects this passage to a three-
fold analysis: 1) discover the range of traditions with the passage; 2)
seek the author's train or movement of thought in assimilating the
diverse traditions; and 3) examine the function of the passage in the
epistle as a whole. Concludes that Ephesians functions to persuade
Gentile believers not to reject, or at least question, their continuity
with Jewish Christianity and old Israel. Using OT traditions, the
author calls his readers to return to their place in God's overall
purposes that extend from creation to the eschaton.

952. Schelkle, K. H. "Eph 5,22-33." In *Der Geist und die Braut. Frauen
       in der Bibel.* Düsseldorf: Patmos, 1977, 121-24. ET *The
       Spirit and the Bride.* Collegeville, MN: Liturgical Press, 1979,
       117-21.

Selected analysis of key texts depicting the role of women in
marriage and the family through the Bible. On the Ephesian passage,
explains how marriage was elevated to the level of sacrament in the
Catholic church.

953. Schlier, H. *Christus und die Kirche im Epheserbrief.* BHTh 6.
       Tübingen: Mohr, 1930, 1966, 50-75.

954. Schnackenburg, R. "'Er hat uns mitauferweckt.'" *Liturgisches
       Jahrbuch* 2 (1952) 178-83.

955. _____. "Die Taufe als Bad der Reinigung (1 Kor 6, 11; Eph 5,
       26)." In *Das Heilsgeschehen bei der Taufe nach dem Apostel
       Paulus.* München: Zink, 1950, 1-8.

956. Schürmann, H. "Neutestamentliche Marginalien zur Frage nach der
       Institutionalität, Unauflösbarkeit und Sakramentalität der Ehe."
       In *Kirche und Bibel.* FS B. E. Schick, ed. A. Winter et al.
       Paderborn: F. Schöningh, 1979, 409-430.

A discussion of marriage in the NT.

957. Schüssler-Fiorenza, E. *In Memory of Her: A Feminist Theological*

Reconstruction of Christian Origins. New York: Crossroad, 1983, 266-70.

Studies the Ephesian *Haustafel* in the section on "Christian Mission and the Patriarchal Order of the Household." Finds that the paradigm of husband-wife relation presented in Ephesians reinforces the cultural-patriarchal pattern of male domination. So whereas Jewish Christians need not submit to Gentiles who dominate the congregation, wives must submit to husbands. Their role is submission and inequality, and the author justifies it Christologically. At the same time the code moderates the husband's role of leader by giving the example of Christ's love as the pattern of leadership.

958. Skrzypczark, O. "'Eu, porém digo...' De Genese 2, 24 para Efésios 5, 32." *RCB* 6/12-13 (1969) 103-14.

959. Small, D. H. *Marriage as Equal Partnership.* Grand Rapids: Baker, 1980.

Expressing a strong support for "Christian feminism," this constitutes popular explication of Eph 5:21-33 that seeks to retain the language of headship-submission while seeing that partnership worked out in a pattern of mutual servanthood in love—of equally shared submission to one another.

960. Terrien, S. *Till the Heart Sings.* Philadelphia: Fortress, 1985, 184-88.

A biblical theology of manhood and womanhood that considers a full gamut of gender and role issues. Considers the Deutero-Pauline perspective of Eph 5:21-32 where the author, after faithfully echoing the Pauline perspective of mutual submission in 5:21, retreated to more patriarchal patterns with his call for wives to submit. The ecclesial analogy of submission to Christ led the author astray in his instructions about marriage. "For this follower of Paul, man and woman are not equal in marriage" (188).

961. Theriault, J.-Y. "La femme chrétienne dans les textes pauliniens." *ScEs* 37/3 (1985) 297-317.

This study investigates key Pauline texts on the "women's issue" settling on nine hermeneutical conclusions on understanding women's positions in the texts and their significance for today.

962.   Thistlethwaite, S. B.   "Eph 5:21-33." In *Feministische gelesen. Ausgewählte Bibeltexte für Gruppen und Gemeinden, Gebete für den Gottesdienst.*   2 vols., ed. E. R. Schmidt, et al. Stuttgart: Kreuz, 1988-89.

The first volume of this set contains thirty-two feminist readings of OT and NT texts pertaining to women including this one on Eph 5:21-33. The second volume includes several essays and articles on twenty-eight other biblical texts.

963.   Toews, J. E.   "Paul's Radical Vision for the Family." *Direction* 19/1 (1990) 29-38.

In this text Paul exhorted men (who were the real problem) to love their wives. Discusses the family in the Greco-Roman world of the first century and considers the language, structure, and literary context for the passage. Treats the relations in terms of mutual commitment/submission (5:21); the wife's commitment/subordination (5:22-24); and the husband's commitment/subordination (5:25-33).

964.   Troadec. H.   "Ce mystère est grand (Eph 5, 22-33)." *BVC* 28 (1959) 14-19.

Performs a verse-by-verse exegesis of this passage.

965.   Vonck, P.   "This Mystery Is a Profound One (Ephes. 5:32): A biblical reflection on marriage." *African Ecclesial Review* 24 (1982) 278-88.

Studies Paul's view of marriage expressed in 1 Cor 7:1-15 and Eph 5:21-33 alongside of Genesis 2, The Song of Songs, and Jesus. Adopts a covenantal theological perspective and shows that the ideal of "one flesh," never totally achieved in marital relations, is realized in the church, illuminating "what human marriage is called to be."

966. Walker, W. O., Jr. "The 'Theology of Woman's Place' and the
      'Paulinist' Tradition." *Semeia* 28 (1983) 101-12.

Finds that *all* of the seven NT passages that support the principle of
male dominance and female submission (including Eph 5:22-33)
derive from a single wing of the church, what he calls the "Paulinist"
wing. This view reflects a post-Pauline reaction against Paul's own
"radical egalitarianism." Such views were not Paul's view, do not
derive from the apostolic period, and were not widely held in the
early church.

967. Wall, R. W. "Wifely Submission in the Context of Ephesians."
      Christian Scholar's Review 17/3 (1988) 272-85.

Though agreeing that Eph 5:22-24 employs patriarchal and hierarchal
rhetoric in outlining a wife's relationship to her husband, in fact the
texts may not be used as part of an antifeminist polemic.   The
Ephesian passage presents a mediating point between Gal 3:28 and
the Pastorals. Its message can also serve to help the modern church
mediate among the various positions and poles argued in the
contemporary church.   The root issue is not one of authority or
hierarchy, but the spiritual formation of a relationship. A wife's
submission is informed by the church's submission to Christ.

968. Wells, P. "La famille chrétienne a l'image de Christ: Une étude
      d'Éphésiens 5:22 à 6:4." *RevRef* 38/3 (1987) 11-23.

The author argues that Paul established the family structure in terms
of the person of Christ. Discusses the problem of cultural context,
the issue of equality in Christ, Christ's authority and its
correspondence to the Christian family, and Christ as head. Analyzes
the passage in light of a Christocentric perspective on the family.

969. Wessels, G. F. "Ephesians 5:21-33: 'Wives, be subject to your hus-
      bands...Husbands, love your wives ...'" *Journal of Theology
      for Southern Africa* 67 (1989) 67-76.

Contends that the passage argues differently from the Stoic ethical codes by stressing reciprocity, mutual submission, and the example of Christ.

970. Witherington, B. *Women in the Earliest Churches. SNTSMS* 59. Cambridge: Cambridge University Press, 1988, 54-61, 70-71.

In this larger study, these sections treat the Ephesian *Haustafel* (Eph 5:21-33), especially in comparison to Col 3:18ff. Believes that 5:21 calls for a mutual submission of all Christians to each other including marital partners. Yet there is no abandonment of headship nor does the author deny differences in how wives and husbands live out submission and service. Nor can the view that "head" means "source" be sustained in this passage: clearly Christ is head *over* the church—implying authority and power; the wife submits to her husband *in all things* as her head.

971. _____. *Women and the Genesis of Christianity.* Ed. Ann Witherington. Cambridge: Cambridge University Press, 1990.

Condenses *Woman in the Earliest Churches* (above) and his earlier *Women in the Ministry of Jesus* to make their findings more accessible. Pp. 154-60 comprise a discussion, "The Ephesian Household Table — Eph. 5:21-33," that addresses the interpretive problems and the contribution of the passage to Paul's theology of marriage and Christian women. Stresses the comparison, not identification, of the two relationships specified (husband/wife; Christ/church). "Head" (v. 23) indicates role in a relationship, and "mystery" (v. 32) refers to Christ's relationship with the church. Considers the central theme to be mutual submission in a Christian context (vv. 21-22) that prepares for what follows.

Ephesians 6:1-9

972. Barclay, W. *Educational Ideals in the Ancient World.* London: Collins, 1959. [Repr. Grand Rapids: Baker, 1974.]

Discusses education among the Jews, in Sparta, among the Athenians, among the Romans, the Christian attitude to pagan culture, and the child in the early church. In the NT the only training that matters is given within the home. Includes an appendix that considers various other issues concerning children and their parents in the Roman context.

973. Bertram, G. "παιδεύω κτλ." *TDNT* 5 (1967) 596-625.

Articles on the concept of teaching, direction, education, and instruction, including discipline.

974. Blomenkamp, P. "Erziehung." *RAC* 6 (1966) 502-59.

975. Bonner, S. F. *Education in Ancient Rome.* London: Methuen, 1977.

976. Gärtner, M. *Die Familienerziehung in der alten Kirche.* Cologne: Böhlau, 1985.

A study of how families functioned to train or educate its members during the time of the early church. For example, the household codes expressed the duty of educating Christian children. Considers evidence in the church fathers. Concludes with an extensive bibliography of ancient and modern sources.

977. Jentsch, W. *Urchristliches Erziehungsdenken: Die Paideia Kyriou im Rahmen der hellenistisch-jüdischen Welt.* Gütersloh: G. Mohn, 1951.

978. Lacey, W. K. *The Family in Classical Greece.* London: Thames & Hudson; Ithaca: Cornell, 1968.

Researches various issues that surround the family in ancient Greece including marriage, property, and women. Traces how views on the family differ during the various stages of the evolution of Greece and its city-states. Includes illustrations.

979. Lincoln, A. T. "The Use of the OT in Ephesians." *JSNT* 14 (1982) 37-40.

See on 2:11-22.

980. Lloyd-Jones, D. M. *Life in The Spirit. An Exposition of Ephesians 5:18-6:9.* Grand Rapids: Baker, 1973.

The series of sermons on these texts is continued.

981. Lyall, F. "Roman Law in the Writings of Paul—The Slave and the Freedman." *NTS* 17 (1970-71) 73-79.

Considers Paul's metaphorical use of slavery and the status of freedmen.

982. Marrou, H. I. *A History of Education in Antiquity.* London: Sheed & Ward, 1956.

983. Moule, C. F. D. "A Note on ὀρθαλμοδουλία." *ExpT* 59 (1947-48) 250.

Posits that the term refers to what can be seen or visible, external activity. Slaves ought to seek not merely to work visibly but to have a devoted inward attitude that results in outward work that pleases God who see hearts.

984. Oepke, A. "παῖς κτλ." *TDNT* 5 (1967) 636-54.

Major article concerning child and children.

985. Schrenk, G. "πατήρ κτλ." *TDNT* 5 (1967) 945-1022.

Major article on father and the father concept.

Ephesians 6:10-20

986.   Adai, J. *Der Heilige Geist als Gegenwart Gottes in den einzelnen Christen, in der Kirche und in der Welt.* Frankfurt: Peter Lang, 1985, 134-46; 231-43; 260-72.

   See on 4:17 - 5:20 (# 803).

987.   Arnold, C. E. *Ephesians: Power and Magic.* Cambridge: Cambridge University Press, 1989, 103-22.

   See on 3:14-21 (# 687).

988.   _____. "The 'Exorcism' of Ephesians 6:12 in Recent Research." *JSNT* 30 (1987) 71-87.

   A response and critique of W. Carr's view in *Angels and Principalities* (see below) in which Carr avers that the concept of mighty forces hostile to humans was *not* prevalent in the first century A.D. though this has certainly been the traditional view. For Carr to maintain his stance requires that he "exorcise" Eph 6:12 as an interpolation. Arnold defends the retention of 6:12 in the text, but, more so, that Carr's essential thesis is not valid, though it may signal a needed corrective to an unbalanced view of the powers in the ancient world. Carr omits several crucial data that rebut his thesis and commits numerous *non sequiturs* along the way.

989.   _____. "Giving the Devil His Due." *Christianity Today* 34/11 (1990) 16-19.

   Studying Eph 6:10-20, the author shows how the text concerns primarily Christian conduct. The major weapon is prayer.

990.   Barclay, L. L. "Ephesians 6:14." *ExpT* 2 (1890-91) 117-18.

991.   Beatrice, P. F. "Il combattimento spirituale secondo san Paolo.

Interpretazione di Ef 6, 10-17." *StPa* 19/2 (1972) 359-422.

Though analogous to other ideas of eschatological conflict (e.g., Qumran), Paul's depiction of the Christian's spiritual battle has moved beyond its Jewish forebears. Christians now join the messianic-eschatological battle that Christ wages against the evil powers of the Law.

992. Bonnardiere, A. M. "Le combat chrétien. Exégèse augustinienne d'Ephes. 6, 12." *REA* 11/3-4 (1965) 234-38.

993. Buscarlet, A. F. "The Preparation of the Gospel of Peace," *ExpT* 9 (1897) 38-40.

Explains the meaning of "preparation" (*hetoimasia*) in Eph 6:15 based on an explanation by Bynaeus who writes on shoes mentioned in the Bible. The meaning is "basis, foundation" such that a Christian's *basis* for standing at the end of the battle with spiritual forces is the gospel. The gospel of peace is the foundation for the believer as the sandals were to the warrior. The gospel provides the only firm footing in the evil day.

994. Carr, W. *Angels and Principalities. SNTSMS* 42. Cambridge: Cambridge University Press, 1981, 93-111.

These pages treat the topic of "powers and the spiritual world" in Ephesians, as part of a larger study of the background, meaning and development of the Pauline phrase *hai archai kai hai exousiai*. Considers the heavenly places, the powers, the prince of the power of the air, and the struggle—where he gives special consideration to 6:12ff. Concludes that in Ephesians the powers are primarily conceived in Jewish terms and do not represent in any sense a picture of the pagan thought world in which people struggled against or feared demonic forces or evil powers.

995. Eckel, P. T. "Ephesians 6:10-20." *Int* 45 (1991) 288-93.

An expository article that seeks to draw out implications and applications of this passage while raising questions about the contemporary relevance of being fortified against the demonic powers today.

996. Emonds, H. "Geistlicher Kriegsdienst." In *Heilige Überlieferung.* FS I. Herwegen, ed. O. Casel. Münster: Aschendorff, 1938, 21-50.

997. Erasmus von Rotterdam. *Ausgewählte Schriften I (epistula ad Paulum Volzium; enchiridion militis Christiani),* ed. W. Welzig. Darmstadt: Wissenschaftliche Buchgesellschaft, 1968, xiii-xxv.

998. Fischer, K. M. *Tendenz und Absicht des Epheserbriefs.* Göttingen: Vandenhoeck & Ruprecht, 1973, 165-72.

See on 1:3-14 (# 316).

999. Gregg, J. A. F. "'Ετοιμασία in Eph 6, 15." *ExpT* 56 (1944) 54.

Supports the view of Buscarlet above.

1000. Harnack, A. von. *Militia Christi.* Tübingen: Mohr, 1905. ET: *Militia Christi: The Christian Religion and the Military in the First Three Centuries,* trans. D. Gracie. Philadelphia: Fortress, 1981, 27-64.

The translator pens a fourteen-page introduction to subsequent developments on the main themes of the book: did Christianity adopt a warlike character? Did the church employ a military-type organization viewing believers as soldiers of Christ? And how did the church view the secular military and war?

1001. Jones, P. R. "La Prière par l'Esprit. Ephésiens 6:18." *RevRef* 27/3 (1976) 128-39.

Isa 59:17 has clearly influenced the discussion of the armor of God in Eph 6:14-17. But Isa 59:17 - 60:7 proceeds to describe God's salvation of Gentiles as well as Jews, a theme that looms large in Ephesians and which, therefore, probably derives from Isaiah.

Proceeds to develop the fundamental role that prayer has in using the sword of the Spirit, the one who provides both Jew and Gentile with access to the Father (Eph 2:18).

1002.   Jonker, A. J. Th. "Ἡ ἑτοιμασία τοῦ εὐαγγελίου τῆς εἰρήνης (Ef. 6:15)." *TS* 11 (1893) 443-51.

1003.   Joüon, P. "Notes philologiques sur quelques versets de l'Épître aux Éphésiens (1,12; 2,1-3; 2,15; 3,13.15; 4,28; 5,18.19; 6,9.19-20)." *Recherches science religieuse* 26 (1936) 454-64.

Brief technical notes.

1004.   Kamlah, E. *Die Form der katalogischen Paränese im Neuen Testament, WUNT* 7. Tübingen: Mohr, 1964, 36, 189-96.

A study of the virtue and vice lists in the NT using form critical methods. After organizing them into their different types, he seeks possible sources and parallels and applies the results to the NT use of paraenesis.

1005.   Kinnaman, G. D. *Overcoming the Dominion of Darkness.* Cambridge, MA: Crossway, 1992 (originally Old Tappan, NJ: Chosen Books, 1990).

1006.   Lash, C. J. A. "Where Do Devils Live? A Problem in the Textual Criticism of Ephesians 6.12." *VigChr* 30 (1976) 160-74.

Seeks an answer to the question raised by the rendering of the Syriac version of Severus: How can the spirits of wickedness be said to dwell in the heavenlies which; would seem to refer to Heaven, the dwelling place of God? His conclusion: the spirits reside "in the sky."

1007.   Lincoln, A. T. *Paradise Now and Not Yet.* Cambridge: Cambridge University Press, 1981; Grand Rapids: Baker, 1992, 164-66.

Considers the battle against the powers in the heavenlies, Eph 6:10ff. Forces attacking believers are no longer a threat, for believers fight from the stance of victory. Thus it is a question of actualizing their position in Christ.

1008.   _____. "A Re-Examination of `the Heavenlies' in Ephesians." *NTS* 19 (1972-73) 468-83.

See on 1:3-14 (# 343).

1009.   _____. "The Use of the OT in Ephesians." *JSNT* 14 (1982) 42-43.

See on 2:11-22 (# 577).

1010. Lloyd-Jones, D. M. *The Christian Soldier (Ephesians 6:10-20).* Grand Rapids: Baker, 1977.

Following the format of prior volumes this contains twenty-six sermons on these eleven verses.

1011. Lövestam, E. *Spiritual Wakefulness in the New Testament.* Lund: Gleerup, 1963, 64-77.

Traces Jesus' teaching on spiritual vigilance as it is reflected in both the Synoptics, and the Epistles and Revelation. Eph 6:18 admonishes the readers to "keep alert." This appeal refers to the Christians' possession of the gift of salvation that enables them to live in the freedom from the "sleep" of the world. Prayer that is "wakeful" (ἀγρυπτεῖν) is "in and through the Spirit," and thus has eschatological significance as in 1 Pet 4:7 and Lk 21:34-36.

1012. Murray, J. O. F. *The Christian Armour, being studies in Eph VI, 10-18.* London: SPCK, 1939.

1013. Neufeld, T. R. Y. "God and Saints at War. The Transformation and Democratization of the Divine Warrior in Isaiah 59, Wisdom of Solomon 5, 1 Thessalonians and Ephesians 6." Th.D. thesis, Harvard University, 1989.

1014. O'Brien, P. T. "Principalities and Powers: Opponents of the Church." In *Biblical Interpretation and the Church: The*

Problem of Contextualization, ed. D. A. Carson. Exeter: Paternoster; Nashville: Nelson, 1984, 110-50.

A study that partakes of both exegesis and hermeneutics, it seeks to understand what various NT writers, and especially Paul, meant by the phrase "principalities and powers," and how it has been understood over time. A goal is to understand the various hermeneutical presuppositions of interpreters as well as the interpretive principles they employ. Concludes with a section on "The Christian's Present Responsibilities" which unpacks the salient points of Eph 6:10ff.

1015. Oepke, A. "ὅπλον κτλ." *TDNT* 5 (1967) 292-315.

Major article on the various implements of war such as spears, shields, armor, missiles, et al.

1016. Pfitzner, V. *Paul and the Agon Motif. Traditional Athletic Imagery in the Pauline Literature. NovT Supp.* 16. Leiden: Brill, 1967, 157-64.

The pages comprise the chapter entitled "The Agon Motif and the Military Image in Paul" as it occurs in various Pauline texts.

1017. Pierron, J. "Être armées pour le combat chrétien (Eph 6, 10-17)." *AsSeign* 76 (1964) 14-28.

1018. Rogers, P. "Hopeful in Spite of Chains. The Indomitable Spirit of Paul, in the Captivity Letters." *BTB* 12 (1982) 77-81.

Studies the quality of Paul the hopeful prisoner in his Prison Epistles though it is doubtful that Paul actually wrote Ephesians (à la Mitton and Nineham).

1019. Romaniuk, K. "Le Livre de la Sagesse dans le Nouveau Testament." *NTS* 14 (1967-68) 498-514.

Studies traces of the apocryphal book of Wisdom in the synoptics, John, Paul, the Apocalypse, and the rest of the NT. Concludes that the book of Wisdom greatly influenced the various writers of the NT, especially, Paul. Wisdom 5:18-22 influenced Eph 6:11-17.

1020. Röther, W. "Kritische Bemerkungen über die Stelle Ephes. 6, 12." *TSK* 8 (1835) 970-75.

1021. Rutherford, J. "Our Wrestling: Ephesians 6:12." *ExpT* 2 (1890-91) 181-82.

1022. Travis, A. E. "The Christian's Warfare. An Exegetical Study of Ephesians Six (Ephesians 6:10-18)." *SWJT* 6 (1963) 71-80.

A running explanation of these verses, homiletical in nature, that attempts to find application all along the way.

1023. Vitti, A. "Militum Christi Regis arma iuxta S. Paulum." *VD* 7 (1927) 310-18.

1024. Whiteley, D. E. H. "Expository Problems: Eph 6:12—Evil Powers." *ExpT* 68 (1957) 100-103.

From the premise that Christ has conquered all Evil Powers and that those in Christ are able to share in his victory, proceeds to develop elements of the "demonic" over which Christians may win today. Doubting that moderns can accept that demons are actually "personal or sub-personal entities," he demythologizes them to discover the malevolent forces that seek to dominate people in the modern era. Psychological complexes and adverse circumstances (e.g., autonomy of the economic, nationalism, preservation, and industrial tension) provide ready examples.

1025. Wiersbe, W. W. *What To Wear to the War. Studies from Ephesians 6.* Lincoln, NE: Back to the Bible, 1986.

1026. Wild, R. A. "The Warrior and the Prisoner: Some Reflections on Ephesians 6:10-20." *CBQ* 46 (1984) 284-98.

The study provides three conclusions concerning Eph 6:10-20. It argues, first, that, structurally, 6:12 is the central verse in a ring-type development.   The key issue is the Christian's "fight with the powers."   Second, given non-Pauline authorship, the request for prayer in 6:19-20 cannot be taken literally, but rather presents Paul as an ethical model of the Christian as a "prisoner" in the world. His true status of "freedom" derives from God.   Finally, the ethical concept of the section is world-affirming, not world-denying, despite its evident appeal to subsequent Gnostics.

1027. Wink, W. *Naming the Powers.* Philadelphia: Fortress, 1984, 84-89.

See on 1:15-23 (# 493). On these pages he treats Eph 6:12.

1028. Wittram, R. "Paradoxie und Wahrheit der Rüstung. Eine biblische Besinnung über Eph 6, 10-18." *Monatsschrift für Pastoraltheologie zur Vertiefung des gesamen pfarramtlichen Wirkens.* 53 (1964) 4-11.

1029. Xenakis, C. "The relationship of inner spiritual conflict to the present experiential sanctification of the believer." D.Min. thesis; Denver: Denver Seminary, 1983.

Employing an exegesis of Eph 6:10-18 as a starting point, the thesis argues that a popular view of sanctification as a struggle-free activity requiring little or no human effort does not agree with Paul's presentation. For Paul struggle was necessary to successful Christian living. The practical dimension of the project sought to instruct the members of a local church in a more adequate understanding of sanctification.

Chapter 8

LITERARY AND TEXTUAL ISSUES

STRUCTURE, GENRE, STYLE, VOCABULARY

1030. Albani, J. "Die Metaphern des Epheserbriefes." *Zeitschrift für wissenschaftliche* Theologie 45 (1902) 420-40.

1031. Alexander, P. S. "Epistolary Literature." In *Jewish Writings of the Second Temple Period, Compendia Rerum Judaicarum ad Novum Testamentum.* Section 2 in 3 volumes. Vol. 2, ed. M. E. Stone. Assen: van Gorcum; Philadelphia: Fortress, 1984, 579-96.

A study of the form and function of the letter in the context of Jewish literary activity in the period c. 200 B.C.E. to c. 200 C.E.

1032. Audet, J. P. "Literary Forms and Contents of a Normal Εὐχαριστία in the First Century." *StEv* 1, ed. F. L. Cross. *TU* 86. Berlin: Akademie-Verlag, 1959, 643-62.

1033. Aune, D. E.   *The New Testament in Its Literary Environment.*
       Philadelphia. Westminster Press, 1987.

1034. Barth, M.   "Die Einheit des Galater- und Epheserbriefs."   *TZ* 32
       (1976) 78-91.

1035. Barkhuizen, J. H.   "The strophic structure of the eulogy of Ephesians
       1:3-14."   *Hervormde Teologiese Studies* 46 (1990) 390-413.

       Presents five important approaches to the structure of the eulogy:
       trinitarian, isometric, formulaic, linguistic, and rhetorical. Concludes
       by finding three stanzas in which the theme of praise of God is
       worked out.

1036. Berger, K.   "Hellenistische Gattungen im Neuen Testament."   In
       *ANRW. Geschichte und Kultur Roms im Spiegel der neueren
       Forschung.* II: *Principat.* Band 25 (2. Teilband). Berlin/New
       York: de Gruyter, 1984, 1031-1432, 1831-85.

1037. _____.   *Formgeschichte des Neuen Testaments.*   Heidelberg:
       Quelle & Meyer, 1984.

       An exhaustive catalog and discussion of the various literary forms
       (*Gattungen*) found in the NT. Makes a case for the relevance of
       form critical analysis for the exegesis of NT texts. Considers various
       issues that impinge on the study of NT epistles including paraenesis,
       Haustafel, and hymns.

1038. Bjerkelund, C. J.   *Parakalô. Form, Funktion und Sinn der parakalô-
       Sätze in den paulinischen Briefen.*   Oslo: Universitetsforlaget,
       1967.

       Form-critical analysis of certain structures in the Pauline literature,
       including Eph 4:1-3.

1039. Büchner, V. F.   "A Marcionite Reading in Ephrem's Commentary on
       the Pauline Epistles."   *Bulletin of the Bezan Club* 5 (1927) 37-
       38.

On Eph 2:14

1040. Burgess, T. C. "Epideictic Literature." *Studies in Classical Philology* 3/5 (1902) 89-261.

1041. Cameron, P. S. "The Structure of Ephesians." *Filologia Neotestamentaria* 3 (1990) 3-18.

An analysis of the internal structure of the epistle, finding that it is constructed on an extraordinarily intricate pattern—a conclusion based purely on linguistic grounds, not as the result of the interpretation of the letter. Finds eight parallel panels and a palistrophic structure (what others may term chiasmas or concentric inclusion).

1042. Dahl, N. A. "Interpreting Ephesians: Then and Now." *Theology Digest* 25 (1977) 305-15. [Repr. *CurTM* 5 (1978) 133-43.]

See Introduction.

1043. Doty, W. G. *Letters in Primitive Christianity.* Philadelphia: Fortress, 1973.

A concise treatment of the essential elements of the epistle genre, both within Hellenistic letters in general and, specifically, Paul's letters. Includes discussion of the variety of forms found in NT letters. Briefly considers non-Pauline letter as well. Classifies Ephesians as a pseudo-Pauline letter.

1044. Dove, R. "The Epistle of Paul the Apostle to the Ephesians." In *Incarnation: Contemporary Writers on the NT,* ed. A. Corn. New York: Viking, 1990, 162-74.

One entry in a volume in which various contemporary authors (e.g., J. Updike, A. Dillard, F. Buechner, et al.) comment on the literary aspects of the books of the NT.

1045. Gnilka, J. "Paranetische Traditionen im Epheserbrief." In *Melanges Bibliques.* FS B. Rigaux, ed. A. Descamps and A. de Halleux. Gembloux: Duculot, 1970, 397-410.

1046. Goguel, M. "Esquisse d'une solution nouvelle du problème de l'épître aux Éphésiens." *RHR* 111 (1935) 254-284; 112 (1935) 73-99.

Discovers two strata in Eph: the earlier is Pauline, and the other consists of interpolations added by a disciple of Paul who wrote ten or twenty years later.

1047. Hatch, W. H. P. and Wells, C. B. "A Hitherto Unpublished Fragment of the Epistle to the Ephesians." *HTR* 51/1 (1958) 33-38.

A description, picture, and transcription of a papyrus fragment purchased in Cairo in 1931 containing parts of Eph 4:16-29 and 4:31 - 5:13.

1048. Hendrix, H. "On the Form and Ethos of Ephesians." *Union Seminary Quarterly Review* 42/4 (1988) 3-15.

Includes a section on literary structure: though the form appears to be in the genre of epistle, its form actually follows the general conventions of honorific decrees in which the author recites the universal benefactions of God and Christ.

1049. Jewett, R. *The Thessalonian Correspondence.* Philadelphia: Fortress, 1986.

1050. Johanson, B. C. *To All the Brethren.* Stockholm: Almqvist & Wiksell, 1987.

1051. Joüon, P. "Notes philologiques sur quelques versets de l'Épître aux Éphésiens (1,12; 2,1-3; 2,15; 3,13.15; 4,28; 5,18.19; 6,9.19-20)." *Recherches Sciences Religieuse* 26 (1936) 454-64.

Brief notes on these texts.

1052. Kennedy, G. A. *New Testament Interpretation Through Rhetorical Criticism.* Chapel Hill: University of North Carolina Press, 1984.

> Provides an introduction to rhetorical criticism as it can be practiced on NT texts and several examples from the gospels, the speeches in Acts and several epistles. Though rhetorical criticism can help understand the message and the unity of a letter, it cannot establish its authenticity. So, if Paul did not write Ephesians, the author did possess considerable rhetorical skill who was determined to write a letter that Paul could well have written.

1053. King, A. C. "Ephesians in the Light of Form Criticism." *ExpT* 63 (1951-52) 273-76.

> A brief discussion of the "common" material employed in Ephesians: epistolary elements, benedictory formulae, doxologies, hymn, apologetic-doctrinal material, the "stoneship" of Christ, sealing, ascent and descent of Christ, and various catechetical elements. Draws conclusions about the relation of Ephesians to other parts of the NT.

1054. Kirby, J. C. *Ephesians, Baptism, and Pentecost. An Inquiry into the Structure and Purpose of the Epistle to the Ephesians.* London: SPCK; Montréal: McGill University, 1968.

> Given a Jewish background, the pseudonymous author developed the first part of the letter on a eucharistic prayer to which he appended a discourse connected with the feast of Pentecost.

1055. Lash, C. J. A. "Where Do Devils Live? A Problem in the Textual Criticism of Ephesians 6.12." *VigChr* 30 (1976) 160-74.

> See on texts, 6:10-20 (# 1006).

1056. Lausberg, H. *Handbuch der literarischen Rhetorik.* 2d ed. Munich: Max Hueber 1973.

1057. Malherbe, A. J. "Ancient Epistolary Theorists." *Ohio Journal of*

Religious Studies 5 (1977) 3-77.

A study of the theory and practice of letter writing in both rhetorical theory and the ancient educational curriculum. A second part presents Greek or Latin texts of ancient materials pertaining to letter writing along with English translations.

1058.   Martin, A. G. "Quelques remarques sur le texte syriaque de l'Épître aux Éphésiens." *ETR* 66/1 (1991) 99-103.

Treats issues relating to the textual transmission of Ephesians, comparing the Syriac version of the NT.

1059.   Moir, I. A. "Text of Ephesians exhibited by minuscule manuscripts housed in Great Britain—some preliminary comments." In *Studies in New Testament Language and Text.* FS G. D. Kilpatrick, ed. J. K. Elliott. *NovT Supp,* 44. Leiden: Brill, 1976, 313-18.

Survey of minuscule manuscripts of Ephesians with a view to determining whether they reflect characteristic deviations of the uncials from the Textus Receptus, whether they represent characteristically later forms of the text, and whether there is support for unusual readings of individual manuscripts. Includes tables of results.

1060.   Morton, A. Q. et al. *A Critical Concordance to the Letter of Paul to the Ephesians. The Computer Bible,* Vol. XXII. Wooster, Ohio: Biblical Research Assn., 1980.

Various statistical analyses and tables as are standard for this series. Includes word counts, frequency profile, and concordances.

1061.   O'Brien, P. T. *Introductory Thanksgivings in the Letters of Paul. NovT Supp.* 49. Leiden: Brill 1977.

Studies the role that the thanksgiving sections play in Paul's letters, including the prayers in those sections. The introduction to Ephesians is not a section included in the study considering the widespread conclusion that Eph is not Pauline.

1062. Paxson, R. *The Wealth, Walk, and Warfare of the Christian.* New York: Revell, 1939.

Popular, practical expositions about various topics in Ephesians under the three rubrics in the title. Includes outline chart of the letter.

1063. Robbins, C. J. "The Composition of Eph 1:3-14." *JBL* 105 (1986) 677-87.

Shows how the seeming unwieldy sentences accords with the principles of Greek rhetoric. See on texts, 1:3-14 (# 366).

1064. Roberts, J. H. "Pauline Transitions to the Letter Body." In *L'Apôtre Paul,* ed. A. Vanhoye. Leuven: Leuven University Press, 1986, 93-99.

1065. Roon, A. van. *The Authenticity of Ephesians.* Leiden: Brill, 1974, 100-212.

A detailed analysis of numerous stylistic features in Ephesians as compared to other Pauline epistles including: features absent in Eph, sentence length, adverbial adjuncts, consecutive genitives, parallelism, rhyming of thoughts, monotony and repetition, aesthetic devices, grammatical details, and unusual expressions. Concludes that the stylistic features of Eph and Col do not place one at a greater distance from the acknowledged Paulines than the other. Indeed, all the stylistic features of Eph are also found in the acknowledged Paulines. The style of Eph is identical to that of 1 Cor 1:1-9 and Rom 1:1-10. This leads van Roon to reject the theories of Morton, Goodspeed, and Mitton that suggest pseudonymity.

1066. Sanders, J. T. "The Transition from Opening Epistolary Thanksgiving to Body in the Letters of the Pauline Corpus." *JBL* 81 (1962) 348-62.

See on texts, 1:15-23 (# 471).

1067. _____. "Hymnic Elements in Ephesians 1-3." *ZNW* 56 (1965) 214-32.

See on texts, 1:3-14 (# 371).

1068. Schubert, P. *Form and Function of the Pauline Thanksgivings.* Berlin: A. Topelmann, 1939.

1069. Sellin, G. "Über einige ungewöhnliche Genitive im Epheserbrief." *ZNW* 83/1-2 (1992) 85-107.

Analyzes the genitive constructions in Ephesians providing detailed assessments of twelve genitive syntagms showing how they are distinct from Hellenistic-Jewish and Pauline texts. The specific analyses discuss 1:13c; 2:15; 1:14; 1:17; 2:14; 3:11; 4:13b; 4:16; 4:29; 4:22; 4:24; 4:23.

1070. Souter, A. "The Epistle to the `Ephesians' not a Secondary Production." *Exp,* 8th series, 2 (1911) 136-41.

1071. _____. "The Non-Secondary Character of `Ephesians.'" *Exp,* 8th series, 2 (1911) 321-28.

1072. _____. "An Interpretation of Ephesians 1:15." *ExpT* 19 (1907-08) 44.

A short note on the manuscript tradition for this verse. Interprets as meaning, "the faith which is among you and (the faith which is) among all the saints."

1073. Stowers, S. K. *Letter Writing in Greco-Roman Antiquity.* Philadelphia: Westminster Press, 1986.

An introduction to the phenomenon of letter writing in the world into which Christianity was born. Part two catalogs and explains the various types of letters.

1074. Thyen, H. *Der Stil der jüdisch-hellenistischen Homilie.* Göttingen: Vandenhoeck & Ruprecht, 1955.

1075. Vanhoye, A. "Épître aux Éphésiens et l'épître aux Hebreus." *Bib* 59/2 (1978) 198-230.

Providing first a statistical analysis of the correlations between the vocabulary of Ephesians and Hebrews, the study manifests certain relations (above all, Christological), though no direct connection. These relations indicate that both epistles were written in the same apostolic environment, at about the same time, though Ephesians preceded Hebrews.

1076. White, J. L. *The Form and Function of the Body of the Greek Letter.* Missoula, MT: Scholars Press, 1972.

A structural analysis of the central section or body of Paul's letters in the context of ancient Greek letters. Compares Paul's letters to the papyri.

1077. _____. "Saint Paul and the Apostolic Letter Tradition." *CBQ* 45 (1983) 433-44.

Traces the practice of ancient Greek letter writing and its use and adaptation by Paul to discover why the "letter" became such a significant medium of apostolic authority. Paul was the foundational figure for developing the letter in the direction of an apostolic letter tradition.

1078. _____. "New Testament Epistolary Literature." *ANRW. Geschichte und Kultur Roms im Spiegel der neueren Forschung.* II: *Principat.* Band 25 (2. Teilband). Berlin/New York: de Gruyter, 1984, 1730-56.

1079. Wilson, J. P. "Note on the Textual Problem of Ephesians 1:1." *ExpT* 60 (1948-49) 225-26.

See on texts, 1:1-2 (# 283).

1080. Wilson, R. A. "`We' and `You' in the Epistle to the Ephesians." *StEv* 2, Part 1, ed. F. L. Cross. *TU* 87. Berlin: Akademie-Verlag, 1964, 676-80.

Seeks to test the hypothesis that Ephesians is addressed to newly-baptized converts by seeing whether it sheds light on the perplexing vacillation between 'you' and 'we' in the letter. Concludes that "we" refers to all Christians while "you" always refers to a small group, in some way distinct from other Christians. See further on texts, 1:3-14.

1081. Zwaan, J. de. "Le 'rythme logique' dans l'épître aux Ephésiens." *RHPR* 6 (1927) 554-65.

RELATIONS TO COLOSSIANS AND THE PAULINES

1082. Alexander, G. "The Twin Epistles of Paul's Prison Life." *Methodist Quarterly Review* 59/2 (1910) 359-80.

1083. Benoit, P. "Rapports litteraires entre les épitres aux Colossiens et aux Ephesiens." In *Neutestamentliche Aufsätze*. FS J. Schmid, ed. J. Blinzler, O. Kuss, and F. Mussner. Regensburg: Pustet, 1963, 11-22. [Repr. in *Exégèse et théologie*. 4 vols. Paris: Du Cerf, 1961-82. III (1968): 318-334.]

A study of the literary relationships between Eph and Col with special attention to Eph 2:1-6 that makes us of Col 2:13 and 3:6-7, both of which serve again in the writing of Eph 5:6. Also, Col 3:5 has a parallel to Eph 4:17-24, and Col 1:21 presents a theme that is echoed in Eph 2:11-12. As a result of these studies of the literary form, the author doubts that Eph can be considered authentically Pauline.

1084. Coutts, J. "The Relationship of Ephesians and Colossians." *NTS* 4 (1958) 201-7.

As a follow up to some implications of his NTS 3 (1957) 115-27 article (see on texts, 1:3-14 [# 305]), argues that Colossians is later than and dependent upon Ephesians, though the relation is more complicated than a simple one-on-one dependence. Doubts that Ephesians depends directly on Colossians. Uses three sets of passages in both letters to develop the case, but believes that further passages seem to yield the same result.

1085. Dahl, N. A. "Der Epheserbrief und der verlorene erste Brief des Paulus an die Korinther." In *Abraham unser Vater.* FS 0. Michel, ed. O. Betz, M. Hengel, and P. Schmidt. Leiden: Brill, 1963, 65-77.

Considers the relationship between Ephesians and the lost first letter that Paul wrote to Corinth. Finds remarkable parallels between Ephesians and the Qumran literature suggesting a common pool of tradition that Hellenistic Jews and Christians shared.

1086. Gnilka, J. "Das Paulusbild im Kolosser- und Epheserbrief." In *Kontinuität und Einheit.* FS F. Mussner, ed. P. G. Muller and W. Stenger. Freiburg: Herder, 1981, 179-93.

Considers the image of Paul found in Col and Eph.

1087. Merklein, H. "Eph 4, 1-5, 20 als Rezeption von Kol 3, 1-17." In *Kontinuität und Einheit.* FS F. Mussner, ed. P. G. Muller and W. Stenger. Freiburg: Herder, 1981, 194-210.

See on texts, 4:1-16 (# 770).

1088. _____. "Paulinische Theologie in der Rezeption des Kolosser- und Epheserbriefes." In *Paulus in den neutestamentlichen Spätschriften. Zur Paulusrezeption im Neuen Testament,* ed. K. Kertelge. Freiburg: Herder, 1981, 25-69.

A discussion of attitudes toward Paul and how Paul's theology finds reception in Col and Eph.

1089. _____. *Das kirchliche Amt nach dem Epheserbrief.* Munich: Kösel, 1973, 28-44.

In this larger study of the issue of church, and the contribution of

Ephesians to this discussion, considers the authenticity of Eph and its history-of-religions background.

1090. Mitton, C. L. *Epistle to the Ephesians.* Oxford: Clarendon Press, 1951, 55-158, 280-338.

See section on Commentaries.

1091. Ochel, W. *Die Annahme einer Bearbeitung des Kolosser-Briefes im Epheserbrief.* Würzburg: Konrad Triltsch, 1934.

1092. Percy, E. *Die Probleme der Kolosser- und Epheserbriefe.* 2d rev.ed. Lund: Gleerup, 1964, 360-433.

Provides an extensive investigation of the language, style, and content of Col and Eph leading to a discussion that compares the many parallels and points of contact between the two letters. Concludes with a consideration of the purpose and addresses of Eph.

1093. Polhill, J. B. "The Relationship between Ephesians and Colossians." *RE* 70 (1973) 439-50.

After cataloging the variety of obvious correspondences between Eph and Col—wording, concepts, style, and structure—the author surveys the various solutions proposed to account for them. Provides bibliography for further study but suggests no new solution.

1094. Roon, A. van. *The Authenticity of Ephesians.* Leiden: Brill, 1974, 4-10; 413-37.

Considers Ephesians' relationship to Col, other Pauline epistles, and 1 Peter. Several charts trace the parallels and affinities. Concludes that there is absolutely no evidence to suggest that the author of Eph is a person from a later period whose command of Pauline expressions was solely the result of reading and re-reading the authentic letters of Paul.

1095. Schmid, J. *Der Epheserbrief des Apostels Paulus.* Freiburg: Herder, 1928, 384-457.

RELATIONS TO OTHER WRITINGS AND GENRES

HYMNS

1096. Audet, J. P. "Literary Forms and Contents of a Normal Εὐχαριστία in the First Century." *StEv* 1, ed. F. L. Cross. *TU* 86. Berlin: Akademie-Verlag, 1959, 643-62.

1097. Best, E. "The Use of Credal and Liturgical Material in Ephesians." In *Worship, Theology, and Ministry in the Early Church*. FS R. P. Martin, ed. M. J. Wilkins and T. Paige. *JSNT Supplement* 87. Sheffield: Sheffield Academic Press, 1992, 53-69.

Examines credal and liturgical materials in Ephesians to assess how and why (if at all) the author (who is not Paul) modified them to suit his purposes. Following the approach of R. P. Martin in his *Carmen Christi*, considers: 1:3-14; 1:20-23; 2:4-10; 2:14-18; 2:19-22; 4:4-6; and 5:14.

1098. Burger, C. *Schöpfung und Versöhnung: Studien zum liturgischen Gut im Kolosser- und Epheserbrief*. Neukirchen-Vluyn: Neukirchener, 1975.

A study in two parts: first, the hymn of Col 1:15-20 (its reconstruction and interpretation) plus how it fits its context and allusions to it in Col 2:9-15; second, the hymn of Eph 2:14-18 (see on texts: 2:11-22 [#545]).

1099. Debrunner, A. "Grundsätzliches zur Kolometrie im Neuen Testament." *TB* 5 (1926), 231-33.

1100. Deichgräber, R. *Gotteshymnus und Christushymnus in der frühen Christenheit. SUNT* 5. Göttingen: Vandenhoeck & Ruprecht, 1967.

Assesses the role of hymnic and liturgical material behind portions of the letter.

1101. Gnilka, J. "Christus unser Friede—ein Friedens-Erlöserlied in Eph 2, 14-17: Erwägungen zu einer neutestamentlichen Friedenstheologie." In *Die Zeit Jesu.* FS H. Schlier, ed. G. Bornkamm and K. Rahner. Freiburg: Herder, 1970, 190-207.

A careful consideration of the concept of peace and, especially, "Christ our peace" in what he considers to be a hymn—the peace-redeemer hymn of Eph 2:14-17—in the attempt to understand the NT theology of peace. In seeing the likelihood that this passage reflects a hymn, Gnilka follows G. Schille and J. T. Sanders (see below).

1102. Jörns, K.-P. *Das hymnische Evangelium.* Gütersloh: Mohn, 1971.

A study of the hymnic elements in the Apocalypse.

1103. Käsemann, E. "Ephesians and Acts." In *Studies in Luke-Acts,* ed. L. E. Keck and J. L. Martyn. Nashville: Abingdon, 1966, 288-97.

Compares the two works at the point in which they both display theological patterns representing traditions and tendencies of a particular era. Ephesians, of all NT books, most clearly marks the transition from the Pauline tradition to the perspectives of the early Catholic era. Both Acts and Ephesians span the time of the gospel tradition and its establishment as a normative theological movement. Acts narrates the history of this development and Ephesians reflects on it meditatively. Eph 1:12b-14, though not really a hymn, contains in concentrated form the themes painted broadly by Acts in the Cornelius story.

1104. Lohmeyer, E. "Das Proömium des Epheserbriefs." *TB* 5 (1926), 120-25.

1105. Maurer, C. "Der Hymnus von Epheser 1 als Schlüssel zum ganzen Brief." *EvTh* 11 (1951-52) 151-72.

1106. Mitton, C. L. "The Relationship between I Peter and Ephesians." *JTS* 1 (1950) 67-73.

1107. Norden, E. *Agnostos Theos.* Leipzig: Teubner, 1913, 141-276, 380-87.

1108. Percy, E. "Zu den Problemen des Kolosser- und Epheserbriefes." *ZNW* 43 (1950-51) 178-94.

1109. Rese, M. "Formeln und Lieder im Neuen Testament." *Verkundigung und Forschung* 15. Munich: Kaiser, 1970, 75-95.

Surveys the various studies on the formulas in the NT, isolating the criteria these scholars use to identify these formulas (and hymns). Applies current research to credal formulas and concludes with critical questions of methodology and content.

1110. Robinson, J. M. "Die Hodajot-Formel in Gebet und Hymnus des Frühchristentums." In *Apaphoreta.* FS E. Haenchen, ed. W. Eltester and F. H. Kettler, *BhZNW* 30. Berlin: Töpelmann, 1964, 194-235. Studies the Hodayoth formula in early Christian prayers and hymns.

1111. Sanders, J. T. "Hymnic Elements in Eph. 1-3." *ZNW* 56 (1965) 214-32.

See on texts, 1:3-14 (# 371).

1112. _____. *The New Testament Christological Hymns.* *SNTSMS* 15. Cambridge: Cambridge University Press, 1971.

See on texts, 2:11-22 (# 610).

1113. Schille, G. *Frühchristliche Hymnen.* Berlin: Evangelische Verlagsanstalt, 1965.

With Deichgräber (# 1100) posits the background of hymnic, liturgical material in sections of Ephesians. Focuses on the genre of

"Redeemer Songs" in the NT including Eph 2:14-18 plus "initiation songs" (e.g., Eph 1:3-12 and 2:4-10). Includes an excursus on the eschatology of Ephesians.

1114. Stanley, D. M. "Carmenque Christo quasi Deo Dicere." *CBQ* 20 (1958) 173-91.

Notes two texts from the captivity letters that provide evidence of the early church's use of hymns in public worship: Col 3:16 and Eph 5:18-20. He assesses several of the early Christian hymns that focus on the theme of Christ's divinity: Phil 2:5-11; Rev. 5:9-10, 12, 13; 15:3; Eph 5:14; 1 Tim 3:16; Col 1:13-20; and Jn 1:1-18.

1115. Wengst, K. *Christologische Formeln und Lieder des Urchristentums.* Gütersloh: G. Mohn, 1972.

See on texts, 2:11-22 (# 634).

GNOSTICISM

1116. Bartsch, H. W. *Gnostisches Gut und Gemeindetradition bei Ignatius von Antiochien.* Gütersloh: Bertelsmann, 1940.

1117. Becker, J. *Das Heil Gottes. Heils- und Sündenbegriffe in den Qumrantexten und im Neuen Testament. SUNT* 3. Göttingen: Vandenhoeck & Ruprecht, 1964.

Seeks to shed light on the NT uses of *alētheia* and *dikaiosynē* by studying related terms in the DSS, especially the Hebrew terms *mspt* and *sdq*. The texts show the development of the *sola gratia* nature of salvation further enlarged by Jesus, John, and especially Paul.

1118. Bianchi, U., ed. *The Origins of Gnosticism, Colloquium of Messina.* Leiden: Brill, 1967.

A collection of numerous essays and papers growing out of a

colloquium studying various aspects of the topic of Gnosticism. Topics include, among many others, the various origins of Gnosticism, its phenomena, attempts at definitions, its relationships to Qumran, and relations to various parts of the NT.

1119. Bieder, W. "Das Geheimnis des Christus nach dem Epheserbrief." *TZ* 11 (1955), 329-43.

1120. Böhlig, S. *Mysterion und Wahrheit.* Leiden: Brill, 1968.

1121. Bultmann, R. *Theology of the New Testament.* 2 vols. New York: Scribners, 1951, 1955.

Believing that Gnosticism predated or, at least, was contemporaneous with the rise of Christianity, Bultmann sees influences of the Gnostic movement in the development of Christianity and its writings. See, especially, Vol. 1, pp. 164-83. Sees the fragment of a hymn in Eph 5:14 to be "cast quite in Gnostic terms." Believes, as well, that the descent and ascent of the Redeemer of Eph 4:8-10 grows out of the Gnostic redeemer-myth.

1122. _____. *Primitive Christianity in Its Contemporary Setting.* London: Thames, 1956.

Within the context of Hellenism, Bultmann sees Gnosticism as a religious movement of pre-Christian origin invading the West from the Orient as a competitor of Christianity. Describes elements of various Gnostic myths in the section on Gnosticism and goes on to argue that Christianity was a syncretistic phenomenon that adopted various key elements from its Hellenistic environment so as to make its message intelligible to Hellenistic audiences and their mental outlook.

1123. Burkitt, F. C. *Church and Gnosis.* Cambridge: Cambridge University Press, 1932.

Five chapters attempting to define and describe the various Gnostic phenomena.

1124.   Colpe, C. *Die religionsgeschichtliche Schule.* *FRLANT*, N.F. 80.
        Göttingen: Vandenhoeck & Ruprecht, 1961.

        Following a general survey of Mandean and Iranian texts, studies the
        "Redeemer" in Gnostic texts.

1125.   _____.   "Zur Leib-Christi-Vorstellung im Epheserbrief."   In
        Judentum-Urchristentum Kirche.   FS J. Jeremias, ed. W.
        Eltester, *BhZNW* 26.   2d ed. Berlin: A. Töpelmann, 1964,
        172-87.

1126.   Dupont, D. J.   *Gnosis.   La Connaissance Religieuse Dans Les
        Épitres de Saint Paul.* 2d ed.. Louvain: Nouvelaerts; Paris: J.
        Gabalda, 1960.

        An extensive study of the various aspects of the topic of "knowledge"
        in Paul's writings. Especially in Chapter VII he considers cosmic
        language of fullness in Col and Eph plus concepts such as "body"
        and "*pleroma*" (fullness).

1127.   Eltester, W., ed. *Christentum und Gnosis.*   *BhZNW* 37. Berlin:
        Töpelmann, 1969.

        A collection of essays, in German, on the presence of Gnostic
        elements in the NT.

1128.   Grant, R. M.   *Gnosticism and Early Christianity.*   New York:
        Columbia University Press, 1959.

        Publication of six lectures on the origins of Gnosticism in
        relationship to early Christianity. Attempts to explain Gnosticism "as
        arising out of the debris of apocalyptic-eschatological hopes which
        resulted from the fall or falls of Jerusalem."   Finds that the
        movement toward Gnosticism is almost complete by the time of the
        writing of Ephesians (post-Pauline and post-fall of the Temple of
        Jerusalem). Sees the references in Eph 2:14 (removal of dividing
        wall) and the principalities and powers of 6:12 as evidences of this
        Gnostic background.

1129. _____. *Gnosticism. A Source Book of Heretical Writings from the Early Christian Period.* New York: Harper, 1961.

An anthology of Gnostic writings, each with an introduction and brief bibliography.

1130. Groningen, G. van. *First Century Gnosticism. Its Origin and Motifs.* Leiden: Brill, 1967.

Detailed analysis of the topic covering definitions, literary sources, origins, types, relationship to early Christianity, the spirit behind Gnostic systems, its settings in the Greek world, Judaism, Christianity, Syria, and motivations behind Gnosticism in Scientism. Concludes that this final element—the spirit of scientism—was the basic motif in the origin of Gnosticism.

1131. Haardt, R. *Die Gnosis.* Salzburg: O. Müller Verlag, 1967.

After an introduction to Gnosis—its nature, history, and exegesis—provides an anthology of Gnostic writings. Concludes with sources and descriptions of Gnosis.

1132. Hegermann, H. *Die Vorstellung vom Schöpfungsmittler im hellenistischen Judentum und Urchristentum. TU* 82. Berlin: Akademie-Verlag, 1961.

Studies the cosmological Christus and salvation in Hellenistic Christianity as well as the creation theme in the Hellenistic synagogue. Studies the hymn of Col 1 and Christ the Redeemer as mediator.

1133. Hoppe, R. "Das Mysterium und die Ekklesia: Aspekte zum Mysterium-Verständnis im Kolosser- und Epheserbrief." In *Gottes Weisheit im Mysterium,* ed. A. Schilson. Mainz: Grunewald Verlag, 1989, 81-101.

1134. _____. *The Gnostic Religion.* Boston: Beacon, 1959; rev. ed. 1963.

Following a description of Hellenism in the East and West, proceeds to survey Gnostic literature focusing on its main tenets and symbolic language. Follows by dividing Gnosticism into its main systems of thought and concludes by relating Gnosticism to classical Greek thinking.

1135. Käsemann, E. *Leib und Leib Christi. BHTh* 9. Tübingen: Mohr, 1933.

1136. Koester, H. "GNOMAI DIAPHOROI. The Origin and Nature of Diversification in the History of Early Christianity." *HTR* 58 (1965) 279-318.

Argues for a new set of criteria by which to assess early Christianity that moves beyond earlier but prejudicial labels such as canonical, apostolic, Jewish-Christian, and Gnostic. The touchstone must be that which happened to the historical Jesus—this is the criterion of Christian proclamation and theology. Proceeds to apply this tactic to several Christian developments.

1137. Kraeling, C. H. *Anthropos and Son of Man.* New York: Columbia University Press, 1927.

An inquiry into the nature, origin, and development of a Gnostic figure call "the Anthropos." Among the author's objectives is to search for a connection between this Gnostic motif and the "Son of Man" controversy in NT studies.

1138. Langerbeck, H. *Aufsätze zur Gnosis.* Göttingen: Vandenhoeck & Ruprecht, 1967.

Papers of the author collected following his death on the philological problem of Gnosis. Includes a chapter on Paul and Hellenism.

1139. Munck, J. "The New Testament and Gnosticism." In *Current Issues in New Testament Interpretation.* FS O. A. Piper, ed. W. Klassen and G. F. Snyder. London: SCM, 1962, 224-38.

Surveys the attempts in NT studies to establish the relationship between the advents of Gnosticism and Christianity. Concludes that Gnosticism, despite attempts allege the contrary, was a heretical movement that arose in the second century—following the advent of Christianity.

1140. Norden, E. *Agnostos Theos.* Leipzig/Berlin: Teubner, 1913, 56-115.

1141. Pokorný, P. *Der Epheserbrief und die Gnosis. Die Bedeutung des Haupt-Glieder-Gedankens in der entstehenden Kirche.* Berlin: Evangelische Verlagsanstalt, 1965.

Pursues how the author of Ephesians uses the concept of body comparing it to relevant texts in the mystery religions. Finds that Ephesians seems to go against several Gnostic concepts, particularly in its view of Jesus as sovereign judge, its eschatology, and its view that all growth comes from union with Jesus.

1142. _____. "Epheserbrief und gnostische Mystenen." *ZNW* 53 (1962) 160-94.

1143. Quispel, G. *Gnosis als Weltreligion.* Zürich: Origo, 1951.

1144. _____. "Neue Funde zur Valentinianischen Gnosis." *ZRG* 6 (1954) 289-305.

1145. _____. "Christliche Gnosis und jüdische Heterodoxie." *EvTh* 14 (1954) 474-84.

1146. _____. "Der gnostische Anthropos und die jüdische Tradition." *ErJb* 22 (1953) 195-234.

1147. Reitzenstein, R. *Poimandres.* Leipzig: Tübner, 1904.

1148. _____. *Das iranische Erlosungsmysterium.* Bonn: Marcus, 1921.

1149. Reitzenstein, R. and H. H. Schaeder. *Studien zum antiken Synkretismus.* Leipzig: Tübner, 1926.

1150. Schenke, H.-M. *Der Gott "Mensch" in der Gnosis.* Göttingen:

Vandenhoeck & Ruprecht, 1962.

Challenges the view of Schlier and Käsemann that Paul's concept of the Church as body of Christ was derived from the Gnostic myth of the Heavenly Man. Rather the concept of Church as Body of Christ may go back to the pantheistic view of God (*Allgott*).

1151. Schmithals, W. *Gnosticism in Corinth.* Nashville: Abingdon, 1971.

1152. _____. *Das kirchliche Apostelamt. Eine historische Untersuchung.* *FRLANT,* N.F. 61. Göttingen: Vandenhoeck & Ruprecht, 1961.

Following Lightfoot's lead at the beginning of the century, pursues the origin and nature of the apostolic office in the early Church. Documents extensively from Gnostic texts.

1153. _____. *Paul and the Gnostics.* Nashville: Abingdon, 1972.

Five essays, the first four of which treat Paul's opponents in various communities of believers: Galatia, Philippi, Thessalonica, and those present in Romans 16:17-20. The final essay draws out some of the implications of these studies for the question of the collection of Pauline letters.

1154. Schoeps, H. J. *Urgemeinde-Judenchristentum-Gnosis.* Tübingen: Mohr, 1965.

1155. Unnik, W. C. van. *Newly Discovered Gnostic Writings.* *SBT* 30. London: SCM; Naperville, IL: Allenson, 1960.

Assesses a few of the documents from the Nag Hammadi library so as to draw some understanding of the Gnostic sects that produced them, and of their world-view and spiritual life. Gnosticism became an exceptionally important rival to youthful Christianity, often because its adherents so closely attached themselves to Christianity.

1156. Weiss, H. F. "Gnostische Motive and antignostische Polemik im Kolosser- und im Epheserbrief." In *Gnosis und Neues*

Testament, ed. K.-W. Tröger. Berlin: Evangelische Verlagsanstalt, 1973, 311-24.

Addresses Gnostic motifs and anti-Gnostic polemic in Col and Eph.

1157. Wilson, R. McL. *The Gnostic Problem.* London: Mowbray, 1958.

The subtitle reads, "A Study of the Relations between Hellenistic Judaism and the Gnostic Heresy." Pursues the Jewish contribution to the development of Gnosticism in the second century.

1158. _____. *Gnosis and the New Testament.* Oxford: Blackwell, 1968.

Begins with an assessment of the Gnostic heresy in light of recent research and discovery, proceeding to the questions of "Gnosticism" in the NT and the Gnostic use of the NT. Argues for more consistency in the use of "gnostic" language: Gnosis, Gnostic, Gnosticism.

QUMRAN

1159. Benoit, P. "Qumran and the New Testament." *NTS* 7 (1960-61) 276-96. [Repr. in *Paul and Qumran,* ed. J. Murphy-O'Connor. Chicago: Priory Press, 1968, 1-30.]

Includes reflections on the methods for studying the Qumran documents alongside the NT. Warns against too quickly assuming direct influences: some features may arise independently in both traditions. Though Qumran may have influenced the NT, it may not have done so at the beginning of the Christian movement. That is, one may not say that Qumran served to create the NT. To the extent that the NT writers did borrow from Qumran, the borrowings only occurred at the periphery of Christian theology, not at any of its core doctrines. The article is amply illustrated with NT texts, including those from Ephesians.

1160.   Betz, O. *Offenbarung und Schriftforschung in der Qumranstexte.*
        Tübingen: Mohr, 1960.

        Analysis of the Qumran sect's own self-understanding, particularly
        how they established their special way of life on their understanding
        of special revelation.

1161.   _____. "The Eschatological Interpretation of the Sinai Tradition in
        Qumran and in the New Testament." *RQum* 6 (1967) 89-107.

        Defends that the ancient Israelites considered the Sinai-event as the
        fundamental act of God's self-disclosure. The Qumranians hoped
        again that God's grace might become a powerful reality for them as
        well: that God would come again and usher in the end times. Shows
        how this motif informs various NT passages. Believes that the
        author of Ephesians picks up a Qumran motif of the "breaking
        through the boundary of the Law" in Eph 2:14-16. Christ abolished
        the Law in his flesh by breaking down the wall of hostility dividing
        Jew and Gentile.

1162.   Bieder, W. "Das Geheimnis des Christus nach dem Epheserbrief."
        TZ 11 (1955) 329-43.

1163.   Braun, H. *Qumran und das Neue Testament.* 2 vols. Tübingen:
        Mohr, 1956. Esp. I: 215-25.

        Major study of the community at Qumran, its writings, and their
        possible impact on the NT.

1164.   _____. "Rom. 7:7-25 und das Selbstverständis des
        Qumranfrommen." *ZTK* 56 (1959) 1-18.

1165.   _____. "Spätjüdisch-häretischer und frühchristlicher Radikalismus."
        BHTh 24 (1957) 1-25.

1166.   Brown, R. E. "The Pre-Christian Semitic Concept of Mystery."
        CBQ 20 (1958) 417-43.

Traces the "mysteries" in the OT and Apocrypha, in the Pseudepigraphy and in the Qumran literature.

1167. _____. "The Semitic Background of the New Testament *mystērion.*" *Bib* 39 (1958) 426-48; 40 (1959) 70-87.

In eight sections traces the Semitic background in its synoptic usage, in John's apocalypse, in 2 Thess, 2 Cor, Rom, Col, Eph, and 1 Tim. *Mysterion* occurs six times in Eph. After discussing these uses, Brown shows the Semitic parallels for Eph 1 and 3. Finds that the Qumran literature provides the backdrop for the overarching motif of the Ephesian mystery: that in Christ all things in heaven and on earth are summed up.

1168. _____. *The Semitic Background of the Term "Mystery" in the New Testament.* Philadelphia: Fortress, 1968.

Reprint of the two preceding articles that present the author's findings about the uses of the term "mystery" in the NT. He defends the pre-Christian Semitic background to the concept, showing how that background fits the twenty-eight occurrences of the term in the NT.

1169. Cambier, J. "Le grand mystère concernant le Christ et son église. Éph. 5, 22-33." *Bib* 47 (1966) 43-90, 223-42.

See on texts, 5:21-33 (# 891).

1170. Cerfaux, L. "L'influence des 'Mystères' sur les épîtres de saint Paul aux Colossiens et aux Éphésiens." In *Sacra Pagina,* 2 vols. Paris: Gembloux, 1959. II: 373-79. [Repr. in *Recueil Lucien Cerfaux. Études d'exégese et d'histoire religieuse de Monseigneur Cerfaux.* 3 vols. Gembloux: Duculot, 1954-62. III (1962): 279-85.]

Shows how the presence of the "mysteries" in the Hellenistic religious world led Paul to respond in Col and Eph, presenting Christianity as a kind of "mystery" par excellence. Suggests that

Paul may have found among the Qumranians this fundamental use of the theme of the mystery of God's divine plan.

1171. Coppens, J.   "Le 'mystère' dans la théologie paulinienne et ses parallèles Qumraniens."   In *Litterateur et Theologie Pauliniennes,* ed. A. Descamps. *RechBib* 5. Bruges: Desclee de Brouwer, 1960, 142-65.   ET "'Mystery' in the Theology of St. Paul and Its Parallels at Qumran."   In *Paul and Qumran,* ed. J. Murphy-O'Connor. London: Chapman, 1968, 132-58.

1172. Dahl, N. A.   "Der Epheserbrief und der verlorene erste Brief des Paulus an die Korinther."   In *Abraham unser Vater.* FS 0. Michel, ed. O. Betz, M. Hengel, and P. Schmidt.   Leiden: Brill, 1963, 65-77.

Considers the relationship between Ephesians and the lost first letter that Paul wrote to Corinth.   Finds remarkable parallels between Ephesians and the Qumran literature suggesting a common pool of tradition that Hellenistic Jews and Christians shared.

1173. Daniel, C.   "Une mention pauliènne des Esséniens de Qumran." *RQum* 5 (1966) 553-67.

1174. Ellis, E. E.   "A Note on Pauline Hermeneutics."   *NTS* 2 (1955-56) 127-33.

Addresses the phenomenon that thirty-eight of Paul's citations from the OT vary from both the LXX and the Hebrew MT.   Following K. Stendahl (*The School of St. Matthew* [1954]) who studied the *pesher* interpretive techniques found in the Habakkuk scroll of Qumran, Ellis explains the bulk of Paul's uses of the OT as examples of a similar midrash-pesher method.   These interpretative paraphrases were created ad hoc by Paul or by the early church before him.   Far from being arbitrary eisegesis, this interpretive approach to referencing texts may express a greater fidelity to the meaning of Scripture. Although Paul frequently cited from the LXX, pesher quotations appear "to go behind the Greek to reflect an interpretation of the Hebrew Ur-text."

1175. Hegermann, H. *Die Vorstellung vom Schöpfungsmittler im hellenistischen Judentum und Urchristentum.* *TU* 82. Berlin: Akademie-Verlag, 1961.

See above on Gnosticism.

1176. Johnson, S. E. "Paul and the Manual of Discipline." *HTR* 48 (1955) 157-65.

Traces parallels in some of Paul's letters with concepts present in the Qumran Manual of Discipline. Nothing suggests Paul ever read the Manual; rather the parallels show how much a Jew he was and how his creative mind developed ideas that parallel the kind of thinking at Qumran.

1177. Klinzing, G. *Die Umdeutung des Kultus in der Qumrangemeinde und im Neuen Testament.* Göttingen: Vandenhoeck & Ruprecht, 1971.

Traces the reinterpretation of the Temple cult and the priesthood in the Qumran community. The third part of the study pursues various parallels to this reinterpretation of the Temple in the NT, among which he considers Eph 2:19ff. on pp. 184-91. Eph 2:22 stands in the tradition of 2 Cor 6:16; 1 Cor 3:16; and 1 Cor 6:19.

1178. Kuhn, K. G. "Der Epheserbrief im Lichte der Qumrantexte." *NTS* 7 (1960-61) 334-46. ET "The Epistle to the Ephesians in the Light of the Qumran Texts." In *Paul and Qumran,* ed. J. Murphy-O'Connor. Chicago: Priory Press, 1968, 115-131.

Seeks to discover any connection between the tradition found in the Qumran texts and Ephesians. Analyzes the language and style of Ephesians and concludes that many characteristic features of the letter parallel the characteristic Hebraic style of the Qumran texts. Also investigates the origin of the paraenetic material in the second half of Ephesians. Concludes that the Ephesian admonitions derive specifically from the Essene paraenesis of the Qumran texts.

1179. Murphy-O'Connor, J. "Who Wrote Ephesians?" *BiTod* 18 (1965)
        1201-9.

        Argues that Paul's amanuensis for Ephesians was a converted Essene.
        See on Authorship above.

1180. _____. "Truth: Paul and Qumran." *RB* 72 (1965) 29-76. [Repr. in
        Paul and Qumran, ed. J. Murphy-O'Connor. Chicago: Priory
        Press, 1968, 179-230.]

        Studies the concept of "truth" (the noun *alētheia*) in both the Qumran
        and Pauline texts. Surveys, first, the background of the concept of
        truth in the OT, finding the same essential strands in the Qumran
        writings, showing no evidence of Hellenistic influence. Seeks to
        uncover the origin of Paul's understanding of truth and how that
        plays out in Paul's understanding of the life of faith for Christians.
        Considers knowledge of the truth, and the foundation of truth.

1181. Mussner, F. "Beiträge aus Qumran zum Verständnis des
        Epheserbriefes." In *Neutestamentliche Aufsätze*. FS J.
        Schmid, ed. J. Blinzler, O. Kuss, and F. Mussner. Regensburg:
        Pustet, 1963, 185-97. [Repr. *Praesentia Salutis*. Düsseldorf:
        Patmos, 1967, 197-211.] ET "Contributions Made by Qumran
        to the Understanding of the Epistle to the Ephesians." In *Paul
        and Qumran*, ed. J. Murphy-O'Connor. Chicago: Priory Press,
        1968, 159-78.

        Pursues several recurring themes, concepts, and patterns of thought
        in Ephesians in light of their presence in Qumran texts. Themes
        include: mystery, the bond between the community and heaven, the
        community as temple and city, re-creation, and two minor concepts
        (to make nigh and unitedness). Concludes that certain themes in
        Ephesians have roots in a tradition also represented at Qumran and
        which is far removed from later Gnosticism.

1182. Reicke, Bo. "Traces of Gnosticism in the Dead Sea Scrolls?" *NTS*
        1 (1954-55) 137-51.

        Finds in the DSS evidence for a gradual development of Jewish

Apocalyptic to more philosophical theories such as the Judaistic Gnosticism or "philosophy" mentioned in Col 2:8. Rejects a too simplistic identification of the Qumran views as Gnostic. For example, the use of "knowledge" has more in common with OT connotations than with later Gnostic formulations.

1183. Rigaux, B. "Revelation des Mystères et Perfection à Qumràn et dans le Nouveau Testament." *NTS* 4 (1957-58) 237-62.

Finds points of comparison between the writings of Qumran, the Pauline literature, and the epistle of Hebrews. Traces the concept of perfection via a knowledge of the mysteries at Qumran. Proceeds to assess the use of *teleios* (perfect) in the NT, especially in Matthew and in Paul's writings. Discovers in Ephesians a synthesis of the concepts of mystery found in Paul's references in Col, Rom, 1 Cor, and Phil. Evaluates the "word of wisdom" (λόγος σοφίας) in Paul, again finding in Ephesians a new development and a new synthesis from the earlier Paulines.

1184. Ryrie, C. C. "The Mysteria in Eph. 3." *BSac* 123 (1966) 24-31.

Interpretations of "mystery" in 3:1-13 range from the amillennial understanding of mystery as a furthering, in NT times, of OT revelation, to the "extreme ultradispensationalist" view of mystery as revelation given specifically during Paul's first Roman imprisonment, and not before. An examination of the word's general concept (vis-à-vis secrecy), Ephesian content (cf. 3:6), and relationship to OT revelation and to Paul (the crux is 3:5), suggest that mystery denotes the equality of Jews and Gentiles in the body of Christ, which was known only after the coming of Christ by the Spirit. For more, see on texts, 3:1-13 (# 680).

1185. Schubert, K. "Der gegenwärtige Stand der Erforschung der in Palästina neu gefundenen hebräischen Handschriften." *TLZ* 78 (1953) 495-506.

1186. Schulz, S. "Zur Rechtfertigung aus Gnade in Qumran und bei Paulus." *ZTK* 56 (1959) 155-85.

1187. Smith, D. C. "Cultic language in Ephesians 2:19-22: a test case."
       RestQ 31/4 (1989) 207-17.

       The presence of common themes, e.g., spiritual temple, house,
       foundation, et al., in both the Qumran literature and Eph 2:19-22,
       argues for dependence.

1188. Stendahl. K., ed. *The Scrolls and the New Testament.* New York:
       Harper, 1957.

       A collection of fourteen articles all but three of which were
       previously published in various journals. Cover various themes
       relating the Qumran documents to NT topics.

1189. Vogt, E. "'Mysteria' in textibus Qumran." *Bib* 37 (1956) 247-57.

       This article in Latin traces uses of "mystery" in some of the DSS:
       1QpHab, 1QS, fragments from Cave 1, 1QM, 1QH, and CD.

1190. Wilson, R. McL. "Gnostic Origins." *VigChr* 9 (1955) 193-211.

       Seeks answers to the questions about the origin and nature of
       Gnosticism. It must be considered unchristian. It resulted from a
       fusion of various strands, a syncretism of various Hellenistic tenets,
       some of which were Christian and Jewish. As a system, it is not
       pre-Christian.

1191. _____. "Gnostic Origins Again." *VigChr* 11 (1957) 93-110.

       Attacks several scholars who allege the presence of pre-Christian
       Gnosticism at Qumran (e.g., Kuhn, Schubert, Haenchen). Better to
       see Gnosticism as essentially unchristian, and full-blown Gnosticism
       resulted from a long process to which the Qumran *Manual of
       Discipline* provided some impetus.

1192. _____. "Simon, Dositheus and the Dead Sea Scrolls." *ZRG* 9
       (1956) 21-30.

OLD TESTAMENT

Most of the following works deal more generally with the problem posed by the NT writers' (and especially Paul's) uses of the OT. While many of them make reference to how the book of Ephesians uses the OT at various points, they will go without annotations. Only those that have special significance will be annotated below.

1193. Barth, M. "Traditions in Ephesians." *NTS* 30 (1984) 3-25.

Traces what appear to be eleven (other than Pauline) traditions lying behind Ephesians. The study moves from Christian to Jewish to Gentile, and also what Barth admits to be more to less certain. Extremely suggestive study from this author of a major commentary on Ephesians.

1194. Bonsirven, J. *Exégèse rabbinique et exégèse paulinienne.* Paris: Beauchesne, 1939.

The first part evaluates the exegetical methods of the rabbis in the midrashim and talmuds. Proceeds to evaluate Paul's exegesis by studying how he uses the OT.

1195. Dietzfelbinger, C. "Paulus und das Altes Testament." In *Theologische Existenz heute,* N F. 95. Munich: Kaiser, 1961.

1196. Dodd, C. H. *According to the Scriptures.* New York: Scribner's, 1953.

1197. _____. *The Old Testament in the New.* London: Athlone, 1952.

1198. Ellis, E. E. "A Note on Pauline Hermeneutics." *NTS* 2 (1955-56) 127-33.

1199. _____. *Paul's Use of the Old Testament.* Edinburgh: Oliver & Boyd, 1957.

This important study makes numerous references to texts in

Ephesians. Includes sections on Paul and Judaism as well as Pauline exegesis.

1200. Hunter, A. M. *Paul and His Predecessors.* London: SCM, 1962 and Philadelphia: Westminster, 1969.

Without denying Paul's creative theological genius, seeks to understand what may be considered Paul's sources—those foundations upon which he builds in his formulations of the Christian message. Attempts to isolate traditions, formulae, hymns, "words of the Lord," paraenesis, the OT, baptismal and Lord's Supper traditions, among others.

1201. Lincoln, A. T. "The Use of the OT in Ephesians." *JSNT* 14 (1982) 16-57.

Notes the paucity of studies on the topic, suggests some reasons for this omission, and proceeds to focus on actual quotations from the OT in Ephesians, not allusions. Texts studied are Psa 68:18 in Eph 4:8-10; Isa 57:19 in Eph 2:17; Gen 2:24 in Eph 5:31-32; Exo 20:12 in Eph 6:2-3; Psa 110:1 and Psa 8:6 in Eph 1:20, 22; plus further briefer references. See further on texts, 2:11-22 (# 577).

1202. Lindars, B. *New Testament Apologetic.* Philadelphia: Westminster, 1962, 222-50.

This study on the doctrinal significance of the OT quotations includes a chapter on quotations in Paul, particularly Galatians and Romans (pp. 222-50).

1203. Michel, O. *Paulus und seine Bibel.* Gütersloh: Bertelsmann, 1929.

1204. Schmid, J. "Die AT Zitate bei Paulus und der sensus plenior." *BZ* 3 (1959) 161-73.

1205. Storer, R. "A Possible Link between the Epistle to the Ephesians and the Book of Ruth." *StEv* IV, ed. F. L. Cross. *TU* 102. Berlin: Akademie-Verlag, 1968, 343-346.

Following the suggestion that Ephesians shows connections to the OT lectionary passages read about the time of Pentecost suggests that the phrase from Eph 1:14, "until the redemption of the purchased possession," might have a connection to Ruth, also read at this time of year. Connections noted include: redemption, the filling up of what was empty, bringing near those who were far off, breaking the barrier between Jew and Gentile, analogy of marriage, calling from a dark unmentioned past, redemption as making two into one, and as a reward for loving dealing and virtuous devotion to the Lord. Provides a full table of alleged parallels.

1206. Strack, H. L. *Einleitung in Talmud und Midrasch.* Munich: Beck, 1930. III: 95-109.

1207. Tasker, R. V. G. *The Old Testament in the New.* 2d ed. London: SCM, 1954, 80-102.

In one chapter of this study the author discusses Paul (pp. 80-102), referencing the use of Psa 68:18 in Eph 4:8 as an example of the times Paul departs from both the Hebrew and Greek versions in citing the OT.

1208. Ulonska, H. *Paulus und das Alte Testament.* Münster: Rotraprint, 1964.

OTHER RELATIONS

1209. Barth, M. "Traditions in Ephesians." *NTS* 30 (1984) 3-25.

1210. Hunter, A. M. *Paul and His Predecessors.* London: SCM, 1962 and Philadelphia: Westminster, 1969.

1211. Mitton, C. L. "The Relationship between I Peter and Ephesians." *JTS* 1 (1950) 67-73.

Chapter 9

HISTORICAL ISSUES

AUTHORSHIP AND PSEUDONYMITY

1212. Aland. K.   "The Problem of Anonymity and Pseudonymity in Christian Literature of the First Two Centuries."   *JTS* 12 (1961) 39-49.

Noting the paucity of essays and monographs on the topic, engages in a study of the issues surrounding anonymity and pseudonymity in the NT by considering Christian literature of the first two centuries as a whole. Accounts for pseudonymity as the attempt of those in later periods to put themselves back into the time of the Apostles in order to use them and claim their authority for the demands of present situations through their more or less successful imitation of the Apostles' ways of thinking and writing.

1213. _____.   "Falsche Verfasserangaben? Zur Pseudonymität im frühchristlichen Schrifttum."   *TRev* 75 (1979) 1-10.

As argued in the above study, and in opposition to Brox (see below) and others, insists that the study of pseudepigraphy must consider *all*

Christian literature prior to A.D. 150 and cannot neglect the parallel phenomenon of anonymity. Sufficient attention need be given to the variety of genres of pseudonymous writings and a major shift in the thinking of Christians about A.D. 150. Argues that the early Christian conviction that the Spirit revealed through prophets meant that using an author's *real* name was the exception.

1214. _____. "Noch einmal: Das Problem der Anonymität und Pseudonymität in der christlichen Literatur der ersten beiden Jahrhunderte." In *Pietas*. FS B. Kötting, ed. E. Dassmann. Münster: Aschendorff, 1980, 121-39.

1215. Albertz, M. *Die Botschaft des Neuen Testamentes.* Zollikon-Zürich: EVZ, 1952. I, 2: 165-68.

1216. Allan, J. A. "The 'in Christ' Formula in Ephesians." *NTS* 5 (1958-59) 54-62.

Seeks to study whether the extensive use of the "in Christ" formula in Eph—much higher even than in Col—can be attributed to Paul. Finds in the Ephesian use an entire absence of the deeper and more striking features of Paul's use of the formula. Draws a number of conclusions, the central of which is that Paul could not have written Eph.

1217. Balz, H. R. "Anonymität und Pseudepigraphie im Urchristentum: Überlegungen zum literarischen und theologischen Problem der urchristlichen und gemeinantiken Pseudepigraphie." *ZTK* 66 (1969) 403-36.

Traces the history of the discussion of the issues of pseudonymity and anonymity—mostly chapters or articles—before pursuing the phenomena in the writings of Greek antiquity and Jewish and Christian spheres. Finds that these practices were widespread in the ancient world, though falsely attributing authorship was sometimes condemned, as was plagiarism. Religious communities produced literature that was later attributed to significant individuals of the past. Believes that the early Christians simply adopted this practice, and this accounts for both anonymity (e.g. Gospels, Acts, 1 Jn, and Heb) and pseudonymity in the NT.

1218. Barth, M. "Traditions in Ephesians." *NTS* 30 (1984)

From his analysis of the various traditional elements contained with the epistle, Barth argues that it is more likely that Paul is the author than that the letter derives from a degenerate Paulinism and traditionalism. Traditional elements Barth finds include those from Israel (including the OT, Jewish interpretations, and synagogue worship), the early church (homily, hymns, confessional formulae, paraenesis, and perhaps a Pauline school), and Hellenistic Greek, Roman, and local Asian religions or cults. Less likely, says Barth, are elements of second century Gnosticism.

1219. Bauckham, R. "Pseudo-Apostolic Letters." *JBL* 107 (1988) 469-94.

Seeks to establish fresh criteria for determining the extent of pseudonymity in the NT. Studies the various types of pseudepigraphic letters in antiquity and compares them to accounts of ancient Jewish pseudepigraphic and pseudo-apostolic letters, concluding that there are broad similarities across them all. Hence any pseudepigraphic NT letters will also fit these patterns. Concludes that Eph and James could easily fit one of the types of pseudepigraphic letters.

1220. Baur, F. C. *Paulus der Apostel Jesu Christi.* Stuttgart: Becker & Müller, 1845, 449-55.

1221. Benoit, P. "Ephesiens." *DB Supp.* Ed L. Pirot et al. Paris: Letouzey et Ané, 1928-70. VII (1961) 195-211.

1222. _____. "L'horizon paulinien de l'épître aux Éphésiens." *RB* 46 (1937) 342-61, 506-25. [Repr. in *Exégèse et Théologie.* 4 vols. Paris: Du Cerf, 1961-82, II (1961): 53-96.]

Proffers the hypothesis that under Paul's supervision a disciple produced Ephesians with the help of the recently written epistle of Colossians.

1223. Brox, N. *Falsche Verfasserangaben: Zur Erklärung der
         frühchristlichen Pseudepigraphie.* Stuttgart: Katholisches
         Bibelwerk, 1975.

    Studies the phenomenon of false attributions of authorship in early
    Christian, Jewish, and pagan writings as well as other pertinent issues
    to seek an understanding of the conditions and tendencies of early
    Christian pseudepigraphy.

1224. _____., ed. *Pseudepigraphie in der heidnischen und
         jüdisch-christlichen Antike.* Darmstadt: Wissenschaftliche
         Buchgesellschaft, 1977.

    A collection of fifteen previously published articles (dating from
    1894 to 1972) on the practice of pseudepigraphy in the ancient
    world. Includes Brox's introduction and an eight-page bibliography.

1225. Cadbury, H. J. "The Dilemma of Ephesians." *NTS* 5 (1958-59)
         91-102.

    Recognizing the subjectivity in any discussion of the authorship of
    Ephesians Cadbury asks, "Which is more likely—that an imitator of
    Paul in the first century composed a writing 90 or 95 percent in
    accordance with Paul's style or that Paul himself wrote a letter
    diverging 5 or 10 percent from his usual style?" (101).

1226. Cameron, P. S.   "The Structure of Ephesians."   *Filologia
         Neotestamentaria* 3/5 (1990) 3-18.

    Argues that the extraordinarily intricate structural pattern he discovers
    probably constitutes a weighty argument against Pauline authorship.

1227. Cerfaux, L. "En faveur de l'authenticité des épîtres de la captivité."
         In *Littérature et Théologie Pauliniennes.* Bruges: Desclee de
         Brouwer, 1960, 60-71. [Repr. in *Recueil Lucien Cerfaux.
         Études d'exégese et d'histoire religieuse de Monseigneur
         Cerfaux.* 3 vols. Gembloux: Duculot, 1954-62. III (1962):
         266-78.]

In arguing for the Pauline authorship of the prison epistles, the author establishes the doctrinal homogeneity between Ephesians and the acknowledged Paulines. Traces what he believes to be central as well as subsidiary Pauline themes to develop the case. Concludes with a possible scenario explaining the development of Paul's ideas and letters in the order: Col, Eph, and the Corinthian letters.

1228. Collins, R. F. *Letters That Paul Did Not Write. The Epistle to the Hebrews and the Pauline Pseudepigrapha.* Good News Studies 28. Wilmington, DE: Glazier, 1988.

Discusses the authorship issue of the letters whose Pauline authorship is widely disputed by scholars in what to him is the order of certainty: Hebrews (least likely to come from Paul), the Pastorals, Ephesians, Colossians, and 2 Thess. Beyond authorship, he considers their content, historical setting, theology and the portrait of Paul each portrays.

1229. Conzelmann, H. "Paulus und die Weisheit." *NTS* 12 (1965-66) 231-44.

Pursues the issue of a wisdom tradition in Paul's writings. Posits that, trained as a theologian, Paul probably established a school, most likely at Ephesus, in which "wisdom" was an organizing principle. Evidence of this schooling in wisdom surfaces in the writings of his later followers, e.g., Hebrews, Ephesians, and the Pastorals. Even certain texts within Paul's acknowledged writings (2 Cor 3:7ff.; 1 Cor 1:18ff.; 2:6ff.; 10:1ff.; 11:2ff.; 13; and Rom 1:18ff. suggest that later editors from his school incorporated wisdom traditions into his writings. Suggests further implications of this thesis for the study of Paul.

1230. _____. "Die Schule des Paulus." In *Theologia Crucis—Signum Crucis.* FS E. Dinkler, ed. C. Andresen and G. Klein. Tübingen: Mohr, 1979, 85-96.

1231. Coppieters, H. "Les récentes attaques contre l'authenticité de l'épître aux Éphésiens." *RB*, n.s. 9 (1912) 361-90.

1232. Donelson, L. R. *Pseudepigraphy and Ethical Argument in the Pastoral Epistles.* Tübingen: Mohr, 1986, 7-66.

1233. Dunn, J. D. G. "The Problem of Pseudonymity." In *The Living Word.* London: SCM, 1987, 65-85.

1234. Erasmus, D. *Novum Testamentum Annotationes.* Basel: Froben, 1519, 413.

1235. Fenton, J. C. "Pseudonymity in The New Testament." *Theology* 58 (1955) 51-56.

1236. Fischer, K. M. "Anmerkungen zur Pseudepigraphie im Neuen Testament." *NTS* 23 (1976) 76-81.

1237. Goguel, M. "Esquisse d'une solution nouvelle du probleme de l'épître aux Éphésiens." *RHPR* 111 (1935) 254-85; 112 (1936) 73-99.

1238. Goodspeed, E. J. "Ephesians, the Introduction to the Pauline Collection," in *New Solutions of New Testament Problems.* Chicago: University of Chicago Press, 1927, 11-20.

1239. _____. *The Meaning of Ephesians.* Chicago: University of Chicago Press, 1933.

1240. _____. "Pseudonymity and Pseudepigrapha in Early Christian Literature." In *New Chapters in New Testament Study.* New York: Macmillan, 1937, 169-88.

1241. _____. "Ephesians and the first edition of Paul." *JBL* 70 (1951) 285-91.

1242. _____. *The Key to Ephesians.* Chicago: University of Chicago Press, 1956.

Argues that following the publication of Luke-Acts the letters of Paul were collected and published, probably in the A.D. nineties. Ephesians was composed at this time—drawing its most powerful elements from the nine Pauline letters—as a cover or introductory letter, probably written by Onesimus.

1243. Goulder, M. D. "The Visionaries of Laodicea." *JSNT* 43 (1991) 15-39.

1244. Guthrie, D. "The Development of the Idea of Canonical Pseudepigraphs in New Testament Criticism." In *The Authorship and Integrity of the New Testament,* ed. K. Aland. London: SPCK, 1965, 14-39.

1245. Harmon, N. B. "Did Saint Paul write Ephesians?" *Methodist Quarterly Review* 75/3 (1926) 492-500.

1246. Harrison, P. N. "The Pastoral Epistles and Duncan's Ephesian Theory." *NTS* 2 (1955-56) 250-61.

1247. _____. "The Author of Ephesians." *StEv* 2, ed. F. L. Cross. *TU* 87. Berlin: Akademie-Verlag, 1964, 595-604.

1248. Hengel, M. "Anonymität, Pseudepigraphie und `Literarische Fälschung' in der jüdisch-hellenistischen Literatur." In *Pseudepigrapha,* Vol. 1 ed. K. von Fritz. Vandoeuvres-Genève: Fondation Hardt, 1972, 231-308, 309-29.

1249. Holtzmann, H. J. *Kritik der Epheser- und Kolosserbriefe auf Grund einer Analyse ihres Verwandtschaftverhältnisses.* Leipzig: Engelmann, 1872.

An in depth analysis of the extent of the parallels between Ephesians and Colossians arguing, among other things, that the starting point of the borrowing seems to shift back and forth between the two. Suggests a rather complex theory involving interpolations and redactions to account for this.

1250. Hübner, H. "Glossen in Epheser 2." In *Vom Urchristentum zu Jesus.* FS J. Gnilka, ed H. Frankemölle and K. Kertelge.

Freiburg/Basel/Wien: Herder, 1989, 392-406.

1251. Knox, J. *Chapters in a Life of Paul.* Nashville: Abingdon, 1950.

Adopts a version of Goodspeed's theory suggesting that Onesimus of
Philemon authored Ephesians as an introductory letter at the head of
the entire Pauline corpus.

1252. Knox, W. L. *St. Paul and the Church of the Gentiles.* Cambridge:
Cambridge University Press, 1939, 182-203.

1253. Laub, F.   "Falsche Verfasserangaben in neutestamentlichen
Schriften." *TTZ* 89 (1980) 228-42.

1254. Lincoln, A. T. Review of *The Authenticity of Ephesians,* by A. van
Roon. *WTJ* 40 (1977-78) 172-75.

1255. _____. "Use of the OT in Ephes." *JSNT* 14(1982).

Lincoln supports the case against Pauline authorship on the basis of
how the writer/editor of Ephesians employs the OT in comparison
with how Paul does in the undisputed letters. Evaluating the places
in Ephesians where the writer directly employs the OT, Lincoln
notes: the use of the OT lacks the promise/fulfillment perspective;
and the use of Gen 2:24 departs from how it is used in 1 Cor 6:16,
as does the writer's use of Exo 20:12 from what Paul would say.
The OT plays a far less important role for the writer of Ephesians—
the OT traditions are only one among many the author sees as
authoritative.

1256. Meade, D. G. *Pseudonymity and Canon.* Tübingen: Mohr, 1986,
esp. 139-57.

1257. Mealand, D. L. "Positional Stylometry Reassessed: Testing a Seven
Epistle Theory of Pauline Authorship." *NTS* 35/2 (1989) 266-
86.

Concerning authorship, tests show we need not limit Pauline
authorship to the Hauptbriefe. Also, probably Eph, Col and 2 Tim

should not be put in the same category as the usually agreed-upon seven.

1258. Merklein, H. *Das kirchliche Amt nach dem Epheserbrief.* Munich: Kösel, 1973, 19-54.

In this study of the concept of church office and the contributions of Ephesians to the topic, devotes these early pages to the letter's authenticity—concluding that it was written by some theologian in the post-apostolic age—and its history-of-religions background (it does not derive from the Gnostic *Urmensch* myth).

1259. Metzger, B. M. "Literary Forgeries and Canonical Pseudepigrapha." *JBL* 91 (1972) 3-24.

In an analysis of the phenomenon of pseudepigraphy, considers: whether such writings ought to be considered literary forgeries, the ethics of the practice (compatible with honesty and candor?), the psychology of an author who impersonates an ancient worthy, whether we ought to take him or her seriously, and, theologically, whether a work that involves fraud can be compatible with the character of a message from God. Traces the motives of ancient pseudepigraphers (e.g., financial gain, malice, love and respect, modesty). Raises the key questions in viewing pseudepigraphal documents as canonical by investigating how the ancients themselves viewed the practice, concluding that pseudonymous works were rejected from the canon and placed, instead, on the forbidden lists of apocryphal works, though there were, no doubt, exceptions to this rule.

1260. Mitton, C. L. "Unsolved New Testament Problems: E. J. Goodspeed's Theory Regarding the Origin of Ephesians." *ExpT* 59 (1947-48) 323-27; 60 (1948-49) 320-21.

In the first article, Mitton reviews the essence of the case against Pauline authorship (vocabulary, style, literary relationships, and doctrine), and, how, despite these objections, the case is very much unsettled. In response, he sets out Goodspeed's account of the origin of the Epistle, believing that some version of it presents a defensible alternative for those who are convinced that Paul did not write Ephesians. In the second article, Mitton responds briefly to Moule's observations [see # 1264]. Particularly draws the implications of the words πλήρωμα and μυστήριον.

1261.   _____. *The Epistle to the Ephesians: Its Authorship, Origin, and Purpose.* Oxford: Clarendon Press, 1951.

The presentation of the case against Pauline authorship. The author knew well and had before him in his writing of Ephesians the collected Pauline corpus of letters. Decisive against Pauline authorship are literary investigations and comparisons: an analysis of the close parallels between Eph and Col and the relationship between Eph and the other genuine Pauline letters.

1262.   _____. *The Formation of the Pauline Corpus of Letters.* London: Epworth, 1955.

Pursues key issues surrounding the formation of the collection of letters that are considered Pauline. Why were the letters collected into the corpus we know? When was the collection done and where? What process resulted in its final form? And who was the person responsible for the collection? Though no definitive answers are possible, the short study speculates and hypothesizes "based on a somewhat subjective assessment of possibilities rather than on actual and reliable evidence." Notes that Ephesians gives substantial evidence of acquaintance with the other nine letters of Paul. Chapter Seven (pp. 61-74) considers the place of Ephesians in the Pauline corpus. Surmises that Eph was written by a follower of Paul as a kind of Introductory Letter to the first published collection of Paul's letters. Admits, though, that this is mere conjecture.

1263.   _____. "Important Hypotheses Reconsidered; VII. The Authorship of the Epistle to the Ephesians." *ExpT* 67 (1955-56) 195-98.

A revisit of the issue of Pauline authorship in light of further research subsequent to Mitton's prior work on the problem. Assesses the work of E. Percy, C. Masson, and F. C. Synge. Still convinced of the validity of his analyses, Mitton concedes that the problem as a whole still remains open to discussion, rejecting contentions of some German scholars who accept without any more question that Paul could not have been the author.

1264. Moule, C. F. D. "E. J. Goodspeed's Theory Regarding the Origin of Ephesians." *ExpT* 60 (1949) 224-25.

Reflecting on C. L. Mitton's analysis and essential adoption of Goodspeed's theory of authorship, offers four points against Goodspeed and two points in his favor. Draws no final conclusions on the issue.

1265. Murphy-O'Connor, J. "Who Wrote Ephesians?" *BiTod* 18 (1965) 1201-9.

Though it is extremely unlikely that Paul himself wrote Ephesians, his genius permeates its pages, and, undoubtedly, such passages as 1:3-14, 2:11-22, and 5:22-33 must come directly from him. Offers the suggestion that Paul's amanuensis for the writing of Ephesians was a converted Essene. Shows how, section by section, Essene (or Qumran) influence might well lay behind the thought of the letter.

1266. Nineham, D. E. "The Case against the Pauline Authorship." In *Studies in Ephesians,* ed. F. L. Cross. London: Mowbray, 1956, 21-35.

Not a new or original study, it attempts "to state the grounds on which the Pauline authorship of Ephesians *has been* doubted." Catalogs the usual arguments concluding with a personal note that the references to Paul in Eph do not "ring true."

1267. Patzia, A. G. "The Deutero-Pauline Hypothesis: An Attempt at Clarification." *EvQ* 52 (1980) 27-42.

Attempts to show how the concept—really, the hypothesis—of "Deutero-Pauline" or "Deutero-Paulinist" raises important questions both for NT introduction and early Christian history *and* for the nature of apostolic authority. Catalogs the factors that make up the Deutero-Pauline hypothesis: authorship problems, so-called "early catholicism," the practice of pseudonymity in the ancient world, and the role of Paul's co-workers. The second issue concerns the alleged motives of the Deutero-Paulinist: to commend Paul to a later generation or to appeal directly to Paul's authority to confront heresy and to establish sound doctrine. Then moves to a description of the characteristics of Deutero-Pauline literature: dependence on Paul, theme of church tradition, liturgical style and paraenetic structure, and theological development beyond the apostolic age. The fourth section of the article assesses the problem of the authorship of the Deutero-Pauline letters.

1268. Percy, E. "Zu den Problemen des Kolosser- und Epheserbriefes." *ZNW* 43 (1950-51) 178-94.

1269. _____. *Die Probleme der Kolosser- und Epheserbriefe.* 2d rev.ed. Lund: Gleerup, 1964.

Defends the Pauline authorship of both Col and Eph, though with some misgivings and the admission of certain features that are difficult to explain. After arguing that Col must be Pauline, shows that the differences between Col and Eph can be accounted for assuming a span of time (albeit very minimal) between their origin and the differences in situation and the nature of the arguments.

1270. Rist, M. "Pseudepigraphy and the Early Christians." In *Studies in New Testament and Early Christian Literature.* FS A. P. Wikgren, ed. D. E. Aune. Leiden: Brill 1972, 75-91.

Argues that pseudepigraphy (equivalent to pseudonymity) was a widely-practiced, dishonorable practice used by Greeks, Romans, Jews, and, finally, Christians. Its design is to deceive so as to obtain the authority or credibility of a famous person that the real author does not possess. Discusses the techniques of pseudepigraphers, the problem of textual alterations of manuscripts, and considers several examples of what the author considers pseudepigraphic writings. Concludes that both "orthodox" and "heretical" Christians employed the technique of pseudepigraphy.

1271. Roon, A. van. *The Authenticity of Ephesians.* Leiden: Brill, 1974.

Extensive analysis of the numerous elements requiring consideration if we are to pass judgment on the authenticity of Ephesians. Considers various historical matters, relationships to other NT epistles, peculiarities in the letter's prescript and ending, the letter's various stylistic features, the use and meaning of key expressions that have cosmic or anthropological characteristics, and the letter's teaching about the church. Comes down on the side of Pauline authorship, though he believes that a secretary had considerable influence in the letter's formulation, which accounts for the letter's divergence from various normal Pauline patterns.

1272. Rowston, D. J. "Changes in biblical interpretation today: the example of Ephesians." *BTB* 9 (1979) 121-25.

The study stalks a hypothesis of R. P. Martin, an evangelical British Baptist, who suggested in an article in 1968 (in conversation with P. R. Jones of Southern Baptist Seminary; see # 1325) that Luke wrote Ephesians. This article traces the background of this Martin-Jones hypothesis through various stages in works by J. J. Gunther, J. H. Moulton, G. H. P. Thompson, W. L. Knox, C. L. Mitton, et al.

1273. Sanders, J. N. "The Case for the Pauline Authorship." In *Studies in Ephesians,* ed. F. L. Cross. London: Mowbray, 1956, 9-20.

Sees the question of authorship as of merely academic interest, since, even were the letter not from Paul, its authority of position in the canon would not in the least be affected. Ephesians is not an epistle at all, but Paul's "spiritual testament" to the Church at the end of his imprisonment in Rome. Responds to objections to the redactional view, particularly those of Goodspeed and Mitton.

1274. Schenke, H.-M. "Das Weiterwirken des Paulus und die Pflege seines Erbes durch die Paulus-Schule." *NTS* 21 (1974-75) 505-18.

Addresses the continuing effect of Paul, particularly how his legacy is maintained through his followers.

1275. Schille, G. "Der Autor des Epheserbriefes." *TLZ* 82 (1957) 325-34.

1276. Schweizer, E. "Zur Frage der Echtheit des Kolosser- und
      Epheserbriefes." *ZNW* 47 (1956) 287. [Repr. in
      Neotestamentica. Zürich: Zwingli, 1963, 429.]

      Suggests that the absence of "(my) brothers" from Col, Eph, and the
      Pastorals, frequent in the genuine letters, might suggest their Deutero-
      Pauline status.

1277. Sint, J. A. *Pseudonymität im Altertum: Ihre Formen und ihre
      Gründe.* Innsbruck: Universitätsverlag Wagner, 1960.

1278. Speyer, W. *Die literarische Fälschung im heidnischen und
      christlichen Altertum.* Munich: Beck 1971.

      Distinguishes between literary forgeries and pseudepigraphy as
      separating species from genus. Discusses reasons for forgeries and
      cites examples in pagan, Jewish, and Christian writings. Surveys the
      criteria for authenticity in patristic writers.

1279. _____. "Religiöse Pseudepigraphie und literarische Fälschung im
      Altertum." *JAC* 8/9 (1965-66) 82-125.

1280. Usteri, L. *Die Entwicklung des paulinischen Lehrbegriffs.* Zürich:
      Orell Füssli, 1824, 2-8.

1281. Wette, W. M. L. de. *Lehrbuch des Neuen Testaments.* Berlin:
      Reimer, 1826, 254-65.

HISTORICAL SETTING

1282. Arnold, C. E. *Ephesians: Power and Magic.* Cambridge:
      Cambridge University Press, 1989, 5-40, 123-24, 165-72.

      See on texts, 3:14-21 (# 687). This study of the "power
      environment" of first century Asia sheds important light on the
      historical background for the power terminology of Ephesians.

1283. Bartlett, W. "The Saints at Ephesus." *Exp* 8/107 (1919) 327-341.

1284. Batey, R. "The Destination of Ephesians." *JBL* 82 (1963) 101.

For "to Ephesus," not in the original address of Ephesians, Batey substitutes "the holy ones" which improves the syntax, accounts for the encyclical nature and impersonal tone of the epistle, explains the early currency, and elucidates the similarity between a general letter to Asia and a specific letter to Colossae.

1285. Bauer, W. *Orthodoxy and Heresy in Earliest Christianity.* Trans. and ed. R. A. Kraft and G. Krodel. Philadelphia: Fortress, 1971, 61-94.

Asks whether Ignatius of Antioch was the authoritative interpreter of faith for all Christians in Syria. In Ephesus, bishops gathered a large majority of the local Christians around them and most were allies of Ignatius. Rev. 1-3 does not present an impressive idea of what sought to replace the Pauline gospel at Ephesus (setbacks occurred from struggles with external enemies and internal discord).

1286. Bean, G. E. *Aegean Turkey.* New York: Praeger, 1966.

By the middle of the first century A.D. the whole of Asia Minor was incorporated in the Roman empire in the form of provinces, although the language remained Greek. "Pax Romana" brought Ephesus great wealth and prosperity which promoted the building of temples, theaters, paved marble streets, and markets. Androclus founded the city and adopted the native goddess under the name of their own Artemis. Discussion of the city of Ephesus on pp. 160-184 and includes many pictures.

1287. _____. *Turkey beyond the Maeander.* London: Ernest Benn, 1971.

Concentrates exclusively on the region of ancient Caria (Mylasa, Labraynda, Iasus, Cnidus, and the Rhodian Peraea). As in his other works, includes an extensive chapter on the history of the region. Paul did not visit here, and the only early churches seem to be in Laodicea and Colossae, on the region's extreme fringe.

1288. _____. *Turkey's Southern Shore.* New York: Praeger. 1968.

Nothing specific with regard to Ephesus, but concentrates on the areas of Pamphylia, Pisidia, and Lycia.

1289. Best, E. "Recipients and Title of the Letter to the Ephesians: Why and When the Designation 'Ephesians'?" *ANRW. Geschichte und Kultur Roms im Spiegel der neueren Forschung.* II: *Principat.* Band 25 (4. Teilband): *Religion* (Vorkonstantinisches Christentum: Leben un Umwelt Jesu; Neues Testament [Danonische Schriften und Apokryphen], Forts.), ed. W Haase. Berlin/New York: de Gruyter, 1987, 3247-79.

A comprehensive assessment of the issues that investigates textual evidence and possible deductions therefrom, possible reasons to account for the insertion of "Ephesus," early evidence for the knowledge of the letter, a discussion of the various collections of Paul's letters and how the letters were collected, and variations in the order of the letters in the collections. Believes that "Ephesus" was inserted as a rather late state in the collection of letters, when they were collected in codex form. Offers several plausible reasons why the name "Ephesus" rather than other locations was inserted.

1290. Black, D. A. "The Peculiarities of Ephesians and the Ephesian address." *GTJ* 2/1 (1981) 59-73.

The study argues against the typical explanation of the encyclical nature of the Ephesian letter. A direct Ephesian address could also account for the features often employed (viz., the lack of personal greetings or the statements in Eph 1:15; 3:2; and 4:21) to argue that Ephesians was addressed to a wide area. Black evaluates early scribal habits and the theme of the letter, and concludes (in keeping with early tradition and textual history) that the Ephesian address should be retained.

1291. Bowman, J. W. "The Epistle to the Ephesians." *Int* 8 (1954) 188-205.

Presents five themes from this epistle written by Paul: the

undergirding of intercessory prayer; the hymn of salvation; the old and new person in Christ, the forces of darkness, and ethical resurrection; the administration, education, and evangelistic program of the Church; and the Christian family and the universal church.

1292. Case, S. J. "To Whom was 'Ephesians' Written?" *Biblical World* 38 (1911) 315-20.

Agrees with Marcion that the epistle referred to as "Ephesians" was a letter to the Laodiceans because it is true to the earliest external evidence available, it accounts for the textual history of Eph 1:1, it recognizes the personal element in the letter, it provides a reason for the close resemblances between Eph and Col, and it removes one of the strongest arguments against Paul as author. Argues that the name was changed because Laodicea fell into bad repute.

1293. Chadwick, H. "Die Absicht des Epheserbriefes." *ZNW* 51 (1960) 145-53.

Suggests a possible scenario for the origin of Ephesians. Its author wanted to stress the metaphysical dimensions of the church, particularly its universality as the center of unity for all races in Christ. Though Paul's mission concentrated on Gentiles, the church should not lose sight of its Judean roots and the continuity between the first church at Jerusalem consisting of Jewish Christians and the Gentile-dominated church developing throughout the Roman empire. The church's mission to the world has replaced Paul's expectation of an imminent parousia.

1294. Curran, J. T. "Tradition and the Roman Origin of the Captivity Letters." *TS* 6 (1945) 163-205.

Inquires among the leading Greek and Latin exegetes (fourth to fifth centuries) the character of the traditional interpretation that locates the prison epistles in Paul's first Roman captivity. He concludes there is no clear-cut consensus of tradition locating these letters in Paul's imprisonment in Rome. That is, the early writers do not appeal to tradition to support their views of the Roman origins for the letters. If they argue the case, it is on internal or other grounds.

At the same time Curran admits the possibility that a early tradition did exist, but it must have been vague and indefinite in detail, though he sees no reason to insist on such a possibility.

1295. Dacquino, P. "I destinatari della lettera agli Efesini." *RivB* 6 (1958) 102-110.

1296. Dahl, N. A. "Gentiles, Christians, and Israelites in the Epistle to the Ephesians." *HTR* 79 (1986) 31-39.

Ephesians seems to represent a negative attitude toward non-Christian Gentiles, but it really demonstrates the rich grace and immense power of God. It calls for a clean break with the pagan past. The Israelites appear as heirs of the promise from whom the Gentiles were once separated but with whom Gentiles have been united in Christ. Paul had keen interest in the Jewish roots and origin of the church but failed to show any concern for the relationship of his audience to contemporary Jews. No reference to specific times, places, persons, or events.

1297. Davies, W. D. *Paul and Rabbinic Judaism.* 4th ed. New York: Harper and Row, 1948, 1955, 1970, 1980.

Attempts to set various pivotal aspects of Paul's career against the background of the rabbinic Judaism of his time. Contends that Paul baptized his rabbinic heritage into Christ believing that only this view does justice to Paul as a Pharisee who became a Christian. Puts Ephesians within the purview of Paul's career. The fourth edition adds an essay "Paul and Judaism Since Schweitzer" and an extensive preface to bring the discussion of the state of Pauline studies up to date as of 1980, including the recognition of views of authorship.

1298. Dickey, S. "Some Economic and Social Conditions of Asia Minor Affecting the Expansion of Christianity." In *Studies in Early Christianity,* ed. S. J. Case. New York: Century, 1928, 393-416.

1299. Duncan, G. S. *St. Paul's Ephesian Ministry. A Reconstruction with Special Reference to the Ephesian Origin of the Imprisonment*

Epistles. London: Hodder & Stoughton, 1929; New York: Charles Scribner's Sons, 1930.

Argues that Paul was imprisoned following about two years of ministry at Ephesus during which time he wrote Philippians. About a year later, on parole after the Demetrius riot, Paul wrote Col, Phlm, and Ephesians.

1300. Elliger, W. *Ephesos: Geschichte einer antiken Weltstadt.* Stuttgart: Kohlhammer, 1985.

A literary and archaeological study of the city of Ephesus since its founding c. 1000 B.C.E. up to the Byzantine period. In the chapter on early Christian Ephesus, the author discusses the material in Acts and Paul's letters.

1301. Elliott, J. H. *A Home for the Homeless.* Philadelphia: Fortress, 1981, 59-100.

Generalizations applied from 1 Peter. Christianity offered a way of coping with hardships. It was sectarian because it emerged out of protest, rejected the view of reality that the establishment claimed, it was egalitarian, it offered love and acceptance within a community, it was a voluntary organization, it demanded total commitment, and it was apocalyptic in nature. Addresses geographical locations, ethnic compositions, religious identity, interaction with non-Christians, as well as legal, economic, and social status.

1302. Faust, E. *Pax Christi et pax Caesaris. Religionsgeschichtliche, traditionsgeschichtliche und sozialgeschichtliche Studien zum Epheserbrief.* Freiburg, Schweiz, and Göttingen: Vandenhoeck & Ruprecht, 1993.

Originally the author's doctoral thesis submitted to the University of Heidelberg, 1992.

1303. Filson, F. V. "Ephesus and the New Testament," *The Biblical Archaeologist,* Reader 2, ed. D. N. Freedman and E. F. Campbell, Jr. Garden City, NY: Anchor Books, 1964,

343-352.

Ephesus' wealth stemmed from many sources. Its sea and land trade was the steady source. Other income came from the large territory the city owned, but its most prestigious revenue came from the cult of Artemis, her temple, and trade in cultic souvenirs. Worship concerned fertility in flocks and the human family. Josephus tells of many decrees safeguarding the rights of Jews to practice their ancestral religion in Ephesus. Protection came from both Roman officials and the Ephesians in the first century B.C. Also, compares sources of words in Acts 19 with inscriptions found in Ephesus and Egyptian papyri for their contribution to NT interpretation.

1304. Fischer, K. M. *Tendenz und Absicht des Epheserbriefes.* Göttingen: Vandenhoeck & Ruprecht, 1973.

See on texts, 1:3-14 (# 316).

1305. Gnilka, J. "Identity-crisis of the Ephesians' church." *TDig* 20 (1972) 35-39.

Believes Ephesians was written by a school of Paul's disciples that presents its views of the universality of the Church (the church grows conscious of her responsibility toward the world by coming before it as a unified, integrated unity), its apostolic legacy (the apostles determined the group plan of the living edifice but in their place stand other people with other functions), and its structures which include the relationship between carism and office.

1306. _____. "Das Akkulturationsproblem nach dem Epheser- und Kolosserbrief." In *Fede e cultura alla luce della Biblia.* Urin: Editrice Elle Di Ci, 1981, 235-47.

On the problem of acculturation in Col and Eph.

1307. Godet, F. "The Epistle to the Gentile Churches." *Exp,* 3d series, 5 (1887) 376-91.

1308. Hemer, C. J. *The Letters to the Seven Churches of Asia in their*

Local Setting. Sheffield: JSOT, 1986.

Superb study of the seven churches according to the order in Rev 2-3. Much helpful historical and cultural data for the entire region, particularly if Ephesians was an encyclical to the churches in that same region.

1309. Hendrix, H. "On the Form and Ethos of Ephesians." *Union Seminary Quarterly Review* 42/4 (1988) 3-15.

Includes a section on literary structure: though the form appears to be in the genre of epistle, its form actually follows the general conventions of honorific decrees in which the author recites the universal benefactions of God and Christ.

1310. Johnson, S. E. "Asia Minor and Early Christianity." In *Christianity, Judaism, and Other Greco-Roman Cults,* Part 2, ed. J. Neusner. Leiden: Brill, 1975, 77-145.

Views Asia Minor as a unit with cultural individuality, the major influences coming from Palestine and Syria. Archaeology, Christian literature, and Gnosticism receive stress. The author of Ephesians was steeped in Paul's thought with traces of thinking and language of Qumran literature. The Pastorals build on the foundation laid by Ephesians.

1311. _____. "Early Christianity in Asia Minor." *JBL* 77 (1958) 1-19.

Overview of archaeological finds and literary figures and writings (including accounts of crucifixions) in Asia Minor from the late 1800s on. Art of the region may have been viewed as idolatry rather than beauty.

1312. _____. "Unsolved Questions about Early Christianity in Anatolia." In *Studies in New Testament and Early Christian Literature,* ed. D. E. Aune. Leiden: Brill, 1972, 181-93.

Pursues the fragmentary knowledge of the Christian movements in the early period, surmising that Gentile Christianity was more open to outside influence than Judaism. The principal interest of Anatolian "orthodoxy" was salvation through the cross and resurrection, as well as through faith, baptism, the Eucharist, and obedience. Women in the Jewish communities of Western Asia Minor were prominent as they took important positions in cults and civil life.

1313. Jones, A. H. M. *The Cities of the Eastern Roman Provinces*. 2d ed. Oxford: Clarendon, 1971, 28-94.

An extensive overview of the majority of Asian cities. Ephesus in Lydia was settled by the Greek Ionians. On the Ionian coast, cities were typically larger than in other areas with fewer, smaller communities in between. Inland, Ephesus owned a great portion of the lower Cayster valley (first century B.C.E.). It is not known how Ephesus absorbed its smaller neighbors to build up its enormous territories.

1314. Käsemann, E. "Ephesians and Acts." In *Studies in Luke-Acts*. FS P. Schubert, ed. L. E. Keck and J. L. Martyn. London: SPCK, 1968, 288-97.

See above on "Hymns" (# 1103).

1315. _____. "Paulus und der Fruhkatholizismus." *ZTK* 60 (1963) 75-89.

Finds a contrast between Paul's theology and that of "early catholicism" as represented in Ephesians, Luke, and the Pastorals. These books began to view the church as an enduring institution following the decrease in the expectation of an imminent parousia. *Heilsgeschichte* came to replace an apocalyptic world view. Though Paul wrote only little about the church—the body of Christ served a paraenetic function—in Ephesians we find the beginning of a doctrine of the church.

1316. Koester, H. *Introduction to the New Testament*. Vol. 2. Philadelphia: Fortress, 1982, 241-347.

This chapter considers the transformation of Pauline theology into ecclesiastical doctrine. Accounts for the emergence of Ephesians as a response due to the struggle against Gnosticism.

1317. _____. "The Origin and Nature of Diversification in the History of Early Christianity." *HTR* 58 (1965) 279-318.

Christian groups later labelled "heretical" dominated the first two or three centuries A.D. Raises the problem of the historical Jesus. Discusses the Thomas tradition and its influences on early Christianity. Paul opened the door to competing groups of Christian missionaries in the countries around the Aegean Sea who challenged the religious inheritance of Judaism.

1318. Ladeuze, P. "Les déstinataires de l'épître aux Éphésiens." *RV* 11 (1902) 573-80.

1319. Lightfoot, J. B. "The Destination of the Epistle to the Ephesians." In *Biblical Essays*. London: Macmillan, 1893, 375-96.

Refers to early Church Fathers for omission of the words "to Ephesus." Paul spent almost three years at Ephesus. No significant historical information cited.

1320. Lindemann, A. *Paulus im ältesten Christentum*. Tübingen: Mohr, 1979.

Investigates the image of Paul that is presented in early Christian writings, and how his theology came to be reworked in early Christianity.

1321. _____. "Bemerkungen zu den Adressaten und zum Anlass des Epheserbriefes." *ZNW* 67 (1976) 235-51.

Believes that the words "in Ephesus" in Eph 1:1 represent the oldest reading which were omitted by later scribes who knew that Paul did not write to the Ephesians. The letter is properly a catholic letter, though 6:10ff. hint at a situation of persecution—probably right before A.D. 100. Pseudonymity hoped to gain apostolic authority to support a new theological emphasis on the church gained by synthesizing both Pauline and Gnostic ideas.

1322. Lona, H. E. *Die Eschatologie im Kolosser- und Epheserbrief.*
      Forschung zur Bibel 48. Würzburg: Echter Verlag, 1984, 428-
      48.

      Abbreviated and revised version of a Habilitationsschrift at the
      Catholic theological faculty at Wurzburg; investigates the eschatology
      of selected passages in the two epistles under two headings: the time
      and place of salvation, and eschatology and situation.

1323. MacDonald, M. Y. *The Pauline Churches. A Socio-historical Study
      of Institutionalization in the Pauline and Deutero-Pauline
      Writings.* SNTSMS 60. Cambridge/New York: Cambridge
      Univ. Press, 1988.

      Pursues the process by which the early church became institutional-
      ized into its more tightly organized form of the 2d century. The
      Deutero-canonical letters Col and Eph occur at the second stage of
      community-stabilizing, and prior to the final stage represented by the
      Pastorals—community-protecting.

1324. Magie, D. *Roman Rule in Asia Minor to the End of the Third
      Century after Christ.* 2 vols. Princeton, NJ: Princeton
      University Press, 1950. [Repr. New York: Arno, 1975.]

      An extensive account of the Romans and their influence in Asia
      Minor, and in particular, Ephesus, to the end of the third century C.E.

1325. Martin, R. P. "An Epistle in Search of a Life-Setting." *ExpT* 79
      (1968) 296-302.

      The textual uncertainty of Eph 1:1 does not mean the letter was
      circular nor that it was blank at this point (no precedence for this).
      Ephesians was written after Paul's death as a mosaic of Pauline
      material following the publication of Acts when there was renewed
      interest in Paul. Argues that Luke was the author because of the use
      of verbs, because twenty-five words are found in Luke-Acts only and
      not in the Pauline material, the link between Acts 20:17-38 and Eph
      1, the parallel ecclesiology, and because only in these documents is
      there a distinction drawn between the ascension and the gift of the

Spirit versus the events of Easter. The purpose of Luke and Ephesians is the same—the nature of the Church and the idea that their Jewish heritage should not be disowned.

1326. Meade, D. G. *Pseudonymity and Canon.* Tübingen: Mohr, 1986, 142-48.

Sees Ephesians as a circular letter, occasional in nature, that shows great interest in Judaism and the supplanting of Jewish Christians by Gentiles. Finds evidence that the community is rife with problems of division and aberrant behavior, and thus the epistle emphasizes unity. One problem stems from false teaching, possibly Gnosticism. The letter was written to counter syncretism, individualism, and the ahistorical influences of popular Hellenistic religions.

1327. Meeks, W. A. *The First Urban Christians.* New Haven: Yale University Press, 1983, 42-45.

In a discussion of the cities of Paul considers Ephesus, the governmental center of the province of Asia.

1328. Meeks, W. A. "In One Body: The Unity of Humankind in Colossians and Ephesians." In *God's Christ and His People,* ed. J. Jervell and W. A. Meeks. Oslo: Universitetsforlaget, 1977, 209-21.

The Haustafel occupies a prominent place in the paraenesis of Eph 5:22-6:9. Major focus is on baptism and unity in Colossians.

1329. Meinardus, O. F. A. *St. John of Patmos and the Seven Churches of the Apocalypse.* Athens: Lycabettus, 1974.

Ephesians is the first of the seven churches addressed in Revelation. The beginnings of Christianity of Ephesus are shrouded in mystery, but it was established by the middle of the first century. The state threatened the church from the outside and heresies undermined its stability and unity from the inside. Imperial worship was practiced as well as the worship of Artemis (Cybele). Recounts the history of Christianity in the first centuries after Paul and explains the major

Christian ruins.

1330.   Miltner, F. *Ephesos: Stadt der Artemis und des Johannes.* Vienna:
        Franz Deuticke, 1958.

1331.   Moffatt, J. "The Problem of Ephesians." *Exp,* 8th series, 2 (1911)
        193-200.

        Paul was not the author of Ephesians; it was sub-Pauline. Disagrees
        that the letter was first associated with Laodicea (in opposition to
        Harnack; see on Texts, 1:1-2, # 272).

1332.   Norris, F. W.   "Asia Minor before Ignatius: Walter Bauer
        Reconsidered." *StEv* 7, ed. E. A. Livingstone. *TU* 126.
        Berlin: Akademie-Verlag, 1982, 365-77.

        Takes issue with Bauer's contention (see # 1285) that Ephesus was
        not a center of orthodoxy, i.e., not a large city in which "orthodoxy"
        was influential.

1333.   Oster, R. E. *A Bibliography of Ancient Ephesus.* Metuchen, NJ:
        ATLA and Scarecrow, 1987.

        A list of 1535 sources covering the ancient history, culture, and
        archaeological evidence of Ephesus.

1334.   Parvis, M. M. "Ephesus in the Early Christian Era." In *The Biblical
        Archaeologist Reader,* 2, ed. D. N. Freedman and E. F.
        Campbell, Jr.   Garden City, NY: Anchor Books, 1964,
        331-343.

        One of the greatest cities in Asia, Ephesus had a municipal
        government, its own acropolis, struck its own coins, and divided its
        population into tribes. It also had intimate connections with Egypt
        as a station for the Egyptian fleet and as a recruiting center for
        Egyptian mercenary soldiers. Between A.D. 138-161 Jews had a
        special quarter of the city allotted to them. The article presents an
        archaeological investigation of the temple of Artemis, one of the
        seven wonders of the ancient world.

1335. Percy, E. "Zu den Problemen des Kolosser- und Epheserbriefes." *ZNW* 43 (1950-51) 178-94.

See above, "Relation to Col et al." (# 1092).

1336. Ramsay, W. M. *The Historical Geography of Asia Minor.* Repr. Amsterdam: A. M. Hakkert, 1962.

A study of the various cities and roads, especially of the Roman era, of Asia Minor.

1337. _____. *The Social Basis of Roman Power in Asia Minor.* Repr. Amsterdam: A. M. Hakkert, 1967.

1338. _____. *The Letters to the Seven Churches of Asia.* London: Hodder & Stoughton, 1904. [Repr. Grand Rapids: Baker, 1985.]

Classic study of these cities to which the letters of Rev 2-3 are penned. Stress on archaeological data—of course, more refined in recent years. The discussion of the city of Ephesus and the letter in Revelation occurs on pp. 210-250.

1339. Roberts, J. H. "The enigma of Ephesians: Rethinking some positions on the basis of Schnackenburg and Arnold." *Neot* 27/1 (1993) 93-106.

Noting the new insights offered in Schnackenburg's commentary (# 201-202) and Arnold's, *Ephesians: Power and Magic* (# 687), evaluates their contributions to the understanding of the background and theology of the letter.

1340. Robinson, T. A. *The Bauer Thesis Examined: The Geography of Heresy in the Early Christian Church.* New York: Edwin Mellen Press, 1988, 93-205.

Provides a history of the debate concerning the theological uniformity of early Christianity and the geographical presence of theological diversity. Views Ephesus as a leading center of early Christianity, contrary to Bauer (see # 1285; cf. # 1332), finding grave problems in Bauer's hypotheses. All Bauer has succeeded in doing is showing how certain we are about the true nature of early Christianity in particular areas.

1341. Rogers, C. L. "The Dionysian Background of Ephesians 5:18." *BSac* 136 (1979) 249-57.

The article finds that the worship of Dionysus the wine god provides the general cultural background for the command in Eph 5:18. An analysis of the Dionysian cult and its practices forms the basis of this conclusion. Thus Paul contrasts being under the control of Dionysus—which promised union with the god and the release from problems—with yielding to the control of the Spirit of the true and living God.

1342. Sanders, E. P. *Paul and Palestinian Judaism.* London: SCM, 1977.

The ground-breaking study of the nature of Rabbinic religion, especially as it relates to Paul, that has opened the way for an entirely new perspective on the Law and the Jews' relation to it. For an important critique see, inter alia, S. Westerholm, *Israel's Law and the Church's Faith: Paul and His Recent Interpreters.* Grand Rapids: Eerdmans, 1988.

1343. Schenk, W. "Zur Entstehung und zum Verständnis der Adresse des Epheserbriefes." In *Theologische Versuche*, 6, ed. J. Rogge. Berlin: Evangelische Verlagsanstalt, 1975, 73-78.

1344. Schnackenburg, R. "Der Epheserbrief im heutigen Horizont." In *Massstab des Glaubens.* Freiburg: Herder, 1978, 155-75.

Ephesians in the present-day horizon of the church.

1345. Shearer, W. C. "To Whom Was the So-called Epistle to the Ephesians Actually Addressed?" *ExpT* 4 (1892-93) 129.

1346. Smith, D. C. "The Ephesian Heresy." In *Society of Biblical Literature: 1974 Proceedings,* ed. F. Francis. Missoula:

Scholars Press, 1974, 45-54.

1347. _____. "The Ephesian Heresy and the Origin of the Epistle to the Ephesians." *Ohio Journal of Religious Studies* 5 (1977) 78-103.

A heresy of Gentile-"Jewish"-Christians elicited this response from the author of Ephesians. Thus, the letter grows out of a specific historical situation to which the author responds, not by directly attacking their heretical views, but by reinterpreting their teachings with his own characteristic theological slant.

1348. Vanhoye, A. "Épître aux Éphésiens et l'épître aux Hebreus." *Bib* 59/2 (1978).

Providing first a statistical analysis of the correlations between the vocabulary of Ephesians and Hebrews, the study manifests certain relations (above all, Christological), though no direct connection. These relations indicate that both epistles were written in the same apostolic environment, at about the same time, though Ephesians preceded Hebrews.

1349. Weiss, H. F. "Gnostische Motive und antignostische Polemik im Kolosser- und im Epheserbrief." In *Gnosis und Neues Testament,* ed. K. Tröger. Berlin: Evangelische Verlagsanstalt, 1973, 311-24.

See under "Gnosticism" above (# 1156).

1350. Wink, W. *Naming the Powers.* Philadelphia: Fortress, 1984.

Seeks to understand the concept and terminology of power and "the powers" in the NT. Within the course of the study considers these texts in Ephesians: 1:20-23; 2:1-2; 3:10; and 6:12.

1351. Yamauchi, E. *The Archaeology of New Testament Cities in Western Asia Minor.* Grand Rapids: Baker, 1980.

Studies the history and monuments of twelve cities of the early Roman empire, including Ephesus.

1352. Yates, R. "Principalities and Powers in Ephesians." *New Blackfriars*
       58 (1977) 516-21.

       Principalities and powers symbolize those elements of the creation
       that are "out of control" and which threaten people's lives. Though
       the powers now account for spiritual warfare, Christ has gained
       control over them and will enable his people to be victorious.

SLAVERY

For sources specifically on slavery reflected in Eph, see also on texts,
6:1-9.

1353. Bartchy, S. S. ΜΑΛΛΟΝ ΧΡΗΣΑΙ: *First-Century Slavery and the
       Interpretation of I Corinthians 7:21.* Missoula, MT: Society
       of Biblical Literature, 1973.

       Includes an excursus on "Biblical Scholarship and Slavery in the
       Ancient World," pp. 29-36. Provides other background study on
       slavery in first century Greece.

1354. Buckland, W. W. *The Roman Law of Slavery.* Cambridge:
       Cambridge University Press, 1970.

1355. Finley, M. I., ed. *Slavery in Classical Antiquity.* Cambridge: Heffer,
       1960.

1356. Gayer, R. *Die Stellung des Sklaven in den paulinischen Gemeinden
       und bei Paulus.* Bern: H. Lang, 1976.

       In preparation for the study of slavery and the status of slaves in the
       Pauline communities and letters, assesses citations about slavery in
       philosophers and poets and the religious environment of the early
       stages of the development of Christianity. Pauline texts center on
       Gal, 1 Cor, and Phlm.

1357. Gülzow, H. *Christentum und Sklaverei in den ersten drei Jahrhunderten.* Bonn: R. Habelt, 1969.

1358. Laub, F. *Die Begegnung des frühen Christentums mit der antiken Sklaverei.* Stuttgart: Katholisches Bibelwerk, 1982.

Begins with comments on the institution of slavery in antiquity and proceeds to chapters on various issues: its place in the context of the household, in early Christian house churches, in Pauline communities, in mission and community in view of the *Haustafel* tradition, and an understanding of how the early church developed its attitude toward slavery.

1359. Schweizer, E. "Zum Sklavenproblem im Neuen Testament." *EvT* 32 (1972) 502-6.

Especially a comment on Paul's view of slavery and securing one's freedom as reflected in 1 Cor 7:21-24. As with Phlm, Paul does not demand freedom for slaves; Christian freedom requires that people act from their own hearts and from true faith.

1360. Stuhlmacher, P. *Der Brief an Philemon.* Zurich: Benzinger, 1975.

This commentary on this brief letter provides helpful background on the institution of slavery in the ancient world, esp. 42-48. Provides an excursus on early Christian house churches, pp. 70-75.

1361. Urbach, E. E. "The Laws Regarding Slavery as a Source for Social History of the Period of the Second Temple, the Mishnah and Talmud." *Papers of the Institute of Jewish Studies* (London), ed. J. G. Weiss. Jerusalem, 1964, 1:1-94.

1362. Vogt, J. "The Structure of Ancient Slave Wars." In *Ancient Slavery and the Ideal of Man.* Tr. T. Wiedemann. Cambridge, MA: Harvard, 1975.

Comprehensive study of the various aspects of the institution of slavery among the ancient Greeks. Includes a history of the research on ancient slavery.

1363. Westermann, W. L. *The Slave Systems of Greek and Roman Antiquity.* 3d. ed. Philadelphia: American Philosophical Society, 1964.

1364. Wiedemann, T. *Greek and Roman Slavery.* London: Croom Helm; Baltimore: Johns Hopkins University Press, 1981.

Translates selected texts and inscriptions from ancient Greek and Roman writers that provide key insights into the institution of slavery. Categorizes the citations and provides brief introductions and analyses. Categories include: the slave as property, debt-bondage, manumission, moral status, status symbol or economic investment, sources of slaves, domestic versus rural slaves, state-owned slaves, cruelty, exploitation, and protection, resistance, rebellion, and true freedom: stoics and Christians.

1365. Zeitlin, S. "Slavery during the Second Commonwealth and the Tannaitic Period." *JQR* 53 (1962-63) 185-218.

An examination of slavery and slave law in the first centuries C.E. with references to Josephus, rabbinic, and OT literature. Jewish sages in this period did not condemn the institution itself, but tried to improve slaves' status. Cautions against using later amoraic (third-fifth centuries C.E.) sources to qualify slavery in the Second Commonwealth, deviating methodologically from prior commentators.

HOUSEHOLD CODES

1366. Balch, D. L. *Let Wives Be Submissive: The Domestic Code in I Peter.* Chico, CA: Scholars Press, 1981.

On the code as found in 1 Peter.

1367. _____. "Household Codes." In *Greco-Roman Literature and the New Testament,* ed. D. E. Aune. Atlanta, GA: Scholars Press, 1988, 25-50.

Enlarges on findings of the previous study including data from this larger corpus of literature.

1368. Berger, K. *Formgeschichte des Neuen Testaments.* Heidelberg: Quelle & Meyer, 1984.

In this comprehensive analysis of form criticism and the variety of "forms" in the NT, includes a short section on the household codes, pp. 135-41.

1369. Cannon, G. E. *The Use of Traditional Materials in Colossians.* Macon, GA: Mercer University Press, 1983.

Traces the variety of sources, traditions, behind parts of Col. In chapter 4, the author addresses the topic of the Household Code, pp. 95-131, though, of course, applied directly to the code found in Col 3:8-4:1. There is a comparison of the *Haustafel* in Col 3, Eph 5, and 1 Pet 3. The study extends to the Pastoral Epistles and early Christian non-canonical literature and takes up the question of the source of the *Haustafel.*

1370. Crouch, J. E. *The Origin and Intention of the Colossian Haustafel.* Göttingen: Vandenhoeck & Ruprecht, 1972.

A study of the phenomenon of the *Haustafel* in the ancient world. First sets out the scope of the issue—what is the *Haustafel*: paraenetic unit, Hellenistic code, Jewish code, or specifically Christian code. Studies the Stoic list of duties in the Roman world and proceeds to seek the sources for the Colossian code. Concludes with judgments about the origin and purpose of the Christian *Haustafel.* Provides an extensive bibliography.

1371. Easton, B. S. "New Testament Ethical Lists." *JBL* 5 (1932) 1-12.

1372. Elliott, J. H. *A Home for the Homeless.* Philadelphia: Fortress, 1981.

Subtitled, "A Sociological Exegesis of 1 Peter, Its Situation and

Strategy," the study includes a chapter on the topic of the household, pp. 165-266. Much excellent material, though, of course, devoted specifically to 1 Peter.

1373.   Fiedler, P.   "Haustafel."   *RAC* 13 (1986) 1063-73.

1374.   Gärtner, M.   "Die Haustafeln des Kolosser- und des Epheserbriefes" and "Haustafeln."   In *Die Familienerziehung in der alten Kirche.*   Cologne: Böhlau, 1985, 32-38, 54-63.

See on texts, 6:1-9 (# 976).

1375.   Gielen, M.   *Tradition und Theologie neutestamentlicher Haustafelethik. Ein Beitrag zur Frage einer christlichen Auseinandersetzung mit gesellschaftlichen Normen.*   Athenaums Monografien, Theologie: Bonner biblische Beitrage 75. Frankfurt: Hain, 1990.

Evaluates the tradition and theology of the household codes in light of various scholarly approaches.   Considers their sociological background in terms of the ancient household and the Pauline mission.   Concludes that the household codes resulted from the church's encounter with the ethical norms of the larger society.   Four excurses end the study: one that considers *kephale* and *soma* in Ephesians.

1376.   Gnilka, J.   "Paränetische Traditionen im Epheserbrief."   In *Mélanges bibliques,* FS B. Rigaux, ed. A. Descamps and A. de Halleux. Gembloux: Duculot, 1970.

See pp. 397-410, especially, 407-10.

1377.   _____.   *Der Kolosserbrief.*   Freiburg: Herder, 1980, 205-16.

On the Household Code in Col.

1378.   Goppelt, L.   "Jesus und die 'Haustafel'-Tradition."   In *Orientierung an Jesus.* FS J. Schmid, ed. P. Hoffmann.   Freiburg: Herder, 1973, 93-106.

1379. Grielen, M. *Tradition und Theologie neutestamentlicher Haustafelethik: ein Beitrag zur Frage einer christlichen Auseinandersetzung mit gesellschaftlichen Normen.* Frankfurt am Main: Hain, 1990.

1380. Hartman, L. "Code and Context: A Few Reflections on the Paraenesis of Col 3:6-4:1." In *Tradition and Interpretation in the New Testament.* FS E. Earle Ellis, ed G. F. Hawthorne and 0. Betz. Grand Rapids: Eerdmans, 1987, 237-47.

Seeks to find the possible source and the function that the household code plays in Col.

1381. Herzog, W. R. "The 'Household Duties' Passages: Apostolic traditions and contemporary concerns." *Foundations* 24 (1981) 204-15.

An examination of Col 3:18 - 4:1 and Eph 5:21 - 6:9 based on P. Berger's and T. Lackman's three-stage model of socialization in *The Social Construction of Reality* (1966): primary (childhood), secondary (post-childhood), and resocialization (major events causing paradigm shifts). The resocialized community of the church sought new primary and secondary socialization through adapting existing Greek and Jewish responsibility lists. Insofar as the author (Paul?) was influenced by his own primary and secondary socialization, the codes are patriarchal; however, these texts evidence the struggle towards resocialization by affirming mutuality and creation intent, among other things. The true revelation of the codes may lie more in the struggle they evidence rather than in their explicit content.

1382. Hunter, A. M *Paul and His Predecessors.* 2d ed. Philadelphia: Westminster, 1961; London: SCM, 1962.

This study pursues some of the sources or "pre-Pauline" material found in Paul's letters. Has a brief section on "The Paraenetic Tradition," (pp. 52-57) and another on this topic in the appendix added to this revised edition (pp. 128-31).

1383. Kamlah, E. *Die Form der katalogischen Paränese im Neuen*

Testament. *WUNT* 7. Tübingen: Mohr-Siebeck, 1964.

Studies both the virtue and vice lists in the NT seeking to account for the dualism by tracing possible sources and parallels.

1384.	_____. "Ὑποτάσσεσθαι in den neutestamentlichen Haustafeln." In *Verborum Veritas.* FS G. Stählin, ed. O. Böcher and K. Haacker. Wuppertal: Brockhaus, 1970, 237-43.

A study of how the concept of "submission" fits into the various household code lists in the NT. See on texts, 5:21-33, # 919.

1385.	Lillie, W. "The Pauline House-Tables." *ExpT* 86 (1975) 179-83.

Distinguishes the "house-tables" both from other similar NT paraenetic tradition (e.g., Rom 13:1-7) and Stoic teaching, thus questioning the maxim that the early church simply adopted this ancient form. Speculates on the situations that may account for the inclusion of housetables in apostolic epistles and concludes with five reflections on what these texts teach the contemporary study of Christian ethics.

1386.	Lips, H. von.	"Die Haustafel als 'Topos' im Rahmen der urchristlichen Paränese.	Beobachtungen anhand des 1. Petrusbriefes und des Titusbriefes." *NTS* 40 (1994) 261-80.

Examines the household codes in 1 Pet and Titus in comparison to those in Col and Eph. Concludes that the codes had a fixed place in Christian paraenesis that portrays a topos including a variety of aspects of life (community, household, and public life). Nevertheless the common features in the various codes do not qualify the code to be considered a *Gattung*.

1387.	Lohse, E. *Colossians and Philemon.* Philadelphia: Fortress, 1971.

Devotes a few pages to "Rules for the Household," (pp. 154-57).

1388.	Lührmann, D.	"Neutestamentliche Haustafeln und antike Ökonomie." *NTS* 27 (1980) 83-97.

Attempts to understand the NT household codes by a study of treatises on the "economy" in various Hellenistic writers. *Oikos/oikia* (house/household) is a socio-economic concept growing out of circumstances in the Greek *polis* (city). Follows a trajectory from early Christianity to the *oikos* in Col and Eph eventually to its complex structure in the Pastorals.

1389. MacDonald, M. Y. *The Pauline Churches.* Cambridge: Cambridge University Press, 1988.

The second part of this study is entitled, "Colossians and Ephesians: Community-Stabilizing Institutionalization" and includes several sections devoted to the household codes (pp. 102-22). Concludes that for Ephesians the code guided how authority should be distributed within the community and served to stabilize relations with outsiders.

1390. Maillet, H. "Alla-plen: metaphore et pedagogie de al soumission dans les rapports conjugaux, familiaux, sociaux et autres selon Éphésiens 5:21 - 6:9." *ETR* 55 (1980) 566-75.

1391. Martin, R. P. "Haustafeln." *NIDNTT* 3 (1975) 928-32.

Concise article that sets out the essential elements for understanding the use of the household codes in the ancient world and the NT. Defines the term, discusses virtues and vices, and considers the meaning and background of house-tables.

1392. Motyer, S. "The Relationship between Paul's Gospel of 'All One in Christ Jesus' (Galatians 3:28) and the 'Household Codes.'" *Vox Evangelica* 19 (1989) 33-48.

Cataloguing prior attempts to understand the call for wives' submission, the author seeks a solution in the tensions between the "already" and the "not yet." Creation, transformed in Christ will ultimately be overthrown in the eschaton.

1393. Müller, K.-H "Die Haustafel des Kolosserbriefes und das antike Frauenthema: Eine kritische Rückschau auf alte Ergebnisse."

In *Die Frau im Urchristentum,* ed. G. Dautzenberg et al.
Freiburg: Herder, 1983, 263-319.

In a larger work devoted to various topics about women in antiquity,
Müller discusses women in the ancient world and, specifically, the
household code in Col.

1394. Nash, R. S.   "The Role of the Haustafeln in Colossians and
Ephesians."   Ph.D. thesis, Southern Baptist Theological
Seminary, 1982.

1395. Rengstorf, K. H.   "Die neutestamentlichen Mahnungen an die Frau,
sich dem Manne unterzuordnen."   In *Verborum Dei: Manet in
Aeternum.*   FS 0. Schmitz, ed. W. Foerster.   Witten: Luther
Verlag, 1953, 131-45.

A study of the teaching of the NT concerning a wife's submission to
her husband, especially as found in 1 Cor 14:34; Eph 5:22ff.; Col
3:18; Tit 2:5; and 1 Pet 3:1ff. with special focus on the meaning of
ὑποτάσσεσθαι (submit, be subject).   Considers the wife's
submission as part of the "household codes" of the ancient world and
in the early Christian οἶκος (household).

1396. Sampley, J. P.   *"And the Two Shall Become One Flesh."*
Cambridge: Cambridge University Press, 1971, 17-30.

Attempts to establish the form, content, and extent of the *Haustafel*
in Eph 5:21-33 by providing a general analysis of the form as it
appears in the NT, comparing the *Haustafel* in Col and Eph, and
observing the Ephesian *Haustafel* against other NT occurrences.

1397. Schrage, W. "Zur Ethik der neutestamentlichen Haustafeln." *NTS*
21 (1975) 1-22.

Contrary to various other attempts, finds the best source for the
household codes in the understanding of the redemptive work of
Jesus as Lord, but not confined merely to the religious or church
spheres.   The reality of Christ as Lord governs all of life—singularly,
the social and political spheres.

1398. Schroeder, D. "Die Haustafeln des Neuen Testaments." Dissertation, Hamburg, 1959.

Rejects the possibility of literary dependence of the various *Haustafeln* on each other. Rather, the close parallels suggest that prior to the epistles the early church employed this type of pattern for its moral instruction. They functioned in the church's moral teaching not its worship.

1399. Schweizer, E. "Die Weltlichkeit des Neuen Testaments: die Haustafeln." In *Beiträge zur alttestamentlichen Theologie.* FS W. Zimmerli, ed. H. Donner, R. Hanhart and R. Smend. Göttingen: Vandenhoeck & Ruprecht, 1977, 397-413.

A study of the household codes. In fact, the codes were *paganized* under the cloak of their Christianizing during the process of moving from the first generation of the apostles to the third when they were written in the epistles.

1400. _____. *The Letter to the Colossians.* London: SPCK, 1982.

On the household code in Col (pp. 213-220.).

1401. _____. "Traditional Ethical Patterns in the Pauline and Post-Pauline Letters and Their Development (lists of vices and house-tables)." In *Text and Interpretation.* FS M. Black, ed. E. Best and R. McL. Wilson. Cambridge: Cambridge University Press, 1979, 195-209.

Begins with a catalogue of nine vice lists, including Eph 4:17; 5:3-5. The second section considers "the House-Tables": their origin, the first list in Col 3:18-4:4, how they underwent further development including what we find in Eph 5:22-6:9, where paganizing goes hand in hand with Christianizing. Covers some of the same ground as the "Weltlichkeit" article (# 1399).

1402. Selwyn, E. G. *The First Epistle of St. Peter.* London: Macmillan, 1946.

On the household code in 1 Peter (pp. 419-39).

1403.   Strecker, G.   "Die neutestamentlichen Haustafeln (Kol 3, 18 - 4, 1
        und Eph 5, 22 - 6, 9)."   In *Neues Testament und Ethik.*   FS R.
        Schnackenburg, ed. H. Merklein.   Freiburg/Basel/Wien: Herder,
        1989, 349-75.

        A discussion of these two household codes.   Traces the history of
        research on the issue followed by an attempt to trace the history of
        the phenomenon of the codes.   Then proceeds to consider
        men/women (Col 3:18f.; Eph 5:22-33), children/father (Col 3:20f.;
        Eph 6:1-4), and slaves/masters (Col 3:22-25; 4:1; Eph 6:5-9).

1404.   Strobel, A.   "Der Begriff des 'Hauses' im griechischen und
        römischen Privatrecht."   *ZNW* 56 (1965) 91-100.

        Surveys recent discussions of the term "house" in the writings of K.
        Aland and J. Jeremias.   Finds in Greek and Roman civil law the
        phrase "N.N. and his house" and suggest that it informs NT usage.
        The meaning of the Greek *oikia* is narrower than *oikos;* whereas the
        latter included slaves and minor children, the former was restricted
        to those possessing legal rights.   Latin usage corresponded to the
        Greek.   Concludes that such house formulae cannot alone decide
        whether the early church baptized children.

1405.   Thraede, K.   "Zum historischen Hintergrund der 'Haustafeln' des
        Neuen Testaments."   In *Pietas.*   FS B. Kötting, ed. E.
        Dassmann.   Münster: Aschendorff, 1980, 359-68.

        Analysis of the historical background of the household codes found
        in the NT.

1406.   Verner, D. C.   *The Household of God: The Social World of the
        Pastoral Epistles.*   Chico, CA: Scholars Press, 1983.

        On the household codes in the Pastorals.   First considers prior study
        on both the *Haustafeln* and their presence in the Pastorals.   Then
        addresses the concept of "household" in the Hellenistic-Roman world
        before applying his energies to the codes in the Pastorals.

1407. Weidinger, K. *Die Haustafeln: Ein Stück urchristlicher Paränese.* Leipzig: J. C. Hinrichs, 1928.

1408. Wendland, H.-D. "Zur sozialethischen Bedeutung der neutestamentlichen Haustafeln." In *Botschaft an die soziale Welt.* Hamburg: Furche, 1959, 104-14.

1409. Wicker, K. O. "First Century Marriage Ethics: A Comparative Study of the Household Codes and Plutarch's Conjugal Precepts." In *No Famine in the Land. FS* J. L. McKenzie, ed. J. W. Flanagan and A. W. Robinson. Missoula, MT: Scholars Press, 1975, 141-53.

Examines the two bodies of texts in light of the ethos and social practices of marriage in the first century. Seeks to assess how they affirm, modify, or overturn current marriage practices.

1410. Yoder, J. *The Politics of Jesus.* Grand Rapids: Eerdmans, 1972.

Seeks to argue the philosophical and biblical case for what might be termed the "pacifist" position in the NT. The chapter on "Revolutionary Subordination" considers the Ephesian household code, among other texts (see pp. 163-92). This is an extremely perceptive and well-researched analysis of the overall phenomenon of the Household Codes. Makes much of Schroeder's study (# 1398).

Chapter 10

THOUGHT AND THEOLOGY

1402. Adai, J. *Der Heilige Geist als Gegenwart Gottes: in den einzelnen Christen, in der Kirche und in der Welt.* Frankfurt and New York: Peter Lang, 1985.

Originally the author's doctoral thesis presented to the University of Regensburg, 1983. The text is in German and Greek including the author's German translation of portions of Ephesians. Argues that Ephesians exhibits a Deutero-Pauline pneumatology developed in places in a Lucan direction. The study groups the findings into four headings: (1) the Ephesian author finds the Spirit more independent of Christ than Paul; (2) Ephesians sees the Spirit's coming more related to the dawning of the era of salvation (cf Acts) rather than, as does Paul, the mark of the eschaton; (3) Ephesians stresses the believer's renewal by the Spirit as a continual process, unlike Paul who stresses believers' participation in Christ; and (4) Ephesians presents the universal church as a pneumatic institution with various office-holders (cf. Acts), not Paul's view of the local church as a charismatic community.

1403. Allen, T. G. "Exaltation and Solidarity with Christ: Ephesians 1:20 and 2:6." *JSNT* (28) (1986) 103-20.

The parallel between Christ's exaltation (1:20) and that of believers (2:6) informs other epistolary images (e.g., building and bride) conveying the unity that exists between Christ and his elect. Gives five points clarifying the nature of the believer's exaltation uniquely captured in Ephesians as a past event. Reviews various explanations of the historical and religious background of the inclusive nature of Christ's exaltation and proposes the Semitic understanding of "corporate personality" as the proper one. Developed from the author's 1982 Glasgow dissertation, "The Body of Christ Concept in Ephesians."

1404. Arnold, C. E. *Ephesians: Power and Magic.* Cambridge: Cambridge University Press, 1989, 12-60.

In this study of the concept of power as related to Ephesians, the author discusses the religious climate of western Asia Minor in the first century C.E. (pp. 5-40). The study leads to a set of six conclusions about Paul's response to "power" problems in and around Ephesus: the superiority of God's power and the supremacy of Christ; the believer's access to God's power; a new means of access to divine power; a new perspective on the "powers"; a new posture toward the "powers"; and a new purpose for divine power.

1405. Arthur, K. *Lord, Is It Warfare? Teach Me to Stand.* Portland, OR: Multnomah, 1991.

1406. Baker, N. L. "Living the Dream: Ethics in Ephesians." *SWJT* 22 (1979) 39-55.

A diverse introduction cites laudatory appraisals of Ephesians as a whole, gives reasons for Paul's impact on ethics, identifies some major works on Pauline ethics, and clarifies Paul's approach to ethics as practical rather than systematic in nature. The rest of the article focuses on "the ethical half" of Ephesians under three rubrics: Promote the Church's Unity (4:1-16); Build Christian Homes (5:21-6:9); and Put on the Armor of God (6:10-20). Informally written.

1407. Barth, M. *Israel und die Kirche im Brief des Paulus an die Epheser.* München, Kaiser, 1959.

Investigates the data in Eph 2 concerning the current question about the validity and necessity of Christian missions to the Jews. Whereas there is a valid mission to the Jews, there is no place for anti-semitism in any form.

1408. _____. *The Broken Wall. A Study of the Epistle to the Ephesians.* Chicago: Judson, 1959; London: Collins, 1960.

Assuming Pauline authorship, the author explores key themes in Ephesians: the perfect work of God, the gathering of God's people, and the church in the world. The foreword of the book calls it a study book for evangelism. As such it seeks to explain a theology of evangelism and how the church can perform its mandate to spread the gospel in a theologically defensible manner.

1409. _____. "Conversion and Conversation: Israel and the Church in Paul's Epistle to the Ephesians." *Int* 17 (1963) 3-24.

This four-part article recovers as part of this epistle's ecclesiological foci the church's solidarity specifically with Israel. Part I reexamines 1:11-14, 2:11-20, and 3:5-6 establishing the church's common life with Israel. Part II locates the fundamental reasons for this surprising description in the meaning of "in Christ," not in an enlightenment attitude of egalitarian multiculturalism. The final sections draw out theological and practical applications, touching on hermeneutical concerns and Christian responsibility toward anti-semitism.

1410. Baulès, R. *L'insondable richesse du Christ. Étude des themes de l'Épître aux Ephésiens.* Paris: Cerf, 1971.

Following a brief defense of Pauline authorship and other introductory issues, the author offers a detailed plan of the entire letter. Succeeding chapters analyze key themes in the epistle such as: God the Father, Christ as Lord not only of the church but the entire universe, salvation as a reality to be communicated to others, and the mystery of God revealed in the Gospel.

1411. Bedale, S. F. B. "The Theology of the Church." In *Studies in Ephesians,* ed. F. L. Cross. London: Mowbray, 1956, 64-75.

Ephesians presents the church via three metaphors: the Body, the Bride, and the Temple. In addition, Christ is the "head" of the body, not meaning "head over" or "ruler of." Rather, growing out of the meaning of the Hebrew *rosh*, Bedale argues that "head" means "beginning" and so Paul asserts that Christ is the origin or principle of the church's being. Correspondingly, the husband's headship over his wife is one of origin not rule. So for the church to grow up into Christ involves our maturation until we attain to Christ's archetypal manhood.

1412. Benoit, P. "Body, Head, and Pleroma in the Epistles of the Captivity." In *Jesus and the Gospel,* 2 Vols. Tr. B. Weatherhead. London: Darton, Longman, and Todd, 1974, II: 51-92.

Discusses the theme of the "body of Christ" as it appears in Col and Eph, seeking answers to two problems: the origin of the concept, and whether it is used in Col and Eph differently than in the earlier epistles. Fully consistent with the earlier uses, in Col and Eph Paul speaks of a "body" that is fully personified, distinguished from the individual Christ, and set in a cosmic perspective of salvation. Christ is both head of the powers and head of the body. Understands *plērōma* to cover the idea of the universe as a "fullness" where God is present in all things, the frame for humanity that was encompassed in God's recreative work. See further on texts, 1:15-23.

1413. _____. "L'horizon paulinien de l'épître aux Éphésiens." *RB* 46 (1937) 342-361, 506-525.

1414. Best, E. "Ministry in Ephesians." *Irish Biblical Studies* 15/4 (1993) 146-66.

Traces how Eph presents the theme of ministry in God's overall plan: ministries are fulfilled, continuing, done by saints, by Paul, and by clergy and laity. Believers did tasks through roles open to all members.

1415. _____. "Das Geheimnis des Christus nach dem Epheserbrief." *TZ* 11 (1955) 329-343.

1416. Bony, P. "L'épître aux Éphésiens." In *Le ministère et les ministères selon le Nouveau Testament,* ed. J. Delorme. Paris: Seuil, 1974, 74-92.

See on texts, 2:11-22 (# 543).

1417. Borland, A. "God's Eternal Purpose." *EvQ* 34 (1962) 29-35.

The central theme of Ephesians is God's plan of salvation that sweeps from eternity past (1:4) to "all generations for ever and ever" (3:21).

1418. Bouttier, M. "L'horizon catholique de l'épître aux Ephésiens." In *L'Evangile, hier et aujourd'hui.* FS F. J. Leenhardt, ed. P. E. Bonnard, et al. Geneva: Labor et Fides, 1968, 25-37.

Portrays the catholic dimension of Ephesians.

1419. Breed, J. L. "The Church as the `Body of Christ': A Pauline Analogy." *Near East School of Theology Theological Review* 6 (1985) 9-32.

Investigates the various Pauline texts in 1 Cor, Rom, Eph, Gal, and Col that teach about the church as Christ's body. Some teach that the church is a unity (includes Eph 2:11-22); diverse members experience unity through the sacraments; and while Jesus is the head, the church forms his body (includes Eph 1:22-23; 2:19-22; and 5:21-32).

1420. Brown, R. B. "Ephesians among the Letters of Paul." *RE* 60/4 (1963) 372-79.

Introduction to Ephesians that adopts Pauline authorship.

1421. Brown, R. E. *The Churches the Apostles Left Behind.* New York: Paulist Press, 1984, 47-60.

Attempts to unpack the legacy left by the three great apostles: Paul, Peter, and John. Chapter three discusses "The Pauline Heritage in Colossians / Ephesians, *Christ's Body to Be Loved.*" Judges that eighty per cent of critical scholars deny that Paul wrote Ephesians and sixty per cent deny his authorship of Colossians. Concludes that the letters derive from the period of C.E. 90-100. Draws implications from his study of these letters for contemporary Catholicism and Christians.

1422. Cambier, J. *Vie Chrétienne en Église: L 'Épître aux Ephesiens leu aux chrétiens d'aujourd'hui.* Paris: Desclee, 1966.

1423. Caldwell, E. C. "The Purpose of the Ages." *Princeton Theological Review* 16 (1918) 374-89.

"The Alps of the NT," Ephesians unrolls the divine panorama of the ages, the spiritual view of history. It is the epistle of the heavenlies. Uncritically comments on the key phrases "in the heavenlies," "mystery," "dispensation," "the Gentiles," and "purpose." Concludes, then, from these the theme of the letter: "the formation of one universal and unending Church in Christ Jesus is the purpose of the ages."

1424. Carson, D. A., ed. *The Church in the Bible and the World.* Grand Rapids: Baker, 1987.

In this collection of essays, texts from Ephesians receive numerous mention. See, especially, the chapters on "The Church as a Heavenly and Eschatological Entity" by P. T. O'Brien and "Ministry in the New Testament" by R. Y. K. Fung.

1425. Cerfaux, L. "A genoux en presence de Dieu (la priere d'Eph III, 14-19)" and "Le message chrétien d'après Saint Paul." In *Recueil Lucien Cerfaux. Études d'exégese et d'histoire religieuse de Monseigneur Cerfaux.* 3 vols. Gembloux: Duculot, 1954-62. III (1962): 309-22.

See on texts, 3:14-21 (# 689).

1426. Chadwick, H. "Die Absicht des Epheserbriefes." *ZNW* 51 (1960) 145-153.

Suggests a possible scenario for the origin of Ephesians. Its author wanted to stress the metaphysical dimensions of the church, particularly its universality as the center of unity for all races in Christ. Though Paul's mission concentrated on Gentiles, the church should not lose sight of its Judean roots and the continuity between the first church at Jerusalem consisting of Jewish Christians and the Gentile-dominated church developing throughout the Roman empire.

1427. Colpe, C. "Zur Leib-Christi-Vorstellung im Epheserbrief." In *Judentum-Urchristentum Kirche.* FS J. Jeremias, ed. W. Eltester. *BhZNW* 26. Berlin: de Gruyter, 1964, 172-87.

On the concept of the body of Christ in Ephesians.

1428. Corley, B. "The Theology of Ephesians." *SWJT* 22 (1979) 24-38.

First notes the hymnodic and prayer-like way in which theology is done in Ephesians (esp. chapters 1-3), and then lays out its several theological motifs: the eternal purpose of God; election in Christ; revelation of the mystery; the New People of God; the unity of believers; images of the church; and the sovereign, exalted Christ. A helpful introduction.

1429. Cross, F. L., ed. *Studies in Ephesians.* London: Mowbray, 1956.

In additional to two essays on the question of authorship, this volume includes six essays by various authors on the theology of the letter. Topics include: unity, Christology, the Church, calling of the Gentiles, the Pauline catechesis and mystery.

1430. Cunningham, M. K. "Karl Barth's Interpretations and Use of Ephesians 1:4 in his doctrine of election. An Essay in the Relation of Scripture and Theology." Ph.D. thesis, Yale University, 1988.

1431. Dahl, N. A. "Interpreting Ephesians: Then and Now." *CurTM* 5 (1978) 133-43.

The proper way to read Ephesians is as a letter that congratulates those who have come to believe the gospel, reminding them to reflect on all the benefits of membership in the body of Christ. Its general nature has allowed both early Gnostics and bishops to find its message congenial to their views. Likewise modern interpreters have tended to see its stance growing out of either Gnosticism or early Catholicism.

1432. Dale, R. W. *The Epistle to the Ephesians. Its Doctrine and Ethics.* 9th ed. London: Hodder & Stoughton, 1896.

A compilation of twenty-four popular lectures that move through the epistle section by section.

1433. Dautzenberg, G. "Theologie und Seelsorge aus paulinischer Tradition: Einführung in 2 Thess, Kol, Eph." In *Gestalt und Anspruch des Neuen Testaments,* ed. J. Schreiner. Würzburg: Echter, 1969, 96-119.

A study of theology and pastoral care in the Pauline tradition represented by these three letters.

1434. Denton, D. R. "Inheritance in Paul and Ephesians." *EvQ* 54 (1982) 157-62.

See on texts, 1:3-14.

1435. Didier, G. "Presence de l'éternel: épîtres aux Éphésiens et aux Colossiens." In *Désintéressement du chrétien. La rétribution dans la morale de saint Paul.* Paris: Aubier, 1955, 172-191.

1436. Dodd, C. H. "The Message of the Epistles. Ephesians." *ExpT* 45 (1933-34) 60-66.

An introductory and roughly sequential treatment of the content of Ephesians. States the theme of the epistle and shows how it is developed and maintained throughout. Tinged with Dodd's own reflections of the epistle's most pertinent contribution to the problems "of our time."

1437. Dove, R. "The Epistle of Paul the Apostle to the Ephesians." In

Incarnation: Contemporary Writers on the New Testament, ed.
A. Corn. New York: Viking, 1990, 162-74.

One of the twenty-three novelists and poets who comment on the
NT.

1438.   Dunn, J. D. G. *Baptism in the Holy Spirit.* London: SCM, 1970,
       158-65.

Considers the topic of the study in these Ephesian texts: 1:13f.; 4:30;
2:4-6; 4:1-6; and 5:25-27.

1439.   Elliott, G. "The fullness of God." *Methodist Review* 111 (1928)
       114-26.

1440.   Efird, J. M. *Christ. the Church, and the End. Studies in Colossians
       and Ephesians.* Valley Forge, PA: Judson, 1980.

Starts with a discussion of the key themes of the letters: Jesus'
person and work, the structure and nature of the church, and the
early church's eschatology. Paul wrote Col from Rom about A.D. 60
while one of his admirers wrote Eph around A.D. 90. Provides a
section by section popular explication of the letters.

1441.   Ernst, J. "Von der Ortsgemeinde zur Grosskirche—dargestellt an
       den Kirchenmodellen des Philipper- und Epheserbriefs." In
       Kirche im Werden, ed. J. Hainz. Munich: F. Schoningh, 1976,
       123-42. ET "From the Local Community to the Great Church:
       Illustrated from the Church Patterns of Philippians and
       Ephesians." *BTB* 6 (1976) 237-57.

Finds Christology to be the origin of the metaphors for the church in
these letters. In Eph the church is the institution of salvation in
which people encounter Christ.

1442.   Ervin, H. M. *Conversion-Initiation and the Baptism in the Holy
       Spirit.* Peabody, MA: Hendrickson, 1984.

A systematic critique from a Pentecostal perspective of Dunn's

Baptism in the Holy Spirit (# 1438). Responds to key Ephesian text on pp. 122-128.

1443. Fendt, L. "Die Kirche des Epheserbriefs." *TLZ* 77 (1952) 147-50.

1444. Field, T. "The Epistle to the Ephesians for the City. A Process for Producing a Cultural Translation." Ph.D. thesis, Golden Gate Baptist Theological Seminary, 1986.

1445. Findeis, H.-J. *Versöhnung-Apostolat-Kirche.* Wurzburg: Echter Verlag, 1983.

1446. Frerichs, W. W. "Reconciled in Christ: ministry in light of Ephesians." *Word & World* 8 (1988) 293-300.

Written for clergy, this article introduces broad themes of the letter— unity, counseling (or "soul-care"), and exhortation—to guide a two-month preaching series. Lays out a schedule of texts corresponding to weeks eight to fifteen of the lectionary (Pentecost) and provides a summary for each week's content.

1447. Fung, R. "The Doctrine of Baptism in Ephesians." *SBT* 1 (1971) 6-14.

Sequentially studies all references to baptism (whether explicit or implicit) in Ephesians (1:13 par. 4:30; 2:4-6; 2:11-22; 4:5; 4:22-24 par. 5:8-14; 5:26), concluding that it is a redemptive act performed by Christ by which believers receive the Holy Spirit and enter a new life of holiness and Christian unity. Contains transliterated Greek and interacts with other sources in expansive footnotes.

1448. Gnilka, J. "Das Kirchenmodell des Epheserbriefes." *BZ* 15 (1971) 161-84.

In Ephesians, the term *ekklēsia* denotes the church as a whole not an individual community. The church constitutes the entire body of Christ characterized by unity under Christ's lordship. As well, the church is apostolic for they are foundational to its origin due to their being agents of God's revelation and the recipients of the most important charisms. No hint of ordination or succession; the church still functions under a charismatic hierarchy.

1449. Grob, F. "L'image du corps et de la tête dans l'Épître aux Éphésiens." *ETR* 58/4 (1983) 491-500.

The study pursues the implications of the head/body metaphor in Ephesians in comparison to Romans and Corinthians and asks about its possible significance for the relationship between husband and wife. In Ephesians, in contrast to Romans and Corinthians, the body (or church) consists not of many members (*melos*) but of two parts (*meros*)—Jews and Gentiles—united in (*en*) and towards (*eis*) Christ and eventually through (*dia*) the cross or the ministries. Likewise, the head is not one of the members of the body nor its leader. Rather, in Ephesians, the body comprises the entire person of Christ which is the head as the firstborn (cf. Col 1:18). One is left to ask, how is the husband the head of the wife?

1450. Grudem, W. "Does κεφαλή ('head') mean 'source' or 'authority over' in Greek literature: a survey of 2,336 examples." *TrinJ* n.s. 6 (1985) 38-59.

Surveying 2336 examples of the word κέφαλη in the TLG listing of 36 authors from the 8th century B.C. to the 4th century A.D., the article finds 49 clear instances of the meaning of "authority."

1451. _____. "The meaning of κέφαλη ('head'): a response to recent studies." *TrinJ* n.s. 11 (1990) 3-72.

In the course of his response, the author covers such issues as women in the Bible, Paul's attitude toward women, theology of women, and Paul's teaching about women in 1 Cor 11, 14.

1452. Guillemette, N. "Saint Paul and Women." *East Asian Pastoral Review* (Manila) 26/2 (1989) 121-33.

Discusses Paul's various statements on women, including Eph 5:21-32; these texts reflect the tension between his claim of egalitarianism on the one hand and his patriarchal and anti-feminist background on the other.

1453.   Halter, H. *Taufe und Ethos: Paulinische Kriterien für das Proprium christlicher Moral.* Freiburg: Herder, 1977.

A study of the specifically Christian elements of Paul's moral theology starting with an analysis of twenty-one passages on baptism, including seven from Ephesians (1:3-14; 2:1-10; 4:1-6; 4:17-24; 4:25-5:2; 5:3-14; 5:25-27). Seeks to develop from the indicatives of the passages the imperatives for Paul's ethic. For Paul, baptism was the key element that both caused and revealed God's plan of salvation through Christ.

1454.   Hanson, S. *The Unity of the Church in the New Testament: Colossians and Ephesians.* ASNU 14. Uppsala: Almqvist & Wiksells, 1946.

1455.   Harrell, C. J. *The Word of His Grace: Studies in Paul's Letter to the Ephesians.* New York: Abingdon-Cokesbury, 1943.

1456.   Harris, W. H. "'The heavenlies' reconsidered: οὐρανός and ἐπουράνιος in Ephesians." *BSac* 148 (1991) 72-89.

See on texts, 1:3-14 (# 326).

1457.   Hoch, C. B. "The significance of the syn-compounds for Jew-Gentile relationships in the body of Christ." *JETS* 25 (1982) 175-83.

To shed light on the relationship between the Old and New Testaments, the article studies elements of the continuity and discontinuity of the testaments displayed in the syn-compounds, especially as they appear in Ephesians. The goal is to minimize the current gap between covenant theologians (who stress continuity) and dispensationalists (who stress discontinuity).

1458.   Houlden, J. L. "Christ and Church in Ephesians." *StEv* 6, ed. E. Livingstone. *TU* 112. Berlin: Akademie, 1973, 267-73.

1459. Howard, G. "The Head/Body Metaphors of Ephesians." *NTS* 20 (1974) 350-56.

A grammatical examination of the head/body metaphors (1:22-23 and 4:15-16) reveals that this correlative relationship is secondary to a head/feet conceptualization (1:22). Argues for the middle voice of πληρουμένου (1:23), takes αὐξήσωμεν (4:15) as transitive, and shows that the author syntactically disassociates "head" and "body." Those texts therefore speak to the cosmic rule of Christ and only to a lesser degree deal with the union of Christ and the church.

1460. Humphreys, A. E. *The Spirit of Jesus. A Study of St. Paul's Epistle to the Ephesians: its Missionary and Social Gospel for Today.* London: SPCK, 1918.

1461. Hui, A. W. D. "The Concept of the Holy Spirit in Ephesians and its Relation to the Pneumatologies of Luke and Paul." Unpublished Ph.D. thesis. Aberdeen: University of Aberdeen, 1992.

Seeks to understand the pneumatology of Ephesians, particularly in relation to those found in Luke and Paul. Disagreeing with Adai's analysis [see above], finds telling similarities both in language and concept between Ephesians and Paul, listing these under seven headings or aspects. Finds the pneumatology of Ephesians to be Pauline in character.

1462. Jeal, R. R. "The Relationship between Theology and Ethics in the Letter to the Ephesians." Ph.D. dissertation, University of Sheffield, UK, 1990.

1463. Käsemann, E. *Leib und Leib Christi.* Tübingen: Mohr, 1933.

A study of the concept of "body" especially as it forms the background for the Pauline theological concept of the body of Christ. Major consideration given to the background of the body concept (as compared with "flesh") in the Jewish (Hebrew OT, the LXX, and the rabbis) and the Greek (classical, including Plato and Aristotle and the Stoa) world. Discusses the body concept in Gnostic thought and other "syncretisms" including Philo and the *"Aion-Urmenschen"* myth. The second major part of the book studies the concept of body in Paul's anthropology, including the concepts of "flesh," "body," and "spirit." The final part investigates the "body of Christ" concept in both the Deutero- and the acknowledged Pauline epistles.

1464. _____. "Christus, des All und die Kirche." *TLZ* 81 (1956) 585-90.

1465. _____. "Das Interpretationsproblem des Epheserbriefes." *TLZ* 86 (1961) 1-8. [Repr. in *Exegetische Versuche und Besinnungen*, vol. 2. 3d ed. Göttingen: Vandenhoeck & Ruprecht, 1970, 253-261.]

1466. _____. "Ephesians and Acts." In *Studies in Luke-Acts*. FS P. Schubert, ed. L. E. Keck and J. L. Martyn. London: SPCK, 1968, 288-97.

See above on "Hymns."

1467. _____. *Jesus Means Freedom*. Philadelphia: Fortress, 1972.

Finds that the major focus of the author of Ephesians lies in ecclesiology, in stark contrast to Paul's concern for Christology. This marks the turning point into "early catholicism."

1468. Kirby, J. C. *Ephesians. Baptism and Pentecost.* London: SPCK; Montréal: McGill University, 1968.

An inquiry into the structure and purpose of Ephesians. The Jewish author of Ephesians based the first part of the letter on a eucharistic prayer and the second on a feast of Pentecost address. Surveys recent literature on Ephesians and studies Jewish liturgical worship materials.

1469. Kitchen, M. "The Status of Law in the Letter to the Ephesians." In *Law and Religion*, ed. B. Lindars. Cambridge, UK: J. Clarke, 1988, 141-47.

Thirteen of the essays in this volume concern NT themes. Three focus on the Law and Paul: F. F. Bruce on Paul and the Law; Lindars on the topic in Rom 5-8; and Kitchen on the topic in Ephesians.

1470. _____. "The Ἀνακεφαλαίωσις of all things in Christ: Theology and Purpose in the Epistle to the Ephesians." Ph.D. thesis, University of Manchester, UK, 1988.

1471. Klein, W. W. *The New Chosen People. A Corporate View of Election.* Grand Rapids: Zondervan, 1990, esp. 158-209.

Pursues the thesis that "election to salvation" in the NT is dominantly, if not exclusively, a corporate concept. This is exemplified in Eph 1:4 in which the author affirms that God has chosen the church in Christ—before the foundation of the world. Addresses the texts in Ephesians that concern the topic of election.

1472. Knoch, O. "Die Botschaft des Epheserbriefes." In *Durch die Gnade Gottes bin ich, was ich bin.* Ostfildern: Schwabenverlag, 1984, 74-89.

Translates the message of the Ephesian letter.

1473. Lee, E. K. "Unity in Israel und Unity in Christ." In *Studies in Ephesians,* ed. F. L. Cross. London: Mowbray, 1956, 36-50.

Takes up the topic of unity as a universal human quest, essentially a religious conception, first on the pages of the OT in Israel's corporate existence as the people of God, those involved in the cult of Israel, and under one divine Law. Shows how the epistle of Ephesians presents these same ideas under the rubrics of representation, worship, and sovereignty. All the elements of the OT designed to achieve unity in the world find fulfillment and enrichment in Christ.

1474. Lemmer, H. R. "A multifarious understanding of eschatology in Ephesians: A possible solution to a vexing issue." *HTS* 46/1-2 (1990) 102-19.

Rather than denying a legitimate eschatology for Eph, he sees it as proleptic, in the process of realization, analeptic, and praesentic. If so nuanced, it represents an adaptation, rather than a degeneration of traditional Pauline eschatology.

1475.   Lincoln, A. T. *Paradise Now and Not Yet.* Cambridge: Cambridge University Press, 1981; Grand Rapids: Baker, 1992.

See on texts, 3:1-13 (# 663).

1476.   _____. "The Use of the OT in Ephesians." *JSNT* 14 (1982) 16-57.

See on texts, 2:11-22 (# 577).

1477.   _____. *The Theology of the Later Pauline Letters.* Cambridge, UK: Cambridge University Press, 1993.

Traces the major theological themes in these letters. Includes criticism and interpretation of Colossians and Ephesians.

1478.   Lidgett, J. S. *God in Christ Jesus.* London: Kelly, 1915.

1479.   Lindemann, A. *Die Aufhebung der Zeit: Geschichtsverständnis und Eschatologie im Epheserbrief.* Gütersloh: Gerd Mohn, 1975.

See on texts, 1:15-23 (# 434).

1480.   Lona, H. E. *Die Eschatologie im Kolosser- und Epheserbrief.* Würzburg: Echter Verlag, 1984.

See above on "Historical Setting" (# 1322)

1481.   Luz, U. "Überlegungen zum Epheserbrief un seiner Paränese." In *Neues Testament und Ethik.* FS R. Schnackenburg, ed. H. Merklein. Freiburg/Basel/Wien: Herder, 1989, 376-96.

A reflection on the paraenesis of Ephesians. Addresses the topic of prayer in the letter and Ephesians as a reminiscence on Paul and his writings.

1482. Lyall, R. *Slaves, Citizens, Sons. Legal Metaphors in the Epistles.* Grand Rapids: Zondervan, 1984.

Studies key legal images in the NT contending that Paul was well-acquainted with the terms of his day.

1483. MacDonald, M. Y. *The Pauline Churches. SNTSMS* 60. Cambridge: Cambridge University Press, 1988.

Sets forth two primary theses: (1) there exists an important continuity—a development, not departure from—between the thought of the original Pauline corpus and that of the Deutero-Paulines (Ephesians/Colossians and the Pastoral epistles; (2) all these "Paulines" must be understood in the context of their socio-historical settings in which they originated. The material found in Ephesians serves as a response to Paul's absence from the Pauline communities.

1484. MacDonald, W. G. "The biblical doctrine of election." In *The Grace of God, the Will of Man,* ed. C. Pinnock. Grand Rapids: Zondervan, 1989, 207-29.

Traces the topic through the Bible with a section entitled, "Election Exclusively 'In Christ': Ephesians 1:3-14" that includes a Greek grammatical layout of this passage that underscores the essential elements.

1485. Mackay, J. A. "Church Order, Its Meaning and Implications: a study in the Epistle to the Ephesians." *ThT* 9 (1953) 450-66.

See on texts, 4:1-16 (# 764).

1486. _____. *God's Order. The Ephesian Letter and the Present Time.* New York: Macmillan, 1953.

The written form of the author's Croall Lectures that move topically through the epistle. Asserts that Ephesians is the greatest and maturest of all of Paul's writings. Mackay presents Paul's understanding of the essential structure of spiritual reality as it appears in Ephesians.

1487. MacPhail, J. R. "Ephesians and the Church of South India." *SJT* 10 (1957) 57-75.

Believing Paul to be the author of Ephesians, MacPhail traces the historical situation leading up to the writing of the letter. Proceeds with an overall interpretation of the letter arguing that it is THE Epistle for South India since that church embodies the corporate unity envisioned in Ephesians.

1488. Malevez, L. "L'Église, Corps du Christ. Sens et provenance de l'expression chez s. Paul." *Recherches de Science Religieuse* 32 (1944) 27-94.

1489. Martin, R. P. *Reconciliation: A Study of Paul's Theology.* London: Marshall; Atlanta: John Knox, 1981. [Repr. Grand Rapids: Zondervan, 1990.]

Part three is entitled, "Pauline Theology in a New Situation" which contains the sole chapter, "Reconciliation and Unity in Ephesians" (pp. 157-98). Assumes that Ephesians is not a "letter" in the usual sense and that it was not written to a local community in Ephesus, and, most likely, not by Paul. Engages in a survey of the history of interpretation of the background for the letter. Pays special attention to the important section, 2:11-22 "where the Pauline teaching on reconciliation gains a fresh dimension by being applied to persons-in-community."

1490. Meeks, W. A. "In One Body: The Unity of Humankind in Colossians and Ephesians." In *God's Christ and His People.* FS N. A. Dahl, ed. J. Jervell and W. A. Meeks. Oslo: Universitetsforlaget, 1977, 209-21.

The dominant theme of unity reproduces elements from the baptismal liturgy and catechism of the Pauline churches of Asia. Sees the attention entirely focused on the earthly congregation. The cosmic imagery of the author's tradition serves his concern for the human congregation.

1491. Merkel, H. "Der Epheserbrief in der neueren exegetischen Diskussion." *ANRW*. *Geschichte und Kultur Roms im Spiegel der neueren Forschung*. II: *Principat*, Band 25 (4. Teilband): *Religion* (Vorkonstantinisches Christentum: Leben un Umwelt Jesu; Neues Testament [Danonische Schriften und Apokryphen], Forts.), ed. W Haase. Berlin/New York: de Gruyter, 1987, 3156-3246.

An extensive overview that explores both the history of and the current state of research on exegetical issues surrounding the book of Ephesians. Begins with the background for historical-critical investigation of Ephesians leading to the beginning of this century by considering the key contributors or schools of interpretation. The second section considers the major figures to Ephesian studies in this century divided into studies that focus on the background of the letter in Gnosis, those that find an OT-Jewish backdrop, those who adopt a Hellenistic-Jewish model of interpretation, and, finally, those preferring alternative explanations. The final section of the study considers important works on individual questions of interpretation of the letter divided into five sections: the addressees, liturgical traditions (considers these sections: 1:3-14; 1:20-23; 2:4-10; 2:14-18; 2:19-22; 5:14), the picture of Paul in Ephesians, the concept of church office, and the concept of mission in Ephesians. A bibliographical gold mine of information. A total of 623 footnotes document the article's analyses of important sources.

1492. Merklein, H. *Das kirchliche Amt nach dem Epheserbrief.* Munich: Kösel, 1973.

See on texts, 2:11-22 (# 588).

1493. _____. "Paulinische Theologie in der Rezeption des Kolosser- und Epheserbriefes." In *Paulus in den neutestamentlichen Spätschriften,* ed. K. Kertelge. Freiburg: Herder, 1981, 25-69.

See Chapter 8, "Relation to Colossians" (# 1088).

1494. Metzger, B. M. "Paul's Vision of the Church; A Study of the Ephesian Letter." *ThT* 6 (1949-50) 49-63.

The theme of Ephesians is the church as the initial manifestation of and instrument towards the ultimate unification of the universe. Notes presuppositions that underlie Paul's formulation of this theme, expounds the significance of the images used to describe the church (body, temple, bride), and rounds out the analysis with several especially practical conclusions.

1495. Meyer, R. P. *Kirche und Mission im Epheserbrief.* Stuttgart: Katholisches Bibelwerk, 1977.

Unpacks the central themes of Eph 1:22b-23 that support a theology of mission. The church functions as missionary in its position as *sōma* (body) and *plērōma* (fullness) of Christ.

1496. Moody, D. *Christ and the Church.* Grand Rapids: Eerdmans, 1963.

A popular exposition of the epistle to help average Christians solve their problems.

1497. Mooney, C. F. "Paul's Vision of the Church in 'Ephesians.'" *SCR* 15 (1963) 33-43.

Discusses impersonal and personal sources of Paul's conception of the "body of Christ" to account for the developed ecclesiology in Ephesians. The Christian's unity with Christ's risen body (1 Cor 12; Rom 12) gives way in the captivity letters to the view of the church as the literal body-person of Christ (cf. Cerfaux, Benoit, H. W. Robinson). Demonstrates how the image of the body, temple, and bride serve to emphasize the collective unity of the church and its lack of autonomy.

1498. Moule, H. C. G. *Ephesian Studies.* London: Hodder and Stoughton, 1900.

A series of spiritual studies that work their way through the epistle.

On a popular level.

1499. Mussner, F. *Christus, das All und die Kirche.* 2d ed. Trier: Paulinus, 1968.

See on texts, 1:15-23 (# 451).

1500. _____. "Die Geschichtstheologie des Epheserbriefes." *BibLeb* 5 (1964) 8-12.

The author of Eph develops a theology of history from the confession "Jesus is the Christ." Jesus is Messiah, the eschatological agent and Lord of the nations. The fullness of times comes with Christ's parousia.

1501. Ochel, W. *Die Annahme einer Bearbeitung des Kolosser-Briefes im Epheser-Brief.* Wurzburg: Konrad Triltsch, 1934.

1502. Odeberg, H. *The View of the Universe in the Epistle to the Ephesians.* Lund: Lund Universitets Arsskrift, 1934.

1503. Ogilvie, L. J. *Enjoying God.* Dallas: Word, 1989.

1504. Parker, J. *The Epistle to the Ephesians.* London: Hodder and Stoughton; New York: George Doran, nd.

Various popular expositions on features the author finds in Ephesians.

1505. Packer, J. I. "Godliness in Ephesians." *Crux* 25 (1989) 8-16.

Ephesians presses Paul's concern that believers be godly (1:4; 5:25-27). After undermining three misconceptions about godliness—that it is unimportant, self-generated, and limited in usefulness—the author unpacks four prepositions revolving around "God's grace and power in Christ" that sum up the apostle's epistolary strategy: Godliness (1) starts with acknowledging it, (2) grows by adoring it, (3) demands alteration of behavior through it, and (4) requires aggression against evil through it.

1506. Paradis, H. "Le Christ Tête de l'Église, selon les Épîtres aux Colossiens et aux Éphésiens." In *L'Église dans la Bible*. Bruges: Desclée de Brouwer, 1962, 95-115.

Discussion of Christ as the head of the church in both Eph and Col.

1507. Paxson, R. *The Wealth, Walk and Warfare of the Christian.* New York: Fleming Revell, 1939.

Popular, practical expositions about various topics in Ephesians under the three rubrics in the title.

1508. Penner, E. "The Enthronement of Christ in Ephesians." *Direction* [publication of Mennonite Brethren Schools] 12/3 (1983) 12-19.

Finds Christ's enthronement to be the central theme in Eph—one that controls the entire letter's instruction on the enthronement of believers, eschatology, spiritual gifts, and the church.

1509. _____. "The Enthronement Motif in Ephesians." Ph.D. thesis, Fuller Theological Seminary, 1983.

1510. Percy, E. *Der Leib Christi in den paulinischen Homologoumena und Antilegomena.* Lund: Gleerup, 1942.

Compares the concept of the body of Christ—the Christian community—in both the recognized Pauline writings, especially Rom 12:4-5 and 1 Cor 12:12-27, with that found in Col and Eph. Though the perspectives differ, both can be viewed as thoroughly Pauline, and Pauline authorship can be affirmed for Col and Eph.

1511. _____. "Zu den Problemen des Kolosser- und Epheserbriefes." *ZNW* 43 (1950-51) 178-94.

1512. _____. *Die Probleme der Kolosser- und Epheserbriefe.* 2d rev. ed. Lund: Gleerup, 1964.

See above on Relation to Col and Pauline corpus (# 1092).

1513.   Perels, O. "Kirche und Welt nach dem Epheser- und Kolosserbrief."
        TLZ 76 (1951) 391-400.

1514.   Pokorný, P. "Σῶμα Χριστοῦ im Epheserbrief." *EvT* 20 (1960) 45-
        64.

        See on texts, 1:15-23 (# 458).

1515.   Reuss, J. "Die Kirche als 'Leib Christi' und die Herkunft dieser
        Vorstellung bei dem Apostel Paulus." *BZ* 2 (1958) 103-27.

        Lists and seeks to address the central problems surrounding a
        consideration of the concept of "the Body of Christ": the meaning of
        the term in the key texts; its meaning in 1 Cor and Rom in contrast
        to Eph-Col; and its source as an identification of the church. Finds
        Paul's own theology as the most likely source for the concept of the
        Church as the Body of Christ. In the Eph-Col letters Paul adds two
        ideas to what he taught previously: the entire community as the body
        of Christ, and Christ as the Head of the Church.

1516.   Reynier, C. *Évangile et mystère. Les Enjeux théologiques de
        L'Épître aux Éphésiens.*   Paris: Éditions du Cerf, 1992.

        Based on the author's doctoral thesis submitted to the theological
        faculty of Centre Sevres, 1990.

1517.   Ridderbos, H. *Paul: An Outline of His Theology.* Tr. J. R. de Witt.
        Grand Rapids: Eerdmans, 1975.

        See on texts, 1:15-23 (# 463).

1518.   Roels, E. *God's Mission: The Epistle to the Ephesians in Mission
        Perspective.* Franeker: Wever, 1962.

1519.   Roon, A. van. *The Authenticity of Ephesians.* Leiden: Brill, 1974,
        213-349; 350-93.

        In the quest indicated by the title, the author inquires into key
        expressions which have a cosmic aspect or are anthropological in

character such as: ἐπουράνιος, τὰ πάντα, the powers, πληροῦν, πλήρωμα, κεφαλή, σῶμα, μέλος, ἀνὴρ τέλειος, ἔσω ἄνθρωπος, παλαιὸς ἄνθρωπος, and καινὸς ἄνθρωπος. In addition, he studies the ecclesiological content of the letter.

1520. Rosado, C. *Broken Walls.* Boise, ID and Oshawa, Ont.: Pacific Press, 1989.

Addresses sociological and religious issues and the implications of Ephesians for race relations.

1521. Rowland, R. *Get a Life! ... and a Faith That Works. What an Early Christian Community Says to Us Today.* San Francisco: Harper, 1992.

1522. Rowston, D. J. "Changes in Biblical Interpretation Today: The Example of Ephesians." *BTB* 9 (1979) 121-25.

Pursues the theory suggested by P. R. Jones and R. P. Martin (see # 1325) that Paul's companion Luke was the author of Ephesians, published either during Paul's final imprisonment or following his martyrdom by Nero.

1523. Scharlemann, M. H. "Human Relations According to 'Ephesians.'" *CTM* 24 (1953) 705-14.

Demonstrates how Ephesians addresses the problem of social relations (especially group segregation), starting with the mention of the dividing Temple-court wall (2:14) and going through the letter. Segregation of Jew and Gentile though initiated by; God, now has been made extinct through the revealed mystery of his will in Christ. The cross has also disturbed the cosmological powers of enmity that foster human hatred. Those who in Christ practice social virtues (4:1-13) come under attack by these powers and must therefore stand in the armor of God (6:14-16).

1524. Schlier, H. *Christus und die Kirche im Epheserbrief.* *BHTh* 6. Tübingen: Mohr. 1930. [Repr. 1966.]

1525. _____. "Die Kirche nach dem Brief an die Epheser," 159-186; and "Die Kirche als das Geheimnis Christi nach dem Epheserbrief," 299-307. In *Die Zeit der Kirche*. Freiburg: Herder, 1956.

1526. Schlier, H. and Warnach, V. *Die Kirche im Epheserbrief.* Münster: Aschendorff, 1949.

1527. Schmid, J. *Der Epheserbrief des Apostels Paulus.* Freiburg: Herder, 1928.

1528. Schnackenburg, R. "Er hat uns mitauferweckt: Zur Tauflehre des Epheserbriefes." *LJ* 2 (1952) 159-83.

A study of what the book of Ephesians teaches about baptism. Baptism is the way to life and dwelling with Christ in the heavenlies (identification with Christ in baptism grows out of the discussion on Rom 6:4-8). Baptism also marks the point of "sealing" with the Holy Spirit. Finally, baptism marks the believer's participation in the salvation of the church (cf. Gal 3:24f.) and the insoluble connection of the church with Christ himself. Baptism provides for us the closest union of the idea and state of the church.

1529. _____. "Gestalt und Wesen der Kirche nach dem Epheserbrief." *Catholica* 15 (1961) 104-120. [Repr. in *Schriften zum Neuen Testament.* Munich: Kösel, 1971, 268-87.]

Paper delivered at a conference on the visible and invisible church. Considers the unity of Jews and Gentiles in the church as an indication of the mystery of salvation. Through the cross both have been brought together into the one body of Christ by the one Spirit and both have access together to the Father. Both service and leadership follow on from Christ—what he did and who he is. The role of apostles and prophets was fundamental in the church as representing Christ. The presence of both Jews and Gentiles shows Christ's victory over the cosmos and the triumph of God's eschatological program.

1530. _____. "Der Epheserbrief im heutigen Horizont." In *Massstab des Glaubens.* Freiburg: Herder 1978, 155-75.

See above on Historical Setting (# 1344).

1531. _____. "L'Idée de 'Corps du Christ' dans la lettre aux Ephesiens:
       Perspective pour nôtre temps." In *Paul de Tarse. Apôtre du
       nôtre Temps*, ed. L. de Lorenzi. Rome: Abbaye de St. Paul,
       1979, 665-85.

       Considers the concept of the Body of Christ in Ephesians, with
       special application to its significance for the modern church.

1532. Smalley, S. S. "The Eschatology of Ephesians." *EvQ* 28/3 (1956)
       152-57.

       Begins by defining eschatology and then discerns three
       "eschatological states" in Ephesians: the mystery of the inclusion of
       Gentiles, the growth of the body in the unity of the spirit, and the
       final summing up of τὰ πάντα (all things) in Christ. Finds
       universalism—which might seem to be raised by this scheme—
       foreign to Paul's thought.

1533. Steinmetz, F.-J. *Protologische Heils-Zuversicht: Die Strukturen des
       soteriologischen und christologischen Denkens im Kolosser-
       und Epheserbrief.* Frankfurt: Josef Knecht, 1969.

       Compares the eschatology of Col and Eph (which tends to be
       "present") with that of the recognized Paulines (which is futurist)—in
       relation to their treatments of Christology and soteriology. Finds that
       Col/Eph grow out of an entirely different thought-world from Paul,
       and no attempt ought be made to harmonize it with Paul's theology.
       See further on texts, 2:1-10 (# 529).

1534. _____. "Parusie-Erwartung im Epheserbrief? Ein Vergleich." *Bib*
       50 (1969) 328-336.

       Studies the use of the categories of *kephalē* and *plērōma* in
       Ephesians, concluding that Paul's uses of them in the letter go a long
       way in explaining the lack of any traditional parousia expectation
       such as is found in the other Paulines. A body does not wait for its
       head; rather the body grows and builds itself up via the fullness of

its head, Christ.

1535. _____. "Jenseits der Mauern und Zäune; somatische Verständnis der kirchlichen Einheit im Epheserbrief." *GeistL* 59 (1986) 202-14.

Cautions against limiting the "we" and "you" in Eph to peoples in antiquity: Jews and Gentiles. The letter stresses "somatic" unity, and the body of Christ reflects the unity of believers with God and each other. The body exists to promote God's glory.

1536. Summers, R. "One Message—Redemption." *RE* 60/4 (1963) 380-98.

A pithy, exegetical study of Eph 1:3-2:10, the segment giving the most sustained attention to the theme of the entire epistle: redemption in Christ. God's provision of redemption guides 1:3-14, while 1:15-2:10 relates the resulting human benefits. Contains several short lists that clarify textual structures and may serve as "seed sermon" outlines.

1537. Tachau, P. *"Einst" und "Jetzt" im Neuen Testament.* Göttingen: Vandenhoeck & Ruprecht, 1972.

See on texts, 2:1-10 (# 531).

1538. Tannehill, R. C. "Ephesians and Colossians." In *Dying and Rising with Christ, BhZNW* 32. Berlin: Töpelmann, 1966, 47-54.

In the section entitled "Dying with Christ as the Basis of the New Life," considers the implications of the data in Eph and Col. The reference to dying with Christ as a past event in Eph/Col disqualify these letters from Pauline authorship. Most of the discussion centers on Colossian texts.

1539. Taylon, W. F. "Speaking the Truth in Love: the congregation as evangelizing community." *Trinity Seminary Review* 7/2 (1985) 39-45.

An address delivered at the 1984 convention of the American Lutheran Church looks at Eph 2 to see why and how the congregation is an evangelizing community. God's love, inclusion of believers in the covenant, and baptism of believers provide the "why." The church's hearing, speaking, including, giving, and being empowered answers the "how."

1540. Taylor, J. V. *The Go-Between God.* London: SCM, 1972.

1541. Theriault, J.-Y. "La femme chrétienne dans les textes pauliniennes." *ScEs* 37/3 (1985) 297-317.

Investigates key Pauline texts on the "women's issue" settling on nine hermeneutical conclusions on understanding women's positions in the texts and their significance for today.

1542. Thurston, B. B. *Spiritual Life in the Early Church. The Witness of Acts and Ephesians.* Minneapolis: Fortress, 1993.

1543. Tillard, J. M. R. "What Is the Church of God?" *Mid-Stream: An Ecumenical Journal* 23 (1984) 363-80; *One in Christ* 20/3 (1984) 226-42.

The study links the more developed Johannine notion of *koinonia* and the Pauline idea of *mysterion,* even though Paul does not develop *koinonia* to the extent the Johannine literature does nor does the Johannine literature use the word *mysterion.* The Christian community realizes the *mysterion* in that it brings together in *koinonia* a divided humanity—God's secret plan achieved through Christ's death and resurrection.

1544. Usami, K. *Somatic Comprehension of Unity: The Church in Ephesus.* AnBib 101. Rome: Biblical Institute Press, 1983.

The author studies the meaning and quality of the unity taught in Ephesians. "Old" and "New" Christians now dwell together in the church (Eph 2:1-13). Being "in Christ" establishes a "Christ-agogical" way of unity (1:3-14). Addresses Paul's role as the spiritual master and his role in the unfolding of God's mystery in the world. The concept of "body" conveys the dynamic character of the Christian community in relation to both its members and its surroundings. The final chapter, an epilogue, draws out extensive implications of Paul's teaching for the modern world and Christians.

1545. Van Engen, C. "The Holy Catholic Church: on the road through Ephesians." *Reformed Review* 37 (1984) 187-201.

In Ephesians, Paul suggests crucial images for understanding both the church's nature and her reason for being, and these, in turn, illuminate the adjectives in the Apostles' Creed: "One, Holy, Catholic." Four elements of the nature of the church emerge: (1) these depictions are received by faith; (2) each requires effort to attain; (3) each individual Christian finds his or her own nature in connection to these adjectives; and (4) becoming each requires continual growth by the church. To be the church comprises both gift and task, indicative and imperative; she can never cease struggling to become what she is by faith.

1546. Ward, W. E. "One Body—the Church." *RE* 60/4 (1963) 399-413.

Against a trend in interpretation (starting with E. Y. Mullins [1931]) that treats Ephesians without reference to ecclesiology, Ward traces the Pauline term "body of Christ" to show that it metaphorically capsulizes Paul's understanding of the church and does not signify, as J. A. T. Robinson holds, Christ's resurrection body. Examines the "one" phrases in 4:4-6 that reinforce the concept of unity in "body." Concludes with an application relevant to the contemporary ecumenical context in which it was written.

1547. Warnach, V. "Taufwirklichkeit und Taufbewusstsein nach dem Epheserbrief." *Liturgie und Mönchtum* 33/34 (1963-64) 36-51. [Also in *Leben aus der Taufe*. FS B. Ebel, ed. T. Bogler. Maria Laach: Ars Liturgica, 1963, 36-51.

Baptismal reality and baptismal consciousness according to Ephesians.

1548. Weiss, H.-F. "Taufe und neues Leben im deuteropaulinischen

Schriftum." In *Taufe und neue Existenz,* ed. E. Schott. Berlin: Evangelische Verlagsanstalt, 1973, 53-70.

Baptism and new life in the Deutero-Pauline writings.

1549. Welch, C. H. *John and the Mystery, or, The Relative Callings of John's Gospel and the Epistle to the Ephesians.* London: Berean Publishing Trust, 1991.

1550. Wendland, H.-D. "Der Epheserbrief. Das Ethos in der Einheit des Leibes Christi." In *Ethik des Neuen Testaments.* Göttingen: Vandenhoeck & Ruprecht, 1970, 90-95.

A study of the topic of ethics in the NT moving rather chronologically from the contribution of Jesus, through the early Christian community, to Paul, to the Deutero-Pauline authors (where he locates Ephesians), then to James, John, and the remaining Johannine literature. Focuses on the ethical paraenesis of 4:1-6:2 and then, more specifically, the *Haustafel* of 5:22-6:9. Sums up the ethic as "walk worthy of your calling."

1551. Wessels, G. F. "The Eschatology of Colossians and Ephesians." *Neot* 21/2 (1987) 183-202.

Refutes the contention that Col and Eph are essentially de-eschatological documents by responding to four arguments used to support their fully realized, hence non-futurist, eschatology: (1) the resurrection and ascension with Christ motif; (2) cosmic powers already subjected; (3) ahistorical spacial categories replace linear time categories; and (4) futurist eschatology is only a marginal phenomenon.

1552. Whiteley, D. E. H. "Christology." In *Studies in Ephesians*, ed. F. L. Cross. London: Mowbray, 1956, 51-63.

Leaving aside the question of authorship, seeks to shed light on the person of Christ through a discussion of the work of Christ as outlined in this letter.

1553. Wild, R. A. "'Be Imitators of God': Discipleship in the Letter to the Ephesians." In *Discipleship in the New Testament,* ed. F. F. Segovia. Philadelphia: Fortress 1985. 127-43.

Sees the pseudepigraphal Ephesians as using Hellenistic categories to present Christianity within a culturally Jewish setting to explain and elaborate the revelation in Christ. Though much of the paraenesis of the letter grows out of the OT, not so the command to "be imitators of God." The study proceeds to explain the origin (the writings of Philo and the Platonic tradition) and nature of the appeal (not Platonic but Christian).

1554. Williams, B. *Encounter Ephesians! Where Is the True Church? The Cosmic Dimension of the Epistle to the Ephesians.* Glastonbury: B. Williams, 1993.

1555. Williams, R. R. "The Pauline Catechesis." In *Studies in Ephesians,* ed. F. L. Cross. London: Mowbray, 1956, 89-96.

Likens Ephesians to a two-part sermon, one a burst of praise and the second the ethical implications. Proceeds to expound Ephesians as an example of NT catechesis. Opines that Ephesians may be a revision of Col, "freely adapted by the primitive Church for use as a baptismal homily."

1556. Williamson, L. *God's Work of Art.* Richmond, VA: CLC Press, 1971.

"IN CHRIST"

1557. Allan, J. A. "The 'in Christ' Formula in Ephesians." *NTS* 5 (1958-59) 54-62.

Surveys the 'in Christ' formula in Ephesians and argues that it functions chiefly in an "instrumental" rather than the usual "corporate" Pauline sense, thus casting doubt on the Pauline authorship of the letter. Attempts to show that 2:15 and 4:15 lack the corporate idea, as do references to dying and rising with Christ (2:5-6).

1558. Bouttier, M. *En Christ.* Paris: Presses Univ. de France, 1962.

Contends that only the translation "in Christ" does justice to the various redemptive aspects of Christ's work contained in the phrase *en Christō* in Paul's writings. Sees the preposition *en* as, at the same time, instrumental (what Christ accomplished), inclusive (what he accomplishes in mystical communion with his people), and eschatological (what he will yet perform).

1559. _____. *La condition chrétienne selon saint Paul.* Nouvelle série théologique 16. Geneva: Labor et Fides, 1964.

Considers *en Christō* to be intensely Pauline and a phrase that colors each text in which Paul uses it. Believers enjoy communion *in* Christ: they live with him through baptism, the Eucharist, death, and life).

1560. Büchsel, F. "In Christo." *ZNW* 42 (1949) 141-58.

1561. Cazelles, H. "Instaurare omnia in Christo (Eph 1, 10)." *Bib* 40/2 (1959) 342-54.

See on texts, 1:3-14 (# 297).

1562. Deissmann, A. *Die neutestamentliche Formel 'in Christo Jesu'.* Marburg: Friedrich, 1892.

1563. Grossouw, W. *In Christ: A Sketch of the Theology of St. Paul.* London: Geoffrey Chapman, 1965.

Written for Catholic laypersons, this quick theological survey understands Paul's thought as consisting of two basic themes: unredeemed existence without Christ and converted existence in Christ. Its five chapters therefore progress through the topics of sin, the provision of the cross, saving faith, being in Christ, and the church (the mystical body).

1564. Kourie, C. E. T. "'In Christ' and related expressions in Paul." *Theologica Evangelica* 20/2 (1987) 33-43.

Considers the Pauline expression 'in Christ.' Surveys the options to explain the expression: mystical, objective, ecclesiological, eschatological, and corporate. Considers its ethical implications and relations to 'in the Lord' and 'in the spirit.'

1565. Lohmeyer, E. *Grundlagen paulinischer Theologie.* Tübingen: Mohr, 1929, 139-40.

1566. Neugebauer, F. "Das paulinische 'In Christo.'" *NTS* 4 (1957-58) 124-38.

Seeks to assess this key Pauline phrase first by analyzing how the preposition *en* occurs with *Jesus, Christus,* and *Kyrios.* Finds "in" means "determined by" and so *en Christo* comes to mean what is determined by the eschatological occurrence of Jesus' death and resurrection—to be drawn into this history.

1567. _____. *In Christus. En Christō. Eine Untersuchung zum Paulinischen Glaubensverständnis.* Göttingen: Vandenhoeck & Ruprecht, 1961.

Assesses prior studies on the phrase, the formula itself, its occurrence in context, and how it fits the Pauline concept of faith. Engages Lüdemann's interpretation of justification and mystic salvation in Paul.

1568. Parisius, H. -L. "Über die forensische Deutungsmöglichkeit des paulinischen *en Christō.*" *ZNW* 49 (1958) 285-88.

Argues that of the 165 occurrences of the phrase in Paul, ten ought be viewed in forensic terms. None occur in Eph.

1569. Reid, J. K. S. "The Phrase 'In Christ'." *ThT* 17 (1960) 353-65.

After summarizing the work of Deissmann (# 1562) and J. Weiss, Reid argues that although the phrase 'in Christ' is characteristically Pauline, the concept it signifies nevertheless has roots in the gospels. Turning to the question of meaning, Reid rejects the conclusion that the phrase indicates a pneumatic Christ and so predominantly has a mystical conception. Rather, its diverse uses cover "the whole range" of the Christian life, connoting not simply a certain relation to Christ but also the basis of that relation.

1570. Schmauch, W. *In Christus.* Gütersloh: Bertelsmann, 1935.

1571. Schweitzer, A. *The Mysticism of Paul the Apostle.* London: A. & C. Black, 1931.

Explains Paul's contribution to early Christianity in keeping with his eschatological understanding of Jesus. Only after Paul did Christianity undergo extensive Hellenization. Thus, the fading of the early eschatological hope led to the adoption of more Hellenistic explanations of their hope. Views the Christians' dying and rising with Christ in mystical terms. To be "in Christ" is another way of saying that Christians are partakers in the Mystical Body of Christ. See especially chapter VI, pp. 101-140.